Praise for Travis Langley's
STRANGER THINGS PSYCHOLOGY

"Look into the psyche of **Stranger Things** and get ready to see the show in a whole new way, uncovering new insights and perspective into the characters, the '80s, and ourselves. Be ready to have your perception turned . . . Upside Down. I really liked it."
— Gail Z. Martin, author of the *Deadly Curiosities* series

About Popular Culture Psychology books

"[Travis Langley's] *Popular Culture Psychology* series . . . aims to make 'boring' science fun by showing how real-life science might explain some of the things we see in films and television."
— *Kirkus Reviews*

"What's great about the books . . . is that they are amenable for both casual reading and deeper study alike." — Pop Mythology

"I'm a really big fan of his work and always wait in anticipation for the next release." — Dimensional Author's Realm

"Always a great, fun read." — Geek at Arms

"Compelling on a multiplicity of levels." — Electric Review

"Absolutely fantastic!" — Retroist

"Super interesting and inspired me." — PBS Braincraft

"The perfect blend of insightful scholarship, pop-culture savvy, and bloody good fun. Highly recommended!"
— Jonathan Maberry, *New York Times* best-selling author

About *Batman and Psychology: A Dark and Stormy Knight*

"Scholarly and insightful.... An intriguing read and a fascinating book."
— Michael Uslan, Batman film series exec. producer

"It is a terrific book." — Dennis O'Neil, comic book writer/editor

"Marvelous." — Adam West, actor

"Definitely a book worth looking for." — Kevin Smith, filmmaker

"A modern classic." — Mark D. White, author of *Batman & Ethics*

"Great read and tremendously insightful into the psyche of The Dark Knight." — Batman-on-Film.com

"This book perfectly balances fiction and non-fiction by using eighty years of Batman's postindustrial mythology as case studies for various psychological conditions." — IPN Top Ten Books

"If you're interested in Batman, psychology, or even inspirational books, I recommend this book. It's entertaining as well." — Knight Light

"You should definitely read this book." — NBU

About *Doctor Who Psychology,* 1st ed. (2nd edition coming soon!)

"A cracking read. They know their Who inside and out, and the science is impeccable. . . . They hit the bullseye every time. . . . An exceptional example of what must how be regarded as a legitimate genre."
— *The Psychologist*, British Psychological Society

"A must-read for every Whovian!" — Night Owl Reviews

"A must-read for Who fans. The diverse range of topics and indepth analysis will have you wanting to watch all the Doctors over again."
— The Beguiled Child

Also by Travis Langley

Batman and Psychology: A Dark and Stormy Knight

The Joker Psychology: Evil Clowns and the Women Who Love Them

Black Panther Psychology: Hidden Kingdoms (with Alex Simmons)

Westworld Psychology: Violent Delights (with Wind Goodfriend)

Daredevil Psychology: The Devil You Know

Supernatural Psychology: Roads Less Traveled (with Lynn Zubernis)

Star Trek Psychology: The Mental Frontier

Wonder Woman Psychology: Lassoing the Truth (with Mara Wood)

Doctor Who Psychology: A Madman with a Box

Game of Thrones Psychology: The Mind is Dark and Full of Terrors

Captain America vs. Iron Man: Freedom, Security, Psychology

Star Wars Psychology: Dark Side of the Mind

The Walking Dead Psychology: Psych of the Living Dead

STRANGER THINGS
PSYCHOLOGY

Life Upside Down

Travis Langley, Editor

WILEY

John Wiley & Sons, Inc.

John Wiley & Sons, Inc.
an imprint of Turner Publishing Company
Nashville, Tennessee
www.turnerpublishing.com

Stranger Things Psychology: Life Upside Down

Cover design by M.S. Corley
Book design by Tim Holtz

Library of Congress Control Number: 2022011184

ISBNs   9781684429080 paperback
        9781684429097 hardcover
        9781684429103 ebook

Printed in the United States of America

to Jamie Walton
and all the other survivors
who try to make this world safer
for those who need paths out of the dark

to Mike Southerland
and all who have introduced us
to strange games that connect us to others
and help us navigate through lives upside down

Contents

I. Friending

II. Fracturing

III. Missing

Acknowledgments

Our Party Members

This book's dedication honors Jamie Walton and Mike Southerland. Jamie has been an advocate for victims and a warrior combating human trafficking. A survivor herself, she became an activist committed to improving public understanding of child exploitation and the trafficking of minors, helping survivors obtain necessary services, and aiding them in their efforts to re-enter society as healthy adults. Jamie has shared her story elsewhere. Her life shows how a person can emerge from the Upside Down, fight monsters, and help others find their way out of the dark. Proceeds from the sale of *Stranger Things Psychology* will be donated to a nonprofit dedicated to rescuing and helping missing and exploited children.

As this book's introduction explains, Mike introduced me and other friends to *Dungeons & Dragons*, and D&D introduced us to much more. People who introduced some of our chapter contributors to (or helped them rediscover) such games include Kevin Casey, Mark Chmura, Fredy Desince II, Robert Duncan, Talya Johnson, Alice Manning, Matt Moran, Don Pitz, Tom Pleviak, Shawn Stone, Rusty Terry, a guy named Hans, and a few too early for our writers to recall. In *Game of Thrones Psychology: The Mind is Dark and Full of Terrors*, I recognized the fantasy adventure game's creators and the many people who played it with us at the beginning, soon after, or across the years since then. A few have left this world along the way, most recently Kevin Robbins—enthusiast of D&D, cigars, friends, family, God, and music, especially Blues Traveler. As friend and fellow gamer Craig Brown put it to Ross Taylor and myself, Kevin "was a passionate man who was argumentative often, opinionated always, lover of all things living, and, most importantly, our friend."

Chapter contributors want to recognize supportive people from their lives: Marit Appeldoom; Iris and Josh Apryasz; Brian Edward Therens; Brittney Brownfield; Hannah Espinoza; Caroline Greco and Ava Stover; Jeffrey Henderson; Katrina Hill; Jimmy Hernandez; Evelyn and Kat La Forgia; Linda Jordan; Travis Sr., Lynda, Nicholas, and Spencer Langley; Elijah Mastin; Dustin McGinnis; Samuel Kolodezh; Lalitha, Ravi, and Keshwan ("the cutest strangest thing") Malla; Angela Petersen; Bethany and Luciano "Luca" San Juan; Diane and Randy Veal; Shannon Velazquez; Amanda, Isaiah, Celeste, Ivy, Caleb, and Hannah Wesselmann; and anyone who has ever joined them in a dungeon. We also thank T. K. Coleman, Danny Fingeroth, Sharon Manning, Gail Z. Martin, Doug Jones, Fred Saberhagen, and J. R. R. Tolkien. To these names, I add my wife and best friend, Rebecca M. Langley, whose company and support I treasure beyond measure.

Because I met many of our contributors and enjoy opportunities through comic cons, I thank the organizers at Comic-Con International (Eddie Ibrahim, Gary Sassaman, Cathy Dalton, Jackie Estrada, Sue Lord, Karen Mayugba, Adam Neese, Amy Ramirez, Chris Sturhan), and many Wizard World and Fan Expo events (Kevin Boyd, Tajshen Campbell, Mike Gregorek, Peter Katz, Bruce MacIntosh, Jerry Milani, Brittany Rivera, Alex Wer). It all begins with the Comics Arts Conference, Comic-Con's conference-within-the-con, which Randy Duncan and Peter Coogan founded, Kate McClancy now chairs, and I help organize.

In addition to my regular course load teaching on the psychology of mental illness, social behavior, and crime, each spring I add something different, usually a story-focused class using film, literature, or other media as a lens through which to examine the science of real human behavior, and I remain grateful to all the students whose participation in those courses inspired me to start writing these books and prods me to carry on. I thank our faculty writers group members (Angela Boswell, Andrew Burt, Maryjane Dunn, William Henshaw, Michael Taylor, Shannon Wittig) for reviewing portions of this material. Latrena Beasley, Sandra D. Johnson, Connie Testa, *Stranger Things* fan Salina Ables, and other staffers have provided invaluable service.

The book would not exist without the efforts of my agent, Evan Gregory with the Ethan Ellenberg Literary Agency; acquisitions editor

Ryan Smernoff and other fine folks at Turner Publishing such as Claire Ong and Tim Holtz; and the countless readers and listeners of all our previous works. The great Connie Santisteban joins us as line editor this time. *Stranger Things* itself would not exist without creators Matt and Ross Duffer, their fellow executive producers Shawn Levy and Dan Cohen, and the show's impressive cast and crew. The actors' portrayals shape the characters' personalities and therefore the psyches into which we now spelunk, and the crew members behind the scenes make it all happen.

And thank you for joining us as we delve into the darkness and hopefully rise back into light as we explore life upside down, right side up, and sometimes topsy-turvy.

Emory University's Briarcliff campus in our world doubles as the fictional Hawkins Research Laboratory in *Stranger Things*. Photo by Counse (2018).

Introduction

Look for the Demogorgon

Travis Langley

Once upon a time, a friend led us into strange adventures. Maybe it happened too early in life for you to remember who got you started, but somebody first showed you the game, the story, the sport, the career, maybe the vice, or other activity that could inspire you, fill your time, and connect you with some birds of that feather. Mike Southerland, my friend since middle school, had been telling us about *Dungeons & Dragons* for two years before several of us finally got together during high school to open rulebooks, draw maps, roll unusual dice, embark on the first adventure, and find out what he'd been talking about all that time. We got hooked. For some of us, it opened up a whole new branch of social life during those years and beyond. Some would leave it behind, some would head off to college thinking they'd never play again only to land in a new campaign while making new friends, and some never let it go at all.

Your strange adventures may never have included the dungeon-crawling game that unites *Stranger Things* characters Will Byers and his friends when they're younger, then gives them language to describe the dangers they face when their world turns upside down. Nevertheless, the bonding activity of their gameplay resonates with viewers, whether from firsthand experience, personal curiosity, or relationships they yearned to have. The gameplay's the thing.

While watching the show's premiere episode and listening to characters worry about whether they might encounter the Demogorgon, a demonic enemy that should be far too powerful for the level game they were playing, I remembered Mike S. singing to the tune of an old Union Label commercial jingle, "Look for the Demogorgon!" As if on cue, Dungeon Master Mike Wheeler holds up a monstrous figurine to reveal the Demogorgon. First the creature gets Will's character within the game, and then a creature that they would name after the Demogorgon catches him on his way home—analogy with analogy as the series turns one crisis after another, great or small, into representations of the chaos in human lives, particularly the turmoil of growing up. We fight monsters out in the world, struggle with the monsters or magic within ourselves, and look for party members with whom to face it all.

Throughout this book, our contributors relate the characters' lives to human experiences, both *interpersonal* (between people) and *intrapersonal* (within the individual). The book's five sections explore characters friending, fracturing, missing, feeling, and healing. Despite common misconceptions, psychology is not only about mental health. It is the science of everything we do, normal or abnormal. It is the science of our stories. Like the characters comparing *Dungeons & Dragons* to describe events in their lives, we can apply examples from their stories to shine light upon the psychology of our own.

Our chapters' authors are therapists and professors plus one criminologist who also knows psychology, along with assistance from another expert co-author or three. We are proud to be full-time nerds even though some still wince at the memory of when the word *nerd* was uttered in junior high classrooms like it was a bad thing. Honestly, writing this kind of book makes us nerds-gone-pro. We are fans of the fantastic, this time discerning parallels between the *Stranger Things* fiction and the real psychology that fills our lives. We look for the Demogorgon, beware the Shadow Monster, and shun the villainous lich Vecna. We form strategies for how to face them no matter where we find the monsters, and we share those strategies with other players in life's adventures. You can too.

Ready to roll?

FRIENDING

–

"Friends Don't Lie"

Friendship Theory and Components

Wind Goodfriend & Andrea Frantz

"A friend is someone that you'd do anything for. You lend them your cool stuff, like comic books and trading cards, and they never break a promise. . . . Friends, they tell each other things."
—Mike to Eleven[1]

"I would rather walk with a friend in the dark, than alone in the light."
—author Helen Keller[2]

"**F**riends don't lie." *Stranger Things* teaches us a lot about bravery, trauma, and the great lengths people will go to in order to save their children or friends. One of the show's most important themes concerns the bond of friendship the main characters share. Rules such as "Friends don't lie" offer explicit reminders of how these burgeoning tweens learn to navigate their social world. The psychology of friendship is a relatively small but important area of study in developmental and social psychology.[3] What does it predict about common friendship patterns in early adolescents, and do the characters in *Stranger Things* reflect these predictions?

Research on Preadolescent Friendships

Establishing friendships with peers plays an important part in growing up. Doing so helps build independence from one's parents and becomes crucial to many children's happiness and self-esteem.[4] For most people, the number of friends we have increases significantly between the ages of ten and eighteen years.[5] Friendships really matter. One study showed that each happy friend in our lives makes us up to 15 percent happier too.[6] Within *Stranger Things*, friendships among Mike, Lucas, Dustin, and Will mature and become more complex. They grow to know, love, and admire new friends such as Eleven, Max, and even Steve. The dynamics shown in this group seem realistic as they argue, make up, and go through shared experiences.

The group's members express explicit awareness of their friendship system, as evidenced by their frequent discussions of how their "party" has its rules: Friends don't lie, friends keep promises, they never leave a friend behind, and they never betray the group's secrets to an outsider. These rules are so explicit that they even have follow-up rules for how to make up for breaches: Whoever has started the breach ("drew first blood") needs to apologize and extend their hand for a handshake. If your friend forgives you, they will shake. (Spitting on your hand first seals the bond even more.)[7]

This type of rule system commonly develops in friendships, both fictional and nonfictional. Psychological research on preadolescent friendships offers additional insight into what we should see throughout the series as the characters share good times and bad times. An important study[8] that explored the psychology of preadolescent friendships set out to identify typical dimensions and rules that arise among friendships at this age. The researchers conducted interviews with boys and girls, asking them to describe the types of expectations and benefits they maintain with their friends. A second group of psychologists[9] coded the children's answers for themes, identifying five key components for preadolescent friendships. All five components are highly visible within the friendship world of *Stranger Things*.

Component 1: Companionship

While companionship can mean different things depending on the context, within friendship theory *companionship* refers to spending time together voluntarily in playful activities. Children who talked about this component of young friendship in research studies[10] mentioned coming up with fun things to do together, going to each other's houses on weekends and evenings, or simply sitting around talking about mutual interests and their lives. From the first episode of *Stranger Things*, it's clear that companionship reigns as a central feature of the kids' friendship.

Playing *Dungeons & Dragons*, biking around town, playing games at the arcade,[11] and trick-or-treating together on Halloween all demonstrate the companionship component of their friendship. One part of companionship is simply the exchange of play. As Mike first gets to know Eleven, he shows her his action figures, dinosaurs, and even how to make their own fun with the La-Z-Boy recliner.[12] At this age, play and the simple pleasure of shared laughter are important parts of making new friends (as Mike and Eleven do) and of maintaining established friendships (as the boys do).

A critical part of companionship at this age involves making sure every member of the friendship group has an important and mutually respected *role* (set of behaviors expected of their position within a setting or group). Friends work together in their respective roles to function together as a team. For example, they work together to prepare tools, weapons, and rations so they can search the woods for Will,[13] or to create a disguise for Eleven so they can take her to school.[14] Everyone contributes to the effort. When they play *Dungeons & Dragons*, members' roles are even more explicit. Locked into categorizing the players' game characters by specific rules-defined roles such as fighter, wizard, and rogue, Mike tells Max there's no room for a "zoomer"[15] (though his perspective on that will mature, expand, and grow). Such teamwork is often needed to solve larger problems, as they must rely on one another to work out how to accomplish a variety of tasks that would be insurmountable without the help of friends—understanding the world of the Upside Down, destroying the Demodogs, and so on.[16]

As the kids grow up, this aspect of their friendship is threatened (which tends to happen in real life as personalities mature, interests change, experiences diverge, roles are outgrown, and other relationships begin). Each character develops independent interests and friendships outside the group. Will sees the weakening of their companionship as Mike and Lucas want to spend time with their girlfriends. He confronts them when they show less interest in *Dungeons & Dragons*, which represents changes common to many childhood friends. Once Mike and Lucas recognize how hurt Will is in that moment, they apologize and make efforts to show they value time with him. When Lucas later joins the basketball team, Dustin and Mike are the ones who feel abandoned, as does Lucas when they don't go to his championship game, and yet Lucas still works to protect and help them despite this apparent rift.[17]

Component 2: Closeness

Closeness refers to how friends feel acceptance, validation, and emotional attachment toward each other.[18] One way to establish and maintain closeness between friends is to exchange *self-disclosures*: telling each other intimate, secret, personal information. When Mike and Eleven are first getting to know each other, she asks him about a cut under his chin.[19] At first he claims he had an accident, but when Eleven says, "Friends tell the truth," he admits he was bullied at school. She solidifies their friendship by simply telling him she understands, helping him feel that she will not judge him negatively for being an outsider. (Nevertheless, she neither discloses the fact that she was previously bullied by other psychic kids in Dr. Brenner's project nor later admits when high schoolers bully her in California—concealments that may hinder feelings of closeness.[20])

Importantly, research on the closeness factor of adolescent friendships finds that friends frequently engage in mutual affirmation of each other's importance and value. There are many instances when the boys validate each other, and this component of friendship is key to the close bond that Mike and Eleven continue to form. Eleven affirms Mike's value after he confesses that he was bullied, and Mike reciprocates on several occasions. When El shows concern about her appearance, as many young girls do, he tells her she's pretty even without makeup or a blond wig.[21] More importantly, Mike assures Eleven that she is not a monster and that she saved them all.[22] This view of herself as a savior may become a self-fulfilling prophecy for Eleven, one that later helps her choose between a life of vengeance versus one of love and friendship.[23] Even when Mike thinks she might be dead, he tries to contact her every day for almost a year.[24]

Max and Lucas solidify their friendship and trust in each other when Max reveals the reasons she and her family moved to Hawkins and the troubled relationships she has with her brother and stepfather.[25] A pivotal point in their relationship occurs when Lucas tells Max all about Will's disappearance and the Upside Down.[26] At first, she thinks he's lying because the story seems too fantastic to be real. This prompts her to cut off the possibility of friendship, clearly showing that closeness and confidences go hand in hand. When she eventually realizes he has told the truth, breaking a rule with the rest of the party in order to welcome her, their friendship is cemented.

Component 3: Security

Mike's assurance to Eleven that she is a savior, not a monster, could also fit into psychologists' third component of preadolescent friendships: *security*, an understanding among friends that they share a "reliable alliance."[27] Children interviewed about security noted that they expect friends to be there for each other if one is having trouble at school or at home. This aspect of friendship is all about trust. *Stranger Things* features many examples of trust among the friends, and their mutual safety and security often depend on that trust.

One way the boys show such trust is that they don't often doubt each other. When Dustin tells them all, at first seemingly at random, to get out their compasses immediately, they do so without asking why.[28] They implicitly trust one another to keep secrets from outsiders, which causes trouble when Lucas self-discloses secrets to Max without the party's permission.[29] Even the adults in the show establish the trust factor within their own friendships, as Hopper and Joyce reciprocally request the benefit of the doubt: "C'mon, how about a little trust here?"[30]

"Friends don't lie" sits at the heart of trust and security. Doubt can drive a wedge between friends, disrupting this component of friendship theory. This happens when Mike implicitly trusts Eleven's claim that Will is lost in the Upside Down, until they find the "body." He is so upset at her perceived betrayal that he yells at her until she provides proof. After this incident, he trusts El and the security of their friendship.

Component 4: Help

The fourth component of friendship, *help*, overlaps in some ways with previous components, such as security and closeness, but is primarily composed of two parts. First, in preadolescent friendships, help includes *aid*, being there when a friend needs you for any reason. Aid arises almost immediately in *Stranger Things* as Mike, Lucas, and Dustin dedicate themselves to finding Will after he disappears. In fact, Lucas believes the appearance of Eleven poses a distraction from helping Will, and he seems to resent her for this reason.[31] Help appears to cover at least one explicit rule the boys have worked out, as Dustin invokes "Code Red" to signal the need for help later (and then feels frustrated by a lack of response, indicating his assumption that his friends would be there for him).[32]

The second part of help is *protection from victimization*.[33] Children interviewed about this aspect of friendship noted that true friends stick up for each other when someone else bullies or bothers them. This aspect of friendship is most evident when Troy victimizes Mike, Dustin, Lucas, and Will at school. When they cannot prevent Troy's bullying from happening, they can at least provide comfort and support afterward.[34] Even more importantly, they directly help one another when possible. This means teaching bullies very public lessons[35] and even potentially sacrificing their own safety (such as Mike jumping off a high cliff) to save a friend.[36]

Component 5: Conflict

It might be surprising to think of friendship as involving *conflict*, and yet that is the fifth component identified by psychological research. Children asked to describe aspects of real friendship noted that conflict is a salient and frequent aspect of their peer relationships.[37] Preteen participants provided an insightful response during interviews: What makes friendships different from other peer relationships is the ability to overcome conflict when it arises and to have the confidence that disagreements—or even fights—won't be the end of a friendship. The young characters in *Stranger Things* display this attitude on several occasions.

Throughout the series, they are willing to point out when they think a member of the party is making a bad decision. Lucas may be the most vocal, as he confronts the others about everything from appearing less dedicated to finding Will[38] to wondering if he's assigned the role of Ghostbuster Winston for Halloween just because of race.[39] Importantly, these conflicts occur frequently, but the boys don't seem particularly concerned that any of the conflicts will permanently end their friendship bond. They know arguments and differences in perspective are accepted in the group. As mentioned before, the party has established rituals for ending conflict through expressions of caring and support, such as mutual handshakes.

Growing Up

The timing of friendship patterns matters. Before adolescence, parent/child relationships are the most important social pairings. Same-sex friendships matter through early childhood and peak in importance just before puberty—but then sexual interest complicates matters.[40] For heterosexual children, cross-sex friendships become complicated by the possibility of attraction in this new, confusing way.

The Complication of Sex

The perplexing social rules of attraction are important to *Stranger Things* when Max moves to town. Two of the boys in the friendship group (Lucas and Dustin) feel their bond strain as they initially compete for her attention and affection, and Eleven becomes jealous of any time Mike spends with Max. In addition, Eleven and Mike struggle with how to show their deepening feelings for each other, unsure whether the other person will return their interest. Getting closer to puberty and adolescence also adds potential sexual attraction into the social interaction mix, adding another complication.[41] The introduction of a girl within a group of boys builds tension, and this happens with both Eleven and Max. The boys struggle with whether girls are "allowed" in the party and with what early romance means for the dynamics among the boys themselves. Same-sex friendships deepen as both the boys and the girls bond over newly discovered differences. Lucas sagely claims that "women are a different species" to comfort and reassure Mike, and Eleven and Max laugh uproariously over the boys' burping and farting when they think they are in private. (Older teens connect similarly, as Robin asserts regarding Nancy and herself, "Us ladies will stick together," adding a taunt to the guys, "Unless you think we need you to protect us.")[42]

Will seems to struggle with sexuality in his own way. He struggles to maintain the bond with his male friends when he declares a "day without girls" and shows a lack of understanding in their interest in kissing.[43] His guilt, grief, and isolation lead him to destroy Castle Byers as he calls himself "stupid," underscoring his confusion about relationships on which he has previously relied. Will's sexual orientation remains to be seen at that point, but peers insensitively judge him for not showing more interest in girls and some tease him on an assumption that he may be gay.[44] Sexuality matters for the young adults in the series as well. When Robin tells Steve she is gay and not interested in him romantically, he accepts that—and her—and their status as friends becomes stronger than ever.[45]

Adult Friendships

Friendships in adulthood have rules of their own regarding needs such as consistent affection, respect, and communication.[46] As *Stranger Things* progresses, the friendship between Joyce Byers and Jim Hopper also grows. They have been friends for years, starting with the shared experience of smoking between classes in high school.[47] Their bond is strengthened when they must work together first to save Will, then Hawkins, then the world, but becomes most personal when Joyce invades a Russian prison despite all odds to bring Hopper back from the dead, to bring him home.[48] Research shows that as we age, our friendship network gets smaller (i.e., we have fewer friends), but the ones we maintain tend to be of high quality.[49] It is certainly possible for heterosexual adult men and women to be close friends in adulthood, but this possibility works best when each is single and doesn't have potentially jealous partners.[50]

Joyce and Hopper's relationship evolves from a platonic friendship into something romantic as they show vulnerability to each other.[51] Hopper invites Joyce to dinner, claiming explicitly that it is not a date—but when Joyce fails to show, he angrily notes the next day that he felt stood up.[52] Hopper reminds Joyce of their shared history, both traumatic and not, which places them squarely in that small network of high-quality friendships.[53] Joyce addresses the dating question on her own terms by inviting him to dinner and calling it an official date, a plan thwarted by his seeming death.[54] The name of the restaurant from the non-date she missed, Enzo's, comes to represent Hopper's rescue from the land of the dead and a prison in the ice, as well as their reunion.[55]

The Importance of Friends

"You said, 'the happiness of your friends.' So does that make us friends, as in officially?"
—Nancy to Robin[56]

The friendships of the young characters in *Stranger Things* appear strong and healthy, and they display all five of the components of friendship identified by psychological researchers. When psychologists[57] asked middle-schoolers to complete a questionnaire measuring all five components in their current friendships, they found that conflict was the factor most likely to end a friendship, but also that friendships with higher quality on all five subscales, even conflict, were the most likely to last over time. They also noted that high-quality friendships provided the opportunity for children to develop in healthy directions and have higher well-being in general.

Researchers further found that there are strong positive correlations among all five components in the closest friendships.[58] This means that within a given friendship, if it's high in companionship, closeness, security, help, or conflict, then it's also likely to be high in the other four factors. Maybe this particular constellation of factors is what determines which friendships become more central to our lives, compared to other more peripheral social bonds. It's clear that the boys have chosen one another as their primary social companions, as their friendship has high levels of all five components. And maybe Mike is right when he tells Dustin it's possible to have more than one "best" friend,[59] as long as everyone in your life who falls in this category honors the five components described here. We should all be so lucky to be surrounded by a party of brave, loyal, and helpful companions. These are our true friends, and they are our home.

"I'm going to my friends. I'm going home."
—Eleven[60]

Wind Goodfriend, PhD, is a professor of psychology, director of the gender studies program, and chair of social sciences at Buena Vista University in Storm Lake, Iowa. She earned her bachelor's degree there, then her master's and PhD in social psychology from Purdue University. Dr. Goodfriend has won the "Faculty of the Year" award at BVU several times. Two of her textbooks each won the "Most Promising Book of the Year" award by the Textbook and Academic Authors Association.

Andrea Frantz, PhD, is a professor of digital media and serves as national executive director of the Society for Collegiate Journalists. She earned her bachelor's degree at Simpson College in Indianola, Iowa, and completed both her master's and PhD degrees in rhetoric and professional communication at Iowa State University. She has won numerous teaching and advising awards, including the national College Media Association Louis Ingelhart Award for First Amendment advocacy.

2

Navigating the Upside Down

Nonnormative and Typical Adolescent Development

Harpreet Malla & Erin Currie

*"People don't spend their lives trying to get a look
at what's behind the curtain. They like the curtain.
It provides them stability, comfort, definition."*
—Murray Bauman[1]

*"Adolescents are not monsters. They are just people trying to learn
how to make it among the adults in the world, who are probably
not so sure themselves."*
—psychotherapist Virginia Satir[2]

The people of Hawkins deny complicated truths about government activity, the Upside Down, and even their own adolescents' awkwardness. Adolescence is commonly a time of significant transition as puberty changes the body, which impacts how people think, feel, and behave. To add to the challenges, cultures carry traditions, norms, and rules about sexual behavior.[3] Cultural standards and rules become apparent by puberty, are heavily influenced by gender, and may involve double standards or illogical equivalences.[4] The whole process becomes more complicated when adults and teens are afraid of having honest conversations about changes during puberty. For teens who do not follow what is considered to be a typical pattern of development, it can be even scarier because they are less likely to get accurate information about their experiences and more likely to feel unnecessarily alone or "abnormal," when in fact they are neither. Emotional and social changes that occur around puberty and emerging sexuality affect the youths of Hawkins both figuratively and literally as they battle the monsters of the Upside Down.

Puberty and Sexuality

When the *Stranger Things* story begins, Eleven and the boys who befriend her are all about twelve years old. They are going through the beginning phases of *puberty*, the physical process that takes us from childhood to adulthood. Along with the visible changes to the body, there are also changes in the brain that impact how we feel and what we do. Testosterone, estrogen, and adrenaline spike during this period and level out later in adulthood. The brain becomes more responsive to physical and emotional excitement and peer approval,[5] especially approval by peers who could be sexual or romantic interests.

With Mike directing his friends as their Dungeon Master while playing *Dungeons & Dragons* (D&D), the boys immerse themselves in this co-created play space, each with their own roles, working together to battle imaginary monsters as they complete their quest.[6] Creating same-sex friend groups based on similar interests occurs commonly across cultures.[7] Yet the same episode hints at the beginnings of romantic feelings or sexual interests as Dustin goes out of his way to take the last slice of their pizza to Mike's older sister, Nancy, who shuts the door in his face. Later in the season, Mike and Eleven share their first kiss, even though Mike has been adamantly denying to his friends that he has feelings for Eleven when they try to exclude her from their friend group.[8] Uncertainty, stress, and confusion are common as members of a peer group experience the physical, emotional, and social changes of puberty at different rates,[9] and new relationships can further challenge the friendship status quo.[10]

The fact that these shifts often come with some embarrassment and self-consciousness makes them even harder to address as direct communication is avoided.

Enmeshed with the changes of body and mind are the changes in social roles and expectations. In the United States and other places, social roles and expectations are commonly based on a *heterosexual script* that includes different expectations and norms for how men and women behave.[11] In order to make her blend in at school, the boys find stereotypic trappings—makeup, a pink dress, and a blond shoulder-length wig—for Eleven to wear. The boys' reactions of speechlessness and renewed awkwardness show that they are seeing Eleven in a new light: as an attractive girl. Even Eleven, who grew up in a lab, is interested in being perceived as pretty.[12] The awe and awkwardness show the degree of change in how the boys see her, even though the changes occur over the course of minutes and are visible on the surface.

As characters progress into their teens, they display some of the more dramatic shifts in emotional response to romantic and sexual interest. Lucas and Dustin compete for Max's attention and romantic interest.[13] Their focus on Max includes watching her from a distance using binoculars, figuring out her schedule, and finding out where she goes.[14] From a biological perspective, the lack of a fully grown prefrontal cortex during puberty means their ability to see the world from someone else's perspective isn't fully developed. Neither is their impulse control, which could be why they continue their behaviors even after Max calls them "stalkers" to their faces.[15] Their behavior follows the heterosexual script, in which men are supposed to compete and win women's attention, and women are passive objects to be won, without much consideration of a woman's feelings about the man.[16]

Boys aren't the only ones behaving poorly due to competitiveness, possessiveness, and heterosexual scripts. Upon seeing Mike hanging out with Max, Eleven uses uses her psychic power to knock Max off her skateboard when a twinge of jealousy hits.[17] Eleven's sudden jealousy response showcases the changes in the teenage brain that strengthen emotions such as anger and insecurity.[18] Nancy feels punished for having sex with Steve while Barb was in danger,[19] and perhaps again with Jonathan.[20] This would be a violation of the heterosexual script's "good girl" tenet that it is okay for men to have sex outside of marriage, but good women must either be chaste or have sex only in a monogamous romantic relationship.[21] Nancy feels shamed by her friend Barb's obvious disapproval,[22] and later is very publicly called a "slut" by Steve's friends, one of whom is also female.[23] The heterosexual script gets reinforced by both men and women through social shaming.[24]

By season three, Mike and Eleven spend much of their time together "making out" and making Hopper, Eleven's adoptive father, anxious and angry. Meanwhile, Joyce, the parent of a teen boy rather than girl, seems okay with Nancy sleeping over with Jonathan.[25] This could simply be reflective of the heterosexual script that normalizes men seeking out sex due to an assumed higher sex drive as a result of testosterone, or it could reflect developmental considerations based on age. Nancy and Jonathan are eighteen years old at this point, therefore adults by US legal standards, whereas Mike and Eleven are in their early teens. So Hopper, like many parents, feels the need to protect Eleven, likely because he's familiar with the heterosexual script that promotes early and active sexuality for boys and punishes women for the same thing.[26]

Caution

Behaviors such as excluding girls and some of the "stalking"[27] the boys engage in can be easy to dismiss as immature or awkward simply because we know that Mike, Lucas, and Dustin are young and oblivious but have good intentions. Some of what they do will follow common patterns we see as children negotiate the physical, emotional, and social changes of puberty. However, some boys don't grow out of these behaviors, and this can have significant consequences. Women in industries such as gaming and computer programming often report higher levels of discrimination and hostility in the workplace than do grown men in these same industries.[28] In its greatest extreme, research on the "incel" (involuntary celibate) movement shows that some self-proclaimed "good guys" objectify and dehumanize women to the point that it leads to violence when denied the female attention to which they feel entitled.[29]

Embracing Diversity

Despite many considerations involved in a typical sexual development process, a number of characters follow developmental patterns deemed nonnormative in 1983 Hawkins, Indiana. For example, although Will Byers is the last in the group who still doesn't have a romantic partner, he nevertheless experiences struggles navigating his evolving teen friend group. When Mike and Lucas have been dumped by Eleven and Max and are obsessing over the "other species" to decode their behavior, Will simply wants to play a game of *Dungeons & Dragons*. He persists in trying to lift his friends' spirits, but they ignore his attempts at cheer and tease him instead. He feels left out when teased for wanting to play a game that once bonded them together (and later brokenhearted over feelings unrequited).[30] Before Dustin meets Suzie, Steve tries to protect his younger friend from the perils of dating by saying, "She's only gonna break your heart, and you're way too young for that."[31] Dustin feels excluded as he watches his peers Lucas and Mike move forward in the dating game without him. This feeling of rejection is commonplace in "late bloomers," who may delay their entry into the dating world for a variety of reasons: intentional choice, risk-aversive feelings in the risky business of love, the need to heal from trauma that disrupted their development, or a lack of opportunity in their peer or social group. Their development may be complicated simply by being different from the norm, which can be the case for queer or asexual folk.

A helpful concept in visualizing development that is outside the norm is psychologist/sex therapist Vivienne Cass's *identity model* of development.[32] In this model, anyone who doesn't follow the normative or majority development of puberty experiences *identity confusion*, a period of discomfort in which individuals recognize that they differ from others' expectations for opposite-sex love. They can then compare themselves to their peers and see how they stack up in *identity comparison*, as Dustin does with Steve in trying to approximate his desirability. After simply accepting oneself as different, an individual may experience *identity tolerance*, a time in which an individual admits to *themselves* they are different—as we see Will painfully acknowledge when he destroys Castle Byers.[33] Will's quip, "Welcome to my world," reflects his views regarding his second-class status as a non-coupled person as he and recently dumped Mike are relegated to the back of the station wagon.[34] Will grieves the loss of his identity as "Will the Wise," feeling like the party member others are starting to leave behind, left out for not moving along with the crushes and opposite-sex dalliances that Lucas, Max, Eleven, Mike, and even "Dusty-Buns" have.

Hopefully, with social support and self-acceptance, individuals can move healthily into *identity acceptance* in which they increase contact with their own community while also finding ways to feel supported in the mainstream community.[35] A great depiction of this is the ease with which Robin and Steve's relationship snaps back into a snarky back-and-forth after Robin expresses to Steve that she has feelings for women. After a simple clarifying remark ("But she's a girl?"),[36] Steve finally understands Robin, then simply accepts her and moves on. It can be difficult to "come out" for many, and this stage is the healthiest that many individuals reach. Coming out is a complex, case-by-case decision that should involve considerations such as trust, timing, consequences, identity validity, and safety—a process Will may be initiating with his brother as he builds trust in their relationship.[37]

Identity pride, a stage that not everyone reaches in the queer identity development process, requires an environment supportive enough that an individual is able to feel positively about their membership as a queer individual and may even engage in activism efforts. *Identity synthesis* differs from this as the sharp dichotomy between "queer" and "straight" dissolves, allowing for a more nuanced view of sexuality and identity across settings and life stages without downplaying its importance. Robin explores her identity and how to honor it in small-town Hawkins, Indiana, where she fears potential rejection and becoming "a town pariah."[38]

Different people develop at different rates. When peers' relationship interests make him feel left out, it is possible that Will simply hasn't reached the stage of puberty at which sexual attraction occurs. However, at that point, it is also possible that his development has been delayed due to his repeated trauma in facing and hosting the Shadow Monster. Will's flashbacks, nightmares, and a desire to initially run from anything related to the Upside Down are all consistent with symptoms of *post-traumatic stress disorder*.[39] People grappling with survival or crisis are often distracted from pursuing the pleasures of life that others who aren't focused on survival are able to strive for.[40] When Will experiences regular disturbances he hasn't grown up with, his reactions are more detrimental to him than Eleven's are to her. She grew up in an environment where darkness such as that of the Shadow Monster, although scary, was more normalized by her "Papa." In either case, allowing the individual to set their own timelines for relationship and sexual milestones is the best thing for professionals, parents, and peers to do.

Fans have speculated that for the younger Byers brother may be *asexual*, a sexual orientation in which an individual rarely or never experiences sexual attraction or desire regardless of whether they may or may not engage in physical sexual activity for other reasons. Asexual individuals can also experience other forms of interpersonal attraction even without sexual interest, which could be the case even as Will's feelings for Mike are shifting from simple friendship to include aching for romance.[41] Psychological and health sciences research have shown that this orientation can be functional and healthy. Like real individuals who identify as gay or asexual, Will may face some unique challenges in their peer groups. While the excitement of dating, courtship, and sex commonly kick in during the teen years, those who never experience it can feel like they are being left out or made fun of when their peers share experiences completely foreign to them. The pressure to pretend to enjoy heteronormative or dating-adjacent activities may push some to act out of alignment with who they truly are, leaving them feeling worse than before. The difficulty explaining their preferences or attitudes toward sex and dating can be a complicated task requiring self-esteem and a foundational knowledge of how to describe one's emotional experience around sex and dating, so a number of individuals consider never coming out at all. When someone is lucky enough to be accepted by their peer group regardless of their differences from them, they are able to express themselves more fully. Feeling a sense of belonging, they can cultivate meaningful, close relationships based on mutual trust, shared interests and activities, and commitment to the bond, whether with a sexual flair or not.[42]

The importance of not being consumed by new romance, although the initial bubbly stages of love (termed *limerence*[43]) make that tempting, is apparent among the teens of Hawkins. When the bubble of bliss bursts for El and Mike after he breaks their cardinal friendship rule of not lying, it is Max who saves the day with a trip to the mall. That helps Eleven connect with peer support and "zoom out" enough to gain perspective that there is more to her at this point than romance with Mike.[44] Similarly, the boys bond over their frustrations in "decoding" the girls and trying to find healthy ways to communicate about more complex topics when the stakes of a romantic relationship and trust are on the line. Successfully navigating transitions of any kind, including transitions from childhood to adulthood and friendship love to romantic love, rely on balance.[45]

As arguably the most sex-positive character in the show shows us in his own lovably direct way, Murray Bauman helps people go beyond their insecurities, self-doubt, and hesitancy to reveal their deeper feelings for one another—with Nancy and Jonathan[46] and again later with Joyce and Hopper.[47] While the rest of the town shies away from complicated truths about the government's involvement in experiments gone wrong with the Upside Down, and avoids seemingly obvious truths regarding their love lives, Murray acts as a champion of truth and a paragon of healthy communication. Without his not-so-gentle nudges and frank assessment of the situation, it's hard to know how long some of the more shy, hesitant residents of Hawkins would take to confess their true feelings or act upon them.

In It Together

Ultimately, whether the residents of Hawkins, Indiana, battle hormones, dating dilemmas, or Demogorgons, they find ways to help one another with advice and to provide space to vent and not feel so alone. Although the changes of adolescence can be challenging and even scary, knowing what you are facing ahead of time and having people who support you can make all the difference. Denying the complicated truths of adolescence and sexual development can leave a person vulnerable to societal monsters like shame, isolation, and victimization. However, talking about it all can give us the tools we need to win our battles. Having proper access to information and education about adolescence and sexual development is as key as the right roll of twenty-sided dice in *D&D*, as is the party or company you keep. Those whose development, gender expression, or sexual attractions are perceived as different from cultural scripts especially need information, connection, and support. Just as they come together to defeat the town's other-worldly monsters, the heroes of Hawkins get through the trials and tribulations of first kisses, unrequited attractions, and fear of being rejected by doing it together. They allow themselves time to enjoy the meaningful connections they cultivate along the way as they fight their individual battles, romantic or not.

> *"If we're both going crazy, we'll go crazy together, right?"*
> —Mike to Will[48]

> *"I think we're mad fools, the lot of us, but if we don't stop him,*
> *who will? We have to try, right?"*
> —Robin to Steve[49]

Harpreet Malla, PhD, a licensed clinical psychologist practicing in Southern California, works with identity development as it pertains to LGBTQ, bicultural, or immigrant populations. Recently she has seen a rise in couples navigating arranged or other nontraditional marital practices in her work such as poly constellations, "kink" practices, and interracial relationships. She serves as diversity chair for the Los Angeles County Psychological Association, where she advocates for marginalized groups and seeks to promote understanding through education.

Erin Currie, PhD, LP, is a counseling psychologist who is driven to use her psychology superpowers for good. By day, she teaches college students at the University of Portland about how their brains work, why they sometimes don't, and how to develop personal and interpersonal superpowers. By night, she gives her inner geek free reign to write about the psychological factors influencing her favorite characters and adventures. She has written for other Popular Culture Psychology books, including *Game of Thrones Psychology*, *Doctor Who Psychology*, *Wonder Woman Psychology*, *Supernatural Psychology*, and *Westworld Psychology*.

Sexual vs. Romantic Orientation
Sex, Love, and Differing Intimacy Needs
Travis Langley

Can Will Byers be both asexual and gay? Despite his heartbreak over Mike's passion for El, yes. Will's unrequited love does not establish sexual interest before season five. Even though actor Noah Schnapp, who plays Byers, confirms that "Will is gay and he does love Mike,"[50] numerous fans perceive Will as asexual. As one put it, "Homoromantic asexual Will Byers just keeps getting stronger."[51]

Whereas *sexual orientation* indicates the gender or genders to which a person feels sexually attracted, *romantic orientation* refers to the gender(s) with which someone wants a loving or romantic relationship.[52] For example, one *pansexual* person whose sexual activity is unrelated to partners' gender might wish to share a life only with someone of a specific gender—perhaps *heteroromantic* (wanting the "opposite sex"), perhaps *homoromantic* (wanting same-sex love). Likewise, a person can long for an intimate and loving, yet nonsexual, companion.

Hollywood largely fails at depicting asexuality without compromising it. Whether asexual, graysexual, sexual but hiding it, or sexual later than peers, Will does not want to be alone. He fears isolation and worries about rejection. Other people can make it difficult to feel good about oneself or even safe.[53] Acceptance from key figures, allies such as Will's older brother, can help.[54]

3

The Upside (and Downside) of Being Social

Eric D. Wesselmann

*"A party member requires assistance,
and it is our duty to provide that assistance."*
—Dustin Henderson[1]

*"Love and belonging might seem like a convenience we can live
without, but our biology is built to thirst for connection because
it is linked to our most basic survival needs."*
—social neuroscientist Matthew D. Lieberman[2]

Many strange things happen in Hawkins, Indiana, but some of the most engaging events take place in the characters' daily lives, in the ups and downs of their interpersonal relationships. Whether someone grows up in a small town in the middle of Indiana (like Lucas Sinclair) or comes from the sunny, coastal state of California (like "zoomer" Max Mayfield), people share one thing in common with almost everyone else in the world: They need other people. Social psychologists have often, sometimes flippantly, referred to the human being as the *social animal*. But what does this mean psychologically?

Matthew Lieberman, a social neuroscientist and philosopher, has argued that humans' social orientation is an adaptation: The natural selection process helped us develop brains that were hardwired to forge stable connections with others and to form groups that would help individual members survive and ultimately develop the complex cultures we have today.[3] For the citizens of Hawkins, social relationships help them survive the deadly assault of Demogorgons, the arrival of Demodogs, the machinations of the Mind Flayer, and the manipulations of Vecna. Individually, none of the protagonists would likely have survived more than a few encounters with these monsters. However, these characters' relationships provide more than just practical support against demonic onslaught. Their friendships and familial bonds provide them with psychological resources to navigate the complexities of daily life, whether these events are mundane or truly strange.

The Benefits of Belonging to a Party

In the *Dungeons & Dragons*-style campaign called "life," we need party members to help us complete our quests successfully. Social psychologists Roy Baumeister and Mark Leary famously argued that people have an inherent *need* to belong—not just a preference or desire, but an ingrained need that *must* be satisfied for someone to be physically and psychologically healthy.[4] Regular social contacts play part in satisfying this need, but they are not sufficient by themselves. While growing up, even though Eleven has regular contact with Dr. Brenner and his staff during the experiments at the Hawkins National Laboratory, these interactions are not known to be positive, emotionally supportive events for the most part. Eleven is objectified and used as an experimental subject rather than valued for her inherent worth as a human being. Based on her traumatic flashbacks throughout the series and her delayed social development,[5] her need for belonging does not appear to have been satisfied by Dr. Brenner and his associates.

The key aspect for satisfying one's need to belong involves quality over quantity. One does not need many social connections to be psychologically satisfied. Rather, a person tends to need a few stable, intimate relationships that provide social support for dealing with the challenges of life.[6] Multiple studies have established that available social support is a key variable in coping with various stressors, especially traumas involving oneself or loved ones.[7] In *Stranger Things*, whether threats come from the Upside Down, from mundane sources such as Sara Hopper's terminal illness, or from government agents hunting Eleven, social support remains crucial to the characters' well-being.

Joyce Byers provides a great example of the various ways that social support can help someone navigate traumatic stress. She receives *social support*—any type of verbal or nonverbal behavior focused on helping someone in need[8]—from some people but not others, both during Will's disappearance and after his return. Supportive behaviors fall into four basic categories: instrumental, informational, appraisal, and emotional.[9] *Instrumental* support involves giving someone practical help with a situation, such as when Joyce's boss provides her with a paycheck advance.[10] *Informational* support involves giving someone advice that may help them deal with their situation, such as when Chief Hopper shares his experience of parental trauma and how to navigate it.[11] *Appraisal* support involves helping the person evaluate the situation, such as by giving constructive feedback or affirming the person's beliefs or coping behaviors. Bob Newby does this by assuring Joyce that her anxiety when Will is out with friends is understandable, validating her feelings rather than dismissing them.[12] Finally, *emotional* support focuses on providing empathy, love, and reassurance to the individual, which Karen Wheeler does verbally when visiting Joyce after Will's disappearance and telling her that she is there for her in any way she needs. Hopper offers Joyce nonverbal emotional support when hugging her while she grieves Bob's death.[13]

Hopper demonstrates how a lack of social support can be detrimental for coping with trauma. He is often shown seeking solitude instead of solace when coping with his own grief. In his flashbacks to Sara's illness, he is shown crying in a hospital stairwell alone rather than with his wife, who is also at the hospital and also in pain.[14] In early episodes, Hopper purposefully avoids talking about Sara's death directly and seems to distance himself emotionally.[15] Eleven lives in his cabin for a year before he finally mentions Sara.[16] After government agents kill his friend Benny (staging it as a suicide), Hopper spends time alone outside in the cold and resists the coaxing from his date Sandra to come back inside.[17] Occasionally seeking solitude when dealing with negative circumstances can be beneficial psychologically and is preferable sometimes to dealing with potentially awkward social interactions, but those who withdraw too much may deprive themselves of social support resources that relationships provide.[18] *Solitude-seeking* seems to be a common coping mechanism for Hopper, who regularly suffers in silence.

Many studies have linked trauma to subsequent substance use (especially depressants and painkillers) and *misuse*, the latter typically defined as excessive, potentially harmful, and often repeated usage of substances in ways that do not align with medical or general usage.[19] Hopper fits this description. Early in the series, beer cans clutter various rooms of his trailer. He even takes his morning medication with beer.[20] As the series progresses, he talks increasingly more to Joyce and to Eleven about Sara's death. Alcohol seems to become less of a staple for him, and he even tries to eat more healthily.[21] Given that studies suggest social support can be a helpful factor in reducing substance misuse, it is reasonable to assume the burgeoning support network he develops with Joyce and Eleven is helping him negotiate his trauma.[22]

Excluded from the Party

Unfortunately, not all the interpersonal interactions within Hawkins are positive and supportive. Indeed, many of the younger main characters are unpopular among their peers. This difference in social status manifests in various stressful ways, such as when middle-school bullies call Mike, Lucas, and Dustin hurtful names (e.g., "Frogface").[23] Psychologists use the term *social exclusion* as a broad category for any type of behavior in a social interaction that makes someone feel physically or emotionally separated from others.[24] These diverse experiences share a variety of negative psychological outcomes, from hurt feelings and anger to lower self-esteem, a threatened sense of belonging, and even perceptions that life is meaningless.[25] Neuroscience research has demonstrated that social exclusion activates pain-focused brain regions usually active when someone experiences a physical injury, which suggests that people's brains literally experience social exclusion as pain.[26] Findings indicate that exclusion has a stronger impact on children and adolescents than on adults.[27] Thus, although the adults in Hawkins may be aware of the exclusion the young members of their community face, they likely underestimate its full impact. Counter to the popular saying adults often tell their children, it is not just "sticks and stones" that young people must be concerned about. Broken hearts can hurt just as much as, if not more than, broken bones.

Social exclusion behaviors can be divided into two types: rejection-focused and ostracism-focused.[28] *Rejection-focused* behaviors involve verbal or nonverbal cues that explicitly communicate that someone is devalued socially and unwanted. This communication could manifest as direct statements, such as when the middle-school bullies call Dustin and the others "losers," Lucas calls Eleven a "weirdo," or Nancy Wheeler tells Steve Harrington their love is "bullshit."[29] Other research finds that hurtful jokes and mean-spirited laughter can make people feel excluded.[30] Will and his friend endure laughter and jokes at their expense when they discover they are the only ones in Halloween costumes at school and El later suffers more vicious rejection, pranks, and mockery by schoolmates in California.[31]

There are times when people can feel excluded not because of negative attention but by a lack of attention, such as when Will's father skips out on their planned outing and does not seem to take much notice of him generally, or Steve and Nancy kiss at her locker and momentarily forget that Jonathan Byers (who has a crush on Nancy) is standing there.[32] *Ostracism-focused* social exclusion is characterized mainly by the experience of being ignored or otherwise treated as if one does not exist. The unique existential threat of being ignored relates to the truism that "bad attention is better than no attention." Indeed, some data suggest that being completely ignored hurts worse than direct negative attention, such as an insult.[33]

"No more fiendish punishment could be devised," argued early psychologist William James, "than that one should be turned loose in society and remain absolutely unnoticed."[34] Ostracism occurs in its most extreme forms when someone is physically exiled or placed in solitary confinement, which happens to Eleven when she does not comply with Dr. Brenner. These memories resurface traumatically when she remembers her time in the Hawkins National Laboratory.[35] Ostracism can also occur subtly, such as when Eleven refuses to acknowledge Max at their first meeting.[36]

Ostracism occurs not just in face-to-face interactions but also in electronic-based communication including texts, private messages, and social media discussions. Not receiving comments or feedback on posts, for example, can make a person feel excluded.[37] Though such technology does not exist in 1980s Hawkins, one equivalent could be ham radio. Dustin likely feels disconnected when he tries to contact his new girlfriend Suzie but she does not respond, then further ostracized when his longtime friends doubt her existence.[38] People who feel ostracized continuously can develop a sense of social alienation, believing they do not fit anywhere.[39] This may help explain why Byers brothers Will and Jonathan, considered social outcasts by many of their peers and even shunned by their own father, identify as "freaks."[40]

Creating Your Optimal Party

The Byers brothers present a great case study: Though they experience various forms of social exclusion in their daily lives, they find ways to bond. Specifically, Jonathan introduces Will to different bands that he may enjoy (e.g., The Clash and Joy Division), and they bond over the experience.[41] Psychologists who study fandom suggest that these interactions can provide a source of belonging for people because sometimes individuals describe their relationships with other fans in familial terms.[42] Common interests, such as comics and D&D, connect Will with his peers Mike, Lucas, and Dustin. Even when the broader peer culture of Hawkins Middle School devalues or outright shuns them, these four young men have forged a solid bond between one another. This bond extends beyond the gaming realm and into daily life, as Dustin notes when they try to make contact with an alien domain, the Upside Down, to help Will.[43]

The need to belong is important but it's not the only social need that people have. People also want to be recognized for their uniqueness. Social psychologist Marilynn Brewer argues that people are continuously striving to find a balance between fulfilling their need to belong and their need to be valued for their individual characteristics. They are striving to find a state of *optimal distinctiveness*.[44] Small peer groups and fan communities often provide this optimal niche.[45] A wonderful example of this in *Stranger Things* occurs during the close of a D&D campaign at the end of season one. Though it is "Will the Wise" in their game who deals the killing blow to the Thessalhydra with his fireball, it is Lucas who cuts off the monster's myriad heads and Dustin who stores them away, with Mike narrating the event. They all have their unique roles yet need to work together to accomplish the quest.[46] Even if they sometimes disagree and fight, in the end they must transcend their differences to reach their collective goal. Such is the challenge we all face, though the reward definitely is worth the struggle.

 **Eric D. Wesselmann**, PhD, is a professor of psychology at Illinois State University. His published research explores the dynamics of social inclusion and exclusion. He co-curates film programming and writes a blog for his local independent theater (The Normal Theater, Film CULTure). He listened to a lot of Joy Division while preparing this chapter. He has contributed to most of the volumes in the Popular Culture Psychology series—and Bob Newby is his superhero.

FRACTURING II

4

Boys' Party
How to Fail or Save
vs. Toxic Masculinity

Alex Langley

"Every man must decide whether he will walk in the light of creative altruism or the darkness of destructive selfishness."
—Dr. Martin Luther King, Jr.[1]

"A 'heart to heart'? What is that?"
—Chief Jim Hopper[2]

 ike. Lucas. Dustin. Will. Jim. Steve. Jonathan. Billy. Eddie. Scott. Bob. *Stranger Things* has more than its fair share of boys and men, but what, ultimately, does it *mean* to be a boy or a man? Is an interest in science stereotypically masculine? Is playing *Dungeons & Dragons* not masculine enough? Is anger the only acceptable emotion for a man to display? Are women and men so different that they operate on entirely different levels of emotion and logic?[3]

Early psychological views of gender included assertions by psychoanalysts such as Sigmund Freud (positions that were short on scientific rigor) centered around maleness and the male experience as the default, and framed the female experience as the "mutilated" or "supplemental" other.[4] Later research from the Kinsey Institute[5] didn't support Freud's male-centered perspective on gender and contemporary critics outright rebuke it, emphasizing that gender is a socially defined concept, mutable and in need of constant reexamination.[6] *Gender roles*, culturally designated behavior patterns expected of male and female members, shape both individuals and cultures at large, and are, in turn, shaped by individuals and cultures at large.[7] How does being assigned the role of "male" affect someone? What do these concepts mean for the heavily male cast of characters in *Stranger Things*?

The Taint of Toxicity

Psychologists Deborah David and Robert Brannon identified the *traditional masculine ideology* as a multidimensional construct with four tenets regarding the way people traditionally felt men should feel and act.[8]

Stereotypical gender role norms suggest that "real men" should:

- Receive respect for their achievements and status, something Jim Hopper often demands of others through his position as the largest and loudest man in the room.
- Seek risk and adventure, not simply out of necessity like the young protagonists do but also like Billy Hargrove does through his dangerous lifestyle choices.
- Never display vulnerability, unlike Lucas, who frequently expresses his doubts and fears over the constant danger the group faces.
- Never show "feminine" qualities, unlike Mike who at times communicates his feelings honestly and empathizes with those around him.

These tenets together create an unhealthy concoction able to poison any man who slavishly devotes himself to them—*toxic masculinity*.[9] A combination of traditional masculine traits that are either inherently harmful or have been heightened to the point of harmfulness—essentially men who have taken the idea of being a man too far.

One of the most harmful manifestations of toxic masculinity comes from the combination of its dismissal of vulnerability and femininity: *alexithymia*,[10] problems identifying and describing one's own emotions,[11] or *normative male alexithymia*, subclinical alexithymic difficulties among men conforming to cultural gender roles.[12] The adage, "Boys don't cry," succinctly reflects these significant deficits in cognitive and affective processing. The boys of *Stranger Things* all have their moments of struggling to understand and express their emotions, but these moments seem rooted in their newly burgeoning emotional intelligence rather than in alexithymia. After all, Max and Eleven have such difficulties too. It's in the show's men and older teens where we see this painful condition manifest.

Jim Hopper fits many criteria for alexithymia, given that his trauma over the loss of his daughter has stunted his ability to process and express what he's feeling. When reaching out to his ex-wife, he cuts off the conversation before voicing too much sentiment.[13] On several occasions with his adoptive daughter, Eleven, he struggles to find the words to communicate his emotions with her. He can only do so through indirect communication via radio or by writing a letter with the aid of Joyce Byers, placing the burden of unpacking his emotions on his closest female friend because he has such difficulty doing so himself.[14] He has moments of emotional clarity, generally with Joyce, but these moments seem too few and far between.

While Hopper's alexithymic symptoms vary over the course of the series, Billy Hargrove's start off severe and stay that way. Men with alexithymia are described as either suppressing or downright dissociating away "unacceptable" emotions. When Hopper suppresses, we can see he is feeling the emotions but isn't expressing them. Billy outright suppresses or dissociates his way through them. Rarely do we ever see Billy express any emotion other than irritation or rage—and occasionally a somewhat *anhedonic* (pleasureless)[15] presentation of lust. Billy's abuse at the hands of his father and his trauma over being abandoned by his mother seem to have created in him a void of emotional expression. Whether he's interacting with Steve, his stepsister Max, Lucas, or any random passerby, Billy's inner emotion tends to have two modes: flat or furious.

The lust Billy apathetically expresses ties into another common aspect of toxic masculinity: *hypersexuality*, problematic sexual excess.[16]

In this case, this hypersexuality presents in the form of an exaggerated obsession with proving one's heterosexuality: To be a "man," one needs to engage in promiscuity and avoid anything too "girly," which can include everything from clothing choices to hobbies to the aforementioned emotional expression. Billy flirts with girls, and numerous references are made to his success with them, and yet there's a certain joylessness to him belying deeper issues beyond hypersexuality.

The most personal interest of any kind we ever see from Billy is directed at Steve. Whether they're at a keg-chugging party, playing basketball, cleaning up in the gym showers, or locked in an intense fistfight, Billy repeatedly focuses on Steve more than anyone else, and that's when we see him most charged. Perhaps surprisingly, the only person to whom Billy expresses non-predatory kindness also happens to be Steve, such as when Billy advises him to plant his feet in basketball and in a few other too-brief instances. Both Billy's preoccupation with Steve and his anhedonic hyper-heterosexuality could potentially be interpreted as his trying to avoid admitting to himself his feelings of attraction for Steve and men in general, pushing his feelings away from conscious acknowledgment through suppression, dissociation, or reaction formation.[17] Given that Billy's father both physically and psychologically abuses him for not meeting his standards of masculinity for and not perfectly responding to his authoritarian rule, Billy could conceivably suppress same-gender sexual feelings as a survival response. Though such feelings might explain some of Billy's behavior, he dies[18] before exhibiting further behaviors that would explicitly confirm or refute this notion. It remains *fanon* (fan canon, a.k.a. head canon) for viewers who perceive this in him, some of whom contemplate the "shipping" (relationship-ing) of Billy and Steve.[19] Additional interpretations for his behavior include possible primitive dominance behavior, displaced aggression in seeking a target for either self-loathing or his resentment toward his father, or an overcompensating attempt to build his paternally damaged self-esteem by tearing someone else down—in this case, the person who has the farthest to fall, Steve.

Steve, also known as "King Steve" or Steve "The Hair" Harrington, has to face challenges to his ego and masculinity thanks to newcomer Billy's aggressive magnetism and Scoops Ahoy's mojo-deflating work uniform. Steve becomes a protective, older brother figure to the younger kids, particularly Dustin. One of the few times he seems truly bothered by his curly-haired apprentice occurs when Dustin's success with his camp-girlfriend Suzie reminds Steve of his own summer failures with the opposite sex.[20] Steve's confidence (and hair) had granted him success with girls, and his success with girls (and hair) granted him even more confidence. Eventually, both his confidence and dating success return by seemingly decoupling the two. When conversing with Robin about her attraction to Vickie, he both credits Robin's advice for his renewed status and gives her advice with almost detached wisdom and unusual insight thanks, in part, to removing his own ego from the equation.[21]

Troy and Dante, the bullies of junior high, exemplify the anti-feminist attitudes of toxic masculinity. They mock Mike, Lucas, and Dustin, whose interest in science renders them feminine in the eyes of their bullies, and Will, whose frail shape and sensitive nature render him the most feminine-seeming to them. At the school assembly to memorialize Will, Troy and Dante openly mock others for expressing their feelings.[22]

Will and Jonathan's wayward father, Lonnie, also discourages anything less than stereotypical masculinity in his sons. Jonathan recounts the story of his father forcing him to go hunting and kill a rabbit, an activity that left ten-year-old Jonathan in tears for a week. With no understanding of his sons' *interiority*, of either one's thoughts or desires, Lonnie remains privy only to his own attempted hypermasculinity. To him and the bullies, the worst thing a person could be is feminine.

The toxically masculine male sees girls and women not as friends, partners, or equals, but instead as beings or even items to be dominated and controlled, to be dehumanized and objectified.[23] Hopper engages in sometimes controlling behavior over the women in his life. When he first finds Eleven, lost in the woods, he takes her to his cabin and flatly says it will be her new home without asking her opinion on the subject.[24] While it may be inferred that a child, on the run and lost in the woods, would welcome a warm home, it is telling that he doesn't ask her feelings first. He enforces strict rules preventing travel or even going outside, stating that these rules are for her safety. Hopper's paranoia, much like his alexithymia, is an understandable manifestation of his trauma over losing his daughter. However, this results in an eventual rebellion from El, putting her much closer to harm's way than a simple stroll through the neighborhood ever could have.[25]

Once Eleven and Mike become a couple, Hopper's need for control worsens. Many of his interactions with her consist of shouting commands through a door.[26] El's autonomy is an afterthought: She is now his daughter and, as he sees things, her fate is his to decide. He becomes similarly possessive of Joyce, dismissing her opinions and feelings—a stark turn from his understanding and empathetic interactions with her when Will goes missing. Though he claims to pursue only friendship with Joyce and genuinely appreciates her company, he does not know how to be friends with a woman. He gets angry and aggressive when she misses dinner, as if she'd stood him up when they'd scheduled a date, suggesting he'd always expected to turn the dinner to romance.[27] Hopper also leans heavily into substance abuse through alcohol, cigarettes, and prescription medication—another common trait found in toxic masculinity as a self-soothing remedy for perceived failures to live up to impossible standards.[28]

When Hopper drunkenly, angrily shouts orders at Eleven through the door after his failed attempt at dating Joyce,[29] the moment seems to be played for levity when any beyond-the-surface examination may deem the scenario chillingly reminiscent of situations experienced by many survivors of parental and domestic abuse. While we, as the audience, trust that Hopper is ultimately a good person, examining his behavior through real-world psychology might tell another story. His affective lability, emotional blackmail in the form of guilt trips, inconsistent authoritarian parenting style, and substance abuse would all be kindling for potentially explosive danger to any children in his home.

Small amounts of friendly competition can bring out the best in people, acting as a crucible to sharpen performances that may have otherwise lain dull.[30] With toxic masculinity, though, the desire for competition and domination escalates to unhealthy degrees. We see numerous examples of dominance-focused behavior through Billy and Hopper. The moment Billy arrives in Hawkins, he becomes obsessed with proving his superiority to resident Big Man on Campus Steve Harrington.[31] Hopper's dominating behavior manifests as a tendency toward using physical intimidation, violence, and sheer vocal volume as deciding factors in disagreements. This drive to be number one and in charge at all costs can result in incredible loneliness and depression on not only the part of the losers of such contests, but the winners as well.[32] Acting like a jerk at every basketball game isn't going to keep the invites coming for long.

Mike, Dustin, Lucas, and Will usually present a refreshing opposite to the toxically dominant lone wolf behavior shown by Billy and Hopper. The boys are collaborative in their discussions and their problem solving, whether it's dealing with a Demogorgon, figuring out their own feelings, or gabbing about girls. They have established rules for reconciling behaviors, and they apologize to each other when they're wrong. Finding themselves both attracted to Max, friends Lucas and Dustin separately try to connect with her but at no point do they sabotage, undermine, or discourage each other from pursuing her. The boys work together and are a far stronger force collectively than they could ever be individually.

The Power of the Positive

This willingness, this desire, to work together exemplifies the counteragent to toxic masculinity: *positive masculinity*.[33] Positive masculinity broadly refers to the idea of men and boys who work together, serve their communities, and care for and provide for others. They are men whose egos are not tied to their maleness, men who do not flee from traditionally feminine qualities or from opportunities to protect others. Positive masculinity emphasizes emotional expression, the acknowledgment and understanding of the feelings of others, the importance of understanding oneself, and a willingness to understand and admit to their own mistakes.[34]

Will is a caring, sensitive boy, going so far as to ask if his brother's cut hand is okay when *he's* the one awakening from a coma in a hospital bed. Yet, while Will is often described as the sensitive member of the party, Mike and Lucas deserve credit for their own sensitive behavior as well. When the boys initially meet Eleven out in the rain and cold, Mike is the first to understand her needs and to decipher her minimalist communications. He's also the first to notice Will's worsening symptoms of trauma (and Mind Flayer possession) and sits with him to have an honest conversation about both Will's trauma and Mike's feelings of sadness and grief over missing El.[35] Lucas, meanwhile, is adept not only at sorting through his own feelings but also noticing the feelings of others. He is the first to notice El exhibiting guilty behavior when she deliberately misleads the group through the woods. After fighting with Mike and El about this deception, he sorts through his emotions on his own and makes the mature move by apologizing first. After Billy dies, he sees the depression and isolation tormenting Max and reaches out to her time and again, trying to keep her from "disappearing" (and blaming himself when he feels he didn't try hard enough).[36]

Hopper has moments of exceptional empathy as well, particularly in his dealings with Joyce when Will goes missing and is presumed dead. Hopper speaks calmly, respectfully, and supportively to her, never dismissing her claims once the severity of the situation becomes clear. He capably intuits her feelings when she has yet to process those feelings herself. When Will's fake body turns up in the water even though Joyce hears him speaking from the Upside Down, Hopper commiserates on hearing his own daughter's voice after she has passed. When he and Joyce cross into the Upside Down to rescue her missing son, he senses her oncoming panic attack and helps her cope with it before it becomes debilitating.[37] As they discuss Will's trauma in season two, Hopper supportively references posttraumatic stress disorder—and during the 1980s, merely referencing its existence would have been a revelatory move for a small-town cop adhering to masculine gender norms.[38] Although his interactions with Mike at the time involve intimidating him, Hopper has also shown himself capable of extending his empathy. Upon finding out that Hopper has harbored Eleven for an entire year without telling him, Mike flies into a rage, shouting obscenities at him and striking him. Hopper simply endures this abuse, wrapping Mike in an understanding embrace while telling him it's okay, and emphasizing for Mike not to be angry with El because she didn't choose to hide. After Hopper later returns from Russia, his warm greeting with Mike hints at growth for them both.[39]

Despite a tendency to suppress emotions until he explodes, Hopper shows himself to be, at times, capable of great empathy, patience, and willingness to accept blame.[40] The ability to shoulder blame and own up to mistakes is another trait of positive masculinity, a good thing—something Mike, Lucas, and Steve all do well. Mike and Lucas are both frequently the first to end feuds with friends (and girlfriends) by expressing their remorse. When the boys feud over Eleven's misleading them away from the Department of Energy, Lucas apologizes to Mike and El without prompting, having worked through his issues during a lengthy trek through the forest.[41]

Steve, known for often doing the wrong thing first, keeps piecing together his own shortcomings, admitting to them, and trying to do better. Whether it's after one of his numerous arguments with Nancy, his fistfight with Jonathan Byers, or any of his other frequent mistakes, Steve time and time again realizes his own wrongness and works to correct it. He also acknowledges others' help, such as when he says listening to Robin has helped him revive his dating life.[42] Unlike toxic masculinity in which the person may refrain from thanking others as though needing help implies weakness or femininity, positive masculinity includes healthy recognition, gratitude, and appreciation toward others.[43]

Positive masculinity also places importance on male figures acting as guardians and mentors in their community. Hopper may be lacking a bit in the mentorship area, but he certainly acts as a guardian to his community and especially to the kids of *Stranger Things*. He's constantly putting himself into dangerous situations to eliminate the danger. He pursues neither glory nor credit for a job well done, not even the thrills of adventure itself, but simply that those around him stay safe—a stark contrast to the thrill-seeking demands of the *traditional masculine ideology*.

Steve takes this guardianship one step further by also providing a valuable presence as a mentor. Despite his need to seem "cool," he readily provides what guidance and advice he can to the kids, particularly when it comes to the areas he feels he knows best: hair and girls.[44] And despite his occasional blundering and frequently received beatings, Steve willingly, automatically shields others from harm by endangering himself first. Against the Demogorgon, against the Demodogs, in the Mind Flayer's tunnels, in the secret Starcourt labs, into the mysterious Creel house, and through a watery gate in Lover's Lake, Steve is usually first in and last out.[45] He physically shields the kids and peers from danger, tells them to get behind him, and makes sure they get out first even if it means he might not. He may be a doofus, but he's one brave doofus. The reason he seems to get beaten up so often is because he goes first to take the hits so others don't.

Steve turns out to be a good friend, even in situations where others might fall back on their wounded pride. After he and Nancy break up, he continues having romantic feelings for her, and yet when he sees the connection between her and Jonathan, he's able to let go of his own ego for her benefit. Even more strikingly, he again shuffles his own ego to the back burner in his heart-to-heart conversation with Robin after a drug-induced vomiting session.[46] Steve, in his classic Eighties cool-guy way, admits that he has feelings for her. Robin, in a classically un-eighties way, discloses that she's gay with a heartfelt monologue about one of their mutual classmates. Steve takes a beat to process this information, then immediately sets in to kid Robin about her choice of women and to laugh with her—reassuring her and letting her know that their relationship, their friendship, remains undeterred by this information. Every time, when it's most important, Steve puts others before himself.

Eddie Munson also plays a mentor role to the boys in his *Dungeons & Dragons* group, the Hellfire Club. Eddie, an older senior who has failed to graduate twice, welcomes newcomers Mike, Dustin, and Lucas when they enter high school. With yet another possible graduation on the horizon, he espouses to the boys the importance of fostering the next generation of outsiders to welcome into the group, to bring into this safe and cooperative haven for the socially atypical. Eddie and Steve even connect over their mutual desire to mentor Dustin and the other boys, rather than begrudge or compete against each other for the role.[47] The desire to guide others is so strong for Eddie that, when mortally wounded, the last thing he asks of Dustin is to promise to "look after the little sheep," to take his place as Hawkins High School's peer mentor to the resident misfits.[48]

The most consistent examples of positive masculinity in *Stranger Things* come from Scott Clarke, science teacher, and Bob Newby, "superhero."[49] Mr. Clarke is always ready to help explain a concept to anyone, student or parent alike, and despite his expertise he speaks peer-to-peer with them. When Joyce Byers asks for help to understand what caused the magnets at Melvald's store to demagnetize,[50] the interaction lacks any of the lechery or condescension typically found in a toxically masculine male.[51] He's just excited about science and wants to share valuable information with anyone curious enough to ask. Mr. Clarke also provides comfort when it's needed, such as when the boys are (at least, from his perspective) mourning Will and in need of a distraction via ham radio and transdimensional theory talk, or by explaining the science behind the special effects of John Carpenter's horror movie *The Thing* to help his date feel less afraid.[52]

Bob Newby epitomizes positive masculinity. Despite having had a tough childhood, he has a warm, optimistic outlook on life. He's upbeat, kind, and romantic. He's publicly passionate with Joyce and shares his feelings first. He's chronically un-hip, but with an eager positivity that makes others feel better even as they roll their eyes out of embarrassment. When Will struggles with his posttraumatic stress and ongoing issues with the Mind Flayer, Bob offers advice.[53] Despite the incredible danger of the situation, Bob bravely navigates the Demodog-infested lab building to help get Joyce and the boys to safety. He cares about others and isn't shy about letting them know. Knowing his poor odds of survival does not deter him from safeguarding them—taking a risk to help others, not for thrills or to follow a social role.

Roll for Positive Masculine Roles

The 1980s were a time brimming with rigid reminders of traditional gender roles, particularly through the popular culture of the time, which was inundated with images of muscular men as hardened, emotionless killing machines or sex-craved chain-smoking party animals. And yet, thanks to the mentorship of men such as Mr. Clarke, Bob, Steve, Eddie, and others, the younger heroes of *Stranger Things* seem poised to grow into healthier, more communicative men than many before them.[54] While each may occasionally fall back on gendered perspectives, they're not as slavishly devoted to them as their forefathers had been. They're willing to learn and grow, and they're capable of recognizing women as partners and equals, not "mutilated" or "supplemental" others. These young men work as a team, are emotionally expressive, and love science and reading. Their favorite hobby is one that involves steady communication, imagination, and teamwork. More easily as they mature, they learn to share the hobby with their female friends and even a little sister.[55]

 **Alex Langley**, MS, co-edited the book *Spider-Man Psychology*. His single-author works include The Geek Handbook series, the graphic novel *Kill the Freshman*, and chapters and features in the Popular Culture Psychology series. With Katrina Hill, he coauthored *100 Greatest Graphic Novels*. He teaches psychology, appears on comic con panels, contributes to the Comic Con-Fusion channel on YouTube, and shares both sense and nonsense as @RocketLlama on Twitter.

A "Predator for Good?"
The Toxic Male Maybe without Toxic Masculinity
Travis Langley

Assuming that one individual's toxic qualities are related to that person's gender, race, or other grouping variable could be a mistake involving *stereotyping*, believing that all individuals with a shared characteristic are alike. This may arise due to the *representativeness heuristic*, following a *heuristic* (taking a mental shortcut in forming judgments or decisions)[56] by assuming that one individual is representative of everyone else who belongs to the same group. Whereas viewers witness enough of Hopper's behavior to spot masculine gender role issues swimming among his anger management difficulties, other characters' aggressive or domineering inclinations can arise for other reasons. For example, scientist Martin Brenner, strangely calm in his pragmatic willingness to sacrifice anyone else in the service of his priorities, looks down upon everybody.

The villain whom Dustin dubs Vecna, with his mysterious motivation to be a "predator for good," judges humanity itself even more harshly than Brenner, deciding that the world is broken and that he should reshape it as he sees fit. He preys upon perceived weakness in people, particularly those riddled with guilt over others' deaths. People who lack capacity for guilt[57] or despise it in themselves are prone to belittling and disdaining it in others. Some psychopaths and even some who are not psychopathic see guilt feelings as weakness. Vecna's critique of humanity's chaos, pettiness, and guilt may be gender-free: He looks down on everybody. He kills anyone. Or does he?

In the massacres of both his family and everyone in sight at Hawkins Lab, he leaves the dominant paternal figure alive each time: young Henry Creel's biological father, Victor, and later Dr. Martin "Papa" Brenner. Then again, he initially intends to let Eleven live as well, until she judges him and her reaction to the massacre fails to feed his power fantasy. Although he says he always intended for his father to live framed for the murders, the music that helps Victor survive also helps Max, to Vecna's annoyance.[58] Max's survival indicates that the music, followed by Henry's collapse into a coma, may matter more in sparing Victor than does Henry's choice. Vecna's sheer ego or simply arrested development (lacking a history of normal social development) may lead him to assert, in effect, "I meant to do that." Even if he did choose to frame father while killing mother, his mother was the one who saw the evil in him. This is a convoluted way of pointing out that, while sexism cannot be ruled out for Vecna, it cannot be confirmed as key to his toxicity either and should not be assumed based solely on his gender. His behavior is narcissistic, Machiavellian, psychopathic, and sadistic (all the qualities that, when brought together and extreme, make up the *dark tetrad* of dangerous personality)[59] regardless of the demographics of his prey.

Still, the song that saves Max—or, more accurately, opens the opportunity for her to save herself—happens to be one about gender issues, wishing woman and man could trade lives and better understand each other.[60]

An '80s Daydream or a Comforting Nightmare?

An Examination of Black Racial Representation in Hawkins

Vanessa Hintz

"To be a Negro in this country and to be relatively conscious is to be in a state of rage almost, almost all of the time—and in one's work. And part of the rage is this: It isn't only what is happening to you. But it's what's happening all around you and all of the time in the face of the most extraordinary and criminal indifference, indifference of most White people in this country, and their ignorance."
—author James Baldwin[1]

"There are certain types of people in this world that you stay away from, and that kid [Lucas], Max, that kid is one of them. You stay away from him, you hear me? Stay away."
—Billy Hargrove to Max Mayfield[2]

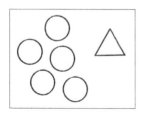

Netflix coined the term *binge racers* to refer to those who watch the entire season of a television series within the first twenty-four hours following its release.[3] In addition to devising new terminology, Netflix and other streaming platforms have revolutionized the experience of engaging with the small screen. Waiting an entire week for the next episode in a series? A lot of people would rather get a root canal or engage in some other less-than-pleasurable activity. In contrast to modernizing the television-watching experience, though, the creatives behind some of Netflix's most popular content continue to rely on some of the most conventional TV tropes.

Stranger Things has been the most-watched show on Netflix.[4] Horror fans rejoiced as the American horror genre received a much-needed reinvigoration from the 1980s-era sci-fi adventures of a diverse(ish) group of teens from the fictional Midwestern town of Hawkins, Indiana. *Stranger Things* employs all the traditional fear-inducing elements to include creepy-crawly things, scary places, suspense, spooky music (cue the intro theme music), and fear of the unusual.[5] Yet still, for many fans of the show who identify as people of color—particularly, Black Americans—perhaps the most horrifying element of the show is the perceived erasure and mishandling of the show's few Black characters. This color-blind approach to diversity on-screen is not unique to the show's creators, the Duffer Brothers, nor is it somehow misaligned to the conventional ways of American life. The United States has continued to identify itself as the world's leading democracy—a nation that values liberty and justice for all. Concerning the issues of racial equity, however, America continues to fall short, and the world has taken notice.[6] Similarly, *Stranger Things'* perceived lack of historical accuracy concerning the experiences of Black citizens in 1980s small-town Indiana not only misses the mark but may unintentionally induce harm to fans in the process.

1980s Nostalgia: One Size Does Not Fit All

One of the most alluring elements of *Stranger Things* is the comforting familiarity of 1980s popular culture. From "stocky televisions with foil-wrapped rabbit ears, poorly lit basement rec rooms lined with half-hearted orange carpet, unwieldy cars shaped like rolling cereal boxes, and cheerfully goofy brown corduroy pants,"[7] it is hard not to get swept up in the neon dream of it all. Nostalgia can serve as a tool for escaping the horrors of the present,[8] but what if the present horrors are merely the most recent manifestations of centuries-old fears maintained by injustice and discrimination? For those of us who are Black, an artistic reimagining of 1980s America can be one wrought with pain and vicarious trauma.

Unlike the "nostalgic daydream" of the Duffer Brothers' recreation of Midwest America in the early 1980s, the decade was one shaped by rigid policies that disproportionately hurt people of color in the United States.[9] In addition to nurturing the concept of "reverse discrimination," or anti-White racism, Ronald Reagan consistently challenged affirmative action programs, and he "fundamentally restructured the composition of the federal courts and the government's civil rights enforcement apparatus."[10] Despite racist governmental, political, and economic forces,[11] many Americans in the 1980s believed racism had been eradicated and that equality and justice prevailed.[12] This belief was likely maintained by the rise of the "new Black middle class" in the 1970s and 1980s, which resulted in a number of Black families moving to suburban neighborhoods.[13]

Lucas Sinclair is one of the few characters of color in *Stranger Things*, with audiences not being introduced to his family in any sort of meaningful way (i.e., with interaction and dialogue) until the show's second season. In their introductory episode, Lucas asks his dad for advice during a family breakfast.[14] While this may be considered unexciting to some in relation to the larger series canon, for African Americans this scene may represent "a regular moment in many black households" and one that celebrates "the ordinary over and above the predominant negative narratives [and] stereotypes."[15]

A 2016 *Saturday Night Live* sketch offered another interpretation of the Sinclair family. Portrayed by Kenan Thompson and Leslie Jones, the Sinclairs educate Lucas on the inherent dangers of the world, telling him, "People who look like us already live in the Upside Down. Let me put it to you this way, Lucas: You don't have to go looking for scary stuff. It's going to find you."[16] Thompson and Jones lift their hands into the air at the arrival of Chief Hopper, to whom they refer as "the monster." Albeit in a sardonic fashion, this sketch points out the pervasive and ideological whiteness of the show. Blinded by the show's charisma and reminiscence, some fans of the show can easily "overlook Lucas's marginalized position as one of the very few African American children in Hawkins."[17]

In essence, the portrayal of America's recent racist past is painfully ambiguous, at best. Instead of tackling these pervasive societal issues head-on, *Stranger Things* adopts an interpretation of 1980s America that is idealized and comfortable. Opportunities exist for this and other fictional accounts of American life to "turn a critical eye to our history" so that we may work to understand how past sins have influenced the present.[18] The mystical creatures of the Upside Down, Eleven's telekinetic abilities, and many of the other Hawkins-exclusive fantastical elements urge fans of the show to "question the nature of our reality, and not take for granted that there is a world beyond our perception."[19] In America, a pervasive reality is one of racial inequity, with the perception of many in the racial majority being that we are now living in a post-racial society. As such, the Hawkins happenings provide opportunities to further understand existing systems of social hierarchy, as well as to consider perspectives and realities different from one's own.

Black America's "Upside Down": Where the Scary Stuff Finds You

Discussions of race, ethnicity, and sexuality are deeply personal matters[20] and are most often challenging to those with privilege. These conversations are often dismissed based on claims that these issues are antiquated.[21] Like many in the 1980s, Americans continue to identify modern society as "post-racial," interpreting the increased enrollment of students of color in higher education institutions, the election of a two-term Black president, and the economic prosperity of people of color in high-profile positions as indications that racial inequity no longer exists. Despite these individual successes, racism continues to be deeply embedded in American society, with a "myriad of legal, cultural, and psychological effects."[22]

The post-racial society has never actually existed.[23] Like *Stranger Things* and its "daydream nostalgia" of a decade long past, the idea of the post-racial world continues to serve as a foundational fantasy of equity that shields those in the racial majority from confronting the horrors of racism.[24] For instance, as aforementioned, Lucas is a Black child in a predominantly White, Midwestern town in the 1980s. Images of Lucas in his element lead viewers to infer that he and his family are economically advantaged. In comparison to the Byers residence, Lucas's home is abundant. For many, Lucas's clothes and premier toys are in obvious congruence with the show's wistful reminiscence. Not made explicit to viewers, however, are the functions of the aforementioned mechanisms for Lucas's survival as the "token Black friend" in his social circle (and perhaps in the entirety of the town of Hawkins).[25] It is not uncommon for people of color in predominantly White spaces to adopt dual identities characterized by ritualized accommodating behaviors as a means to fit in with majority cultural norms.[26] In the case of the Hawkins crew, Lucas's attempts to be *just like everyone else* despite the obvious and apparent physical and cultural differences may be an attempt to offset the pervasive experiences of racism, discrimination, and oppression.

Personal Resistance to Confronting Issues of Racism

The showrunners may have elected to elude explicit commentary on issues of race and racism. Resistance to engagement in conversation and exploration concerning systems of inequity can be categorized as cognitive, emotional, or behavioral.[27] Akin to the façade maintained by claims of a "post-racial society," *cognitive resistance* is characterized by a belief that racism does not exist in modern society, as well as the utilization of specific mechanisms to avoid conversations on the subject. Moreover, people of color are perceived to be exaggerating about reported instances of inequity and discrimination. *Emotional resistance* describes the process of obstructing one's capacity to acknowledge, understand, or make sense of racial injustice. *Behavioral resistance*, similarly, refers to one's reported feelings of helplessness to do anything to eradicate systemic inequities.

As alluded to above, a substantial number of White Americans deny the existence of systemic racism, thus manufacturing an attitude of resentment for people of color who provide evidence to the contrary.[28] *Stranger Things* has been acclaimed as a series that "plays things straight, with heart."[29] Straight for *whom*, in this instance? As previously discussed, rather than confronting issues of past racial tensions head-on, *Stranger*

Things portrays the "1980s as we want it to have been."[30] In essence, the showrunners may have prioritized the maintenance of the pretense of post-racial society over more comprehensive—albeit unpleasant for some—representations of race relations in Reagan-era Indiana.

White Fragility

There seems to be widespread fear that the acknowledgment of culture-specific values by people of color are somehow attacks on White cultural norms and values.[31] *White fragility* is the term most often used to describe this phenomenon, noting when a challenge to racial worldviews is interpreted "as a challenge to our very identities as good, moral people."[32] Moreover, this heightened cultural sensitivity lends itself to a desire for discussions about racial identity that maintain the status quo[33]—whiteness as the norm and preferred way of being.

In the second season of *Stranger Things*, Billy Hargrove arrives with his washboard abs–mullet combination, palpable intensity, and notable anger management issues. In one instance, without an *explicit* reference to his racial identity, Billy instructs his stepsister, Max, to stay away from Lucas.[34] As Billy continues to strike fear into Max and her companions, no one mentions Billy's veiled racism. In fact, Billy's dreadful behavior is in essence "whitewashed." Not only is the audience made aware of Billy's abusive childhood, but he engages in a seemingly "redemptive act" in saving another's life.[35] Both of these could be construed by some viewers to "explain away" Billy's inherent racism.[36] This is not to say that Billy's childhood trauma or personal sacrifice should be dismissed out of hand. Why not highlight *all* of the aforementioned with the same fervor? Billy is a not-so-nice guy with a painful past *and* his actions demonstrate sentiments rooted in racial stereotyping and discrimination. Why is the former so much more acceptable to portray than the latter? How might the show be different had the showrunners elected to investigate the different ways Lucas and his friends were treated in Hawkins?[37] For some, this may merely appear to be an artistic decision made by the show's creative directors. For Black fans, however, this may serve as yet another painful reminder that portrayals of racial *colorconsciousness* on the small screen are in constant competition with larger ideologies of colorblindness.[38]

Black Racial Identity and
the Cross Model of Nigrescence

"No one wants to be Winston, man!"
—Lucas Sinclair [39]

People of color who are fans of *Stranger Things*—particularly Black Americans—have undoubtedly experienced unique points of connection with the characters in the series. Situations in which Black viewers experience further marginalization or an increased devaluing of self-worth, however, can be unintentionally harmful. The dynamics of Black racial identity may serve as useful mechanisms by which to understand these circumstances.

Developed by ethnic-identity researcher William Cross in the early 1970s, the *model of Nigrescence* outlines the identity process of "becoming Black."[40] Cross's model identifies five independent stages—though it is important to note that this is not a linear stage model, in that individuals can move through the stages out of sequence and may return to previous stages based on changes in worldview and/or circumstance.

Pre-Encounter

In the initial stage, *pre-encounter*, Black individuals place little emphasis on their racial identity and are more likely to adopt dominant cultural norms (i.e., White norms). This stage is often marked by feelings of internalized racism, in which they may—consciously or otherwise—inherit dominant cultural values rooted in race-based discrimination.

Cross's pre-encounter stage can induce internalized feelings of anti-Blackness, which may occur when an individual "does not realize that they have been raised with White westernized ideologies, because it is so embedded in their culture."[41] In the second season's Halloween episode, viewers are introduced to the coordinated Ghostbusters-themed costumes of Lucas, Dustin, Mike, and Will.[42] Lucas confronts Mike for insisting that he dress up as Winston. Though Mike does not explicitly pinpoint racial identity as the mitigating factor, Lucas asserts this shouldn't be the mechanism for deciding who dresses as which Ghostbuster. Much like the implied racial undertones seen in Billy's character, this situation is not addressed any further in the series. Perhaps Lucas is in the *pre-encounter* stage of Nigrescence, indicating he—conceivably akin to his White peers—does not want to dress up as Winston because he is "the Black Ghostbuster" (or the least desirable, by majority society's standards). On the other hand, perchance Lucas does not want to be tokenized in this fashion as the sole Black friend in his social circle. Nonetheless, because the show-runners neglected to explore these dynamics further, viewers are left only with speculation.[43]

Encounter

Individuals move into the second stage, *encounter*, following some sort of race-based event that leads to some dissonance concerning pre-viously held beliefs. Feelings of guilt and shame for being "brainwashed" by the majority culture are pervasive as well. Returning to the example of Billy Hargrove, interactions between him and Lucas may serve to transition Lucas into this second stage. Upon realizing that Billy's ani-mosity toward him is more intense than that aimed at Dustin, Mike, or Will, Lucas would then transition into a stage of dissonance, in which believing that he is just like everybody else becomes increasingly difficult.

Immersion-Emersion

The third stage, *immersion-emersion*, is highlighted by an individual's detachment from previously held views, thus adopting a new racial identity informed by newfound understandings about race. This stage consists of two phases, the first of which involves a "strong desire to learn and promote Black culture" while simultaneously rejecting white-ness.[44] People then adopt a more "balanced" view of Black identity in the second phase of this stage. Should Lucas elect to distance himself from his friend group, and instead maintain relationships *only* with other Black people, one could determine this to be an iteration of *immersion*. If Lucas then decides to explore the possibilities of rekindling his relationships with Mike, Will, Dustin, and other White peers, this would be an example of the latter phase of *emersion*.

Internalization

Internalization, the fourth stage of Cross's model, is characterized by a transition period, in which individuals work through the challenges of adopting a new identity.[45] The process by which Lucas may potentially grapple with the personal costs and benefits of maintaining relationships with White peers demonstrates the introspective nature of the internalization stage.

Internalization-Commitment

The final stage, *internalization-commitment*, is focused on cultivating long-term interest in the wellness of Black individuals,[46] ultimately fueled by beliefs about Blackness developed throughout the process of Nigrescence.[47] Following the aforementioned periods of consideration, the internalization-commitment stage would see Lucas again joining with his primary friend group *while* maintaining strong connections not only to his Black peers but also to the prosperity and well-being of the Black community as a whole.

Colorblind Advocacy

One of the most commanding new characters in the series is, undoubtedly, Lucas's spunky younger sister, Erica Sinclair. Many viewers have enjoyed her quick-witted comebacks and feisty attitudes. From a racial identity perspective, though, there are a few problematic undertones inherent in Erica's character arc. In essence, Erica's "annoying little sister persona became a sassy Black woman trope in little girl form"[48] quickly, quintessentially transforming her into a stereotype. Moreover, returning to this idea about the cultural realities of the Reagan era for people of color, Erica's admission concerning the benefits of capitalism seems particularly disconcerting. Erica identifies capitalism as what she loves most about America, further asserting, "Do you know what capitalism is? It means this is a free market system."[49] Referred to as "metaphorical blackface,"[50] having a young, Black girl deliver this message, arguably, perpetuates societal values that maintain systems of inequity. This, like many of the other potentially problematic character portrayals outlined above, seems to adopt a "dangerous" colorblind representational strategy, inviting multiple interpretations from audiences—some of which may be emotionally burdensome for people of color.[51] What responsibility, then, do storytellers have to work toward more *colorconscious* representations of the Black experience?

The Burden of Creative Responsibility

The interpretation of popular media is rooted in a process of bidirectional influence. Societal events influence artistic direction, just as popular representations of the human experience can affect mainstream ways of thinking. Though media does not, in itself, create change, it does "play an important role in the spread of new ideas and demands for change."[52] As such, one could argue that the inability of *Stranger Things* to confront issues of race within its fictional context is, at best, irresponsible. Given the highly individualized nature of Hollywood storytelling,[53] some level of scrutiny concerning the cultural "accuracy" of racially diverse characters is unavoidable. Nonetheless, moving beyond symbolic inclusion is vital. Additional considerations must be given to *how* characters of color are represented on screen and *what kind* of racial messages are being conveyed.[54] Absent this intentionality in storytelling, it is unlikely that significant movements toward racial justice and equity will be made.

 **Vanessa Hintz**, PsyD, a licensed clinical psychologist in Wisconsin, earned her doctorate in psychology from the Chicago School of Professional Psychology. Dr. Hintz has served on panel discussions of the manifestations of psychological concepts in American popular culture. An active proponent of diversity, equity, and inclusion, she works collaboratively with individuals to understand how each person makes meaning of the world within their various cultural contexts. A self-proclaimed "Psych Geek," she incorporates elements of popular culture into her work.

Bullying
What It Is and
What to Do about It

Leandra Parris

"Bullying among schoolchildren is no doubt a very old phenomenon."
—psychologist Dan Olweus[1]

"Mouthbreather."
—Eleven[2]

Many people treat bullying among children as a simple fact of life, sometimes as a rite of passage. Yet research indicates that children can experience drastic negative effects even into adulthood. It is not uncommon for victims of bullying to develop a fear response to bullies parallel to a response to life-threatening events.[3] The fear Mike and Dustin experience when interacting with the school bullies on the cliff overlooking the lake is echoed in the distress Will shows when flashing back to his time in the Upside Down.[4] The distress caused by bullying can lead to depression, anxiety, traumatic stress, poor school performance, and long-term challenges with building relationships.[5]

When high schoolers bully and humiliate El, she reveals it to no one because she has never learned any social coping skills and does not want to seem weak.[6] The negative impact of bullying on children's well-being is concerning, given that approximately 33 percent of youth experience some form of bullying.[7] Further, witnessing bullying can impact academic performance, feelings of safety, and the use of maladaptive coping strategies such as aggression.[8] As more becomes known about bullying and how it influences child development, it becomes clear that bullying should not be treated as a normal stressor that youth must face on their own.

Understanding Bullying

"Look, I'm tired of being bullied. I'm tired of girls laughing at us. I'm tired of feeling like a loser."
—Lucas Sinclair[9]

Bullying behaviors are acts that cause distress in another, are intentionally repeated, and include an imbalance of power between the perpetrator and victim.[10] Four components play critical roles in identifying the degree to which such actions are recognized as bullying: victim perception, intentionality, repetition, and power differential.

Victim Perception

The first component of this definition may be the most crucial, as it requires that the victim perceive the behaviors as being threatening or harmful. For instance, when the boys are playing *Dungeons & Dragons*, Mike gets sarcastic and makes fun of his friends. While this does not seem to bother Dustin or Lucas, Will becomes visibly upset.[11] Therefore, Mike's behaviors toward Dustin and Lucas would not be considered bullying, but those same behaviors toward Will would meet this particular criterion. There is more to bullying than that, though.

Intentionality

The second requirement for bullying is that the behaviors are intentional. For example, when Mike realizes how upset Will is, he genuinely tries to clarify that he was "just messing around" and didn't mean to hurt Will.[12] He cares how Will feels. So while this interaction meets the first criterion of causing distress, it does not meet the second criterion of intentionality.

Repetition

These behaviors must also be repeated. A singular incident of exclusion, fighting, hurting someone's feelings, or spreading a rumor does not mean the child is engaging in bullying. However, repeatedly engaging in behaviors that they know will upset others is clearly bullying. Mike does not repeat his teasing of Will once he realizes it upsets his friend. However, the school bullies repeatedly target Mike, Lucas, Dustin, and Will across time and location.[13]

Power Differential

The fourth component of bullying is a power differential between the perpetrator and the victim. Physical power is typically easy to determine and understand. Physical power, though, is rarely the type of power used in bullying.[14] More often, children who bully have power that comes from social standing, cultural privilege, and lack of accountability from others. This does not mean that the bully feels that they have power; in fact, there is evidence that some children bully others as a means of taking back some perception of control that they lack in other contexts.[15] Bullies Troy and Billy apply power to coerce others, such as when Troy makes Mike jump off a cliff, but Billy also has strength and autonomy as an older teen. While little is known of Troy's mother other than her concern over who hurt her son, Billy's experiences with his father leave him feeling lost and out of control, thus engaging in bullying as a way of balancing out those needs.[16]

Forms of Bullying

Bullying can be physical, verbal, relational, or electronic (i.e., cyberbullying).[17] *Physical bullying* means hitting or forcing another into a situation that can cause physical harm, such as Troy forcing Mike to jump from a high cliff.[18] *Verbal bullying* includes name-calling and verbal threats, such as Billy yelling and threatening Max and Lucas when he finds them together.[19] *Relational bullying* targets social standing, often seeking to damage the victim's reputation, such as when Steve's friends write slurs against Nancy Wheeler on the theater marquee.[20] Behaviors can include spreading rumors, ostracizing someone, or sharing embarrassing information about them. *Cyberbullying* occurs when using electronic devices to bully others, such as sending threatening messages or posting derogatory social media posts. The children of *Stranger Things* do not yet experience incidents of cyberbullying in the 1980s. Yet even as early as the 1990s, youngsters found themselves targets of online peer aggression, and for some, cyberbullying was possible in the 1980s anywhere institutions had in-house networks.

As mentioned before, bullying is different from fighting among friends, teasing, and harassment. When friends fight, they may intentionally hurt each other but rarely mean what they say or experience a power differential, such as when Lucas and Mike argue.[21] This would not be considered bullying. In *teasing*, it may be repeated and include some aspect of a power differential, such as an older sibling teasing a child. However, teasing is not always meant to be hurtful but can be playful or even affectionate in intent. Unfortunately, benign intent may not be easily recognized by the other child, leading them to feel hurt, such as when Mike teases Will. While the targeted child may experience the teasing negatively, if it is not intentionally done to cause harm, then the incident may be seen as a misunderstanding. This intentionality also becomes important when considering *microaggressions*, which are seemingly innocuous statements that are grounded in bias toward the other individuals.[22] Examples include when Mike assumes that Lucas would dress as Winston, the Black character from *Ghostbusters*,[23] or when Nancy's colleagues tell her to get coffee at work.[24]

Because *microaggressive* behaviors (meaning small aggressions) stem from prejudice, ignorance, or both, they can cause discomfort and distress in another. Once microaggressions are repeated and clearly intentional, we often describe these acts as *identity-based bullying* because the child is getting targeted based on one or more of their identities, such as gender, sexual orientation, race, ethnicity, religion, ability, or language.[25] This form of bullying can be extremely harmful as it focuses on who the child is as a person, rather than general and opportunistic bullying. Examples of identity-based bullying include times Troy and James call Dustin "Toothless" and make fun of him because of his *cleidocranial dysplasia* (a rare genetic condition that impairs development of teeth and bones).[26] Identity-based bullying overlaps with harassment, unwanted aggressive actions toward a person based on a protected class (e.g., race, gender), seen as more severe than bullying.[27] Harassment has legal consequences, which is often not true for bullying even when an organization has anti-bullying policies. As such, the difference between identity-based bullying and harassment may come down to how a state or agency defines these two phenomena and what the consequences are for each.

In general, bullying appears to happen most often in environments that do not have clear or consistent consequences for peer aggression, lack mechanisms for peer support, or represent a transition for a group of students.[28] For instance, schools with poor climate—which includes a lack of teacher support, cultural acceptance, connectedness, etc.—tend to have higher rates of bullying.[29] Bullying is also more frequent in schools that lack clear anti-bullying education and do not have policies that promote social support between students.[30] When students enter a new context together, such as the introductions of Eleven and Max, social standings and roles may be reformed, and bullying can be one way of establishing the social hierarchy.[31] Identities begin to develop in early and middle adolescence, the developmental period that almost all the children in *Stranger Things* are initially experiencing. Children become more aware of who they are and how they fit within the larger social context. These developments and growth periods can create tensions that lead to group conflict.

These tensions can be compounded by individual experiences and characteristics. As previously mentioned, bullies often report feeling less control over their environment and report believing that others blame them for things they can't help.[32] Bullying others may be one way to regain some sense of power or control. Another contribution is *hostile attribution bias*, which is the tendency to perceive others' actions as aggressive and threatening, sometimes leading a child to respond in kind.³³ Contexts that model aggression as a form of conflict resolution or emotion regulation can also lead children to engage in bullying behaviors when confronted with something or someone they do not like.³⁴ Billy embodies many of these motivations. As a child, Billy's mother leaves him without giving him the option to go with her, and his father abuses him. These experiences lead Billy to feel powerless and adopt aggression as a means of interacting with others and to interpret others' presence as negative and aggressive.³⁵

Retaliation is another motivator for bullying wherein a child may be a *bully-victim*, someone who gets bullied and in turn bullies others.³⁶ Children who perpetuate aggression toward others when they experience conflict often struggle to develop key social-emotional skills. That is, children who bully may not have developed skills in conflict resolution, empathy, perspective-taking, adaptive coping, acceptance of responsibility, self-management, or interpersonal awareness. It is important for both children and adults to understand that youth do not typically bully each other out of pure malice. Children who bully do need to experience consequences for their behavior, while also getting help with difficulties the child is having and/or skills they have not developed yet. Troy's mother should not excuse her son's behaviors (and, admittedly, we do not know whether she is aware of them),³⁷ yet she must also recognize there are needs (e.g., safe spaces) that are not being met for him.

Addressing Bullying

Strategies for coping with bullying fall into at least four different categories: constructive, externalizing, cognitive distancing, and self-blame.³⁸ *Constructive strategies* directly address bullying and the child's feelings about the experience in what is considered a productive manner, such as talking about situations with friends, avoiding the bully, planning what to do next time, or engaging in self-soothing. When Dustin explains his medical condition or when Mike tries to reason with the bullies, they are engaging in constructive coping. *Externalizing strategies* also directly address the situation and/or resulting emotions, but in ways that are outwardly oriented and often not viewed as positive. An example would be hitting the bully, like Steve does with Billy.[39] *Cognitive distancing* does not directly address the problem but may serve as a protective factor against negative emotions as it involves ignoring the bully, trying to forget about it, and pretending to not care. Mike appears to do this multiple times. While he does not actively avoid the bullies, he does not seem to spend much time thinking on incidents either. *Self-blame* also does not directly address the problem but focuses on inward responsibility, such as the need to do something different or think that the bullying was deserved.

Perhaps surprisingly, constructive strategies are not reported by children as the most effective tools. Children who tell a teacher or try to stand up to the bully often experience increased victimization, while problem-solving does not always help the child cope.[40] Children who engage in these behaviors tend to report more frequent victimization and feel less successful in coping, which may explain why the children of *Stranger Things* continue to experience bullying despite using these strategies. However, there is some evidence that these strategies pay off over a longer period, suggesting the need for continual engagement in order for children to see the benefit of their use.[41] Yet children do not feel better when being told these strategies will eventually work. It is not hard to imagine Will or Dustin's frustration if they were repeatedly told that eventually the bully will stop if they just keep standing up to him, despite a lack of success so far.

In situations in which children do not have control or easily accessible resources (e.g., a supportive adult), avoidant behaviors can be beneficial as an initial response.[42] This may explain why cognitive distancing strategies appear to be common among victims and reported as a more effective response. Ignoring the bully often takes away the power they have in the situation by depriving them of attention and control. There is also a certain amount of detachment that occurs when using cognitive distancing that allows the victim to maintain their positive self-concept and self-image. For example, when Jonathan explains to Will that there is nothing wrong with him and that what other people think is not as important as what we think about ourselves, it allows Will to *cognitively distance* himself from the opinions of others.[43] This goes beyond simply accepting that bullying happens: It is accepting that bullying happens because other people have things to figure out, which does not mean that there is something wrong with the victim. This also highlights the ineffectiveness of self-blame, which internalizes that behavior as being deserved or accurate in some way. Self-blame, another way of seeking to regain control, is the least productive of the coping strategies. It is important that children are taught how to reframe and cognitively distance in the moment to address their psychological needs while working to engage in long-term constructive styles that address the problem more directly.

Bystanders

One of the most effective ways to address bullying is by training bystanders. Bystanders can join in on the bullying, stand up to the bully, or passively support the victim by offering support afterward.[44] For instance, Mike engages in supportive behavior when he tells Dustin that he thinks his medical condition is "like a superpower" after the bullies make fun of Dustin, while Steve engages in active defending of Lucas against Billy.[45] Often, children will passively support the victim or do nothing at all when they see bullying happen.

The risk of becoming a target may explain why children are more likely to stand up for victims if they have a stronger sense of moral responsibility, feel that others expect them to intervene, or have greater empathy.[46] Friendship, caring for each other, and feeling empathetic appear to be enough to outweigh the risk of intervening, such as Eleven actively defending her new friends against Troy in front of a large crowd.[47] Another factor is whether or not the child has experience and success with certain types of coping when they experience bullying. Children who are likely to seek social support when they are victimized are also more likely to provide social support when they see others being victimized.[48] Similarly, students who engage in externalizing behaviors as victims may become more likely to join in when witnessing bullying, while those who use more constructive approaches tend to defend others actively.[49] Interestingly, those who cognitively distance as victims are also more likely to defend others,[50] suggesting that students are able to recognize that what is most effective as a victim isn't always what is most effective as a bystander.

Adult Intervention

Although most children report that they don't think adult intervention is helpful, there are some ways that teachers, caregivers, and mentors can improve the situation. The first is to validate and offer the emotion-focused support that helps mitigate the distress experienced by the victim.[51] Often, adults try to problem-solve for children or deny the need to be sad in ways that overlook their emotional needs, unintentionally dismissing or invalidating those emotions in the process. When discussing the fact that other kids call Will a freak, Jonathan says, "You're not a freak!"[52] Jonathan is trying to convince Will that the bullies are wrong without recognizing that Will does, in fact, feel different and is bothered. Jonathan achieves greater success when he backtracks and focuses on normalizing that experience instead of trying to solve the problem for Will. Sometimes the most effective intervention involves listening, validating, and asking what the child thinks will help the situation before offering our own advice. Helping a victim to distance the behaviors of another from their personal self-worth is key, while helping perpetrators recognize the need for more productive means of communicating and having their needs met also helps.

Mental health interventions are valuable in addressing bullying for both the victim and the bully. Both benefit from *cognitive behavioral therapy* (CBT) approaches that focus on reframing negative thought patterns, establishing behaviors that are helpful and not harmful to others, and practicing skills in conflict resolution, empathy, and adaptive coping with peer stress.[53] An example of CBT *reframing* occurs when Nancy's mom says that she is proud of her only for Nancy to scoff, focusing on the fact that she got fired. Her mom *reframes* the situation by saying it's "because you stood up for yourself."[54] Mrs. Wheeler helps Nancy see how the situation reveals her strength, not her failure. When working with children who engage in bullying behaviors, mental and behavioral health providers tend to focus on approaches that rely on *choice therapy* (e.g., making choices that lead to better outcomes) and accountability while also addressing stress, interpersonal communication, and anger management when working with aggressive children.[55] Were Billy or Troy to receive services at school, the counselor, psychologist, or social worker would likely focus on the fear and distress that fuels their anger, try to help them build empathy toward others, and find productive ways for them to gain a sense of control in their lives.

Adults too often to focus on punishment over understanding. Yet researchers found that *restorative justice practices*, where children are guided through the process of understanding each other and redressing harm they have caused, are more effective in reducing bullying behaviors.[56] In one example of restorative practice, Steve removes the disparaging comments about Nancy from the theater marquee and seeks out Jonathan to apologize, both undoing the vandalism and working toward mitigating damage he has instigated.[57] By helping children understand how their feelings and thoughts contribute to behaviors, actively confront the impact those behaviors have on others, and work toward mitigating the harm they have caused, we provide an intentional, comprehensive method that has a long-lasting impact on behaviors. As such, the effectiveness of restorative justice is twofold: The bully learns to be accountable for the impact of their behavior while the victim is encouraged toward healing.

Prevention

Prevention is most effective when strategies are consistent and universal across a system (e.g., a school) and they emphasize the role of bystanders in helping create safe and supportive climates that do not support bullying behaviors.[58] Prevention programs that teach children to be *upstanders*, those who stand up for others and themselves, are valuable tools as they focus on training youth to engage in productive and assertive behaviors that disrupt bullying. It is important that bullying prevention training and modeling are provided to children early and consistently as part of their weekly education. The presence of positive support systems and mentorship—such as Mr. Clarke's readiness to support inquiring minds, Eddie's guidance for freshman gamers, and Nancy's encouragement from her mom—will be crucial for preventing and reducing bullying. (Despite Brenner's sometimes-gentle encouragement and usually calm manner,[59] his authoritarian control coupled with shortcomings in offering nurturance and healthy guidance in his project may explain why bullying arises there even among youngsters who may have never learned it from outside peers. They learn it from their keepers.[60])

Despite any assumption that children will simply pick up the skills for addressing bullying on their own, the continued presence of bullying and passive bystanding suggest that's not entirely true. Rather than using punishment and blaming victims after bullying occurs, it is more efficient and effective to provide support, guidance, and a positive climate that builds an environment focused on reducing the likelihood of bullying ever occurring. As Hopper notes in his letter to Eleven, people need to "build an environment where we all feel comfortable, trusted, and open to sharing our feelings."[61] Creating a climate wherein bullying is deemed as unacceptable, rather than a fact of life, may be key to reducing bullying so children can learn, grow, and interact together in positive ways. Doing so strengthens not only the individual functioning of the child over the course of their life, but the health and well-being of the community as a whole.

> *"We showed you that school didn't have to be the worst years of your lives, right? Well, I'm here to tell you that there are other lost little sheepies out there who need help. Who need you."*
> —Eddie Munson[62]

Leandra Parris, PhD, NCSP, is an associate professor of school psychology at William & Mary. Her expertise is in socially just and trauma-informed educational practices. She loves sci-fi and popular culture, using both as teaching and healing tools. She regularly guests on Dark Loops Production podcasts, discussing series such as *Lovecraft Country* and *The Expanse*. She coauthored chapters in Popular Culture Psychology books on *Supernatural*, Black Panther, and the Joker.

Missing Children and the Impact on Their Loved Ones

Shelly Clevenger

"I don't care if anyone believes me. I am not gonna stop looking for him until I find him and bring him home!"
—Joyce Byers[1]

"When a person goes missing, the family deserves the truth."
—Families of the Missing, organization motto[2]

Hawkins, Indiana, is a place where, according to Chief Hopper, nothing ever happens.[3] That's what many people from small towns believe until something does happen and it changes the people and the place forever. *Stranger Things* chronicles the stories of characters in this town, with a focus on those who go missing. The first to vanish is Will Byers.[4] Early in the series, the focus is on finding Will, and in the following seasons the viewers see Will's adaptation to his life afterward. Another missing youth story in the first two seasons concerns Barbara (Barb) Holland.[5] The story of Eleven as a kidnapped child is explored throughout the series. These characters' stories, set during the early to mid-1980s in a small town, are relevant to issues of real-life missing children and their loved ones.

Public attention to missing children surged to the forefront of the national consciousness during the 1980s.[6] A series of high-profile cases of missing and murdered children gained considerable media attention and led to national campaigns to raise awareness about missing children. The most notable campaign put missing children's faces and information on milk cartons, pizza boxes, and billboards.[7] People across the country, but particularly in small towns and suburbia, began to worry that their children would be kidnapped. During this time, it seemed that everywhere someone looked, there was a missing child. It was the height of "stranger danger," and the nation was on edge (nations, actually, because the phenomenon by no means remained exclusive to the United States).[8]

Despite their paranormal circumstances, youth disappearances in *Stranger Things* reflect the fears of the nation at that time, as well as the painful issues that loved ones face when a child disappears and their whereabouts are unknown. Each year, close to half a million children are reported missing.[9] (The majority of these are coded as runaways, but the figures include thousands of abductions nevertheless.[10]) When a child goes missing, loved ones experience a range of emotions such as terror, anger, sadness, helplessness, and fear. They also may experience disbelief, numbness, and shock. Loved ones exist in a state between hope for their loved ones' return and complete hopelessness. Many suffer clinical disorders such as depression, anxiety, and posttraumatic stress disorder (PTSD).[11] The stories of Will Byers, Barbara Holland, and Eleven reflect the psychological impact that missing children have on the people who care about them, as well as the challenges that occur when the missing sometimes return.

Boundary Ambiguity

Among the hardest things for the loved ones of missing children to deal with are the change or absence of that person and the lack of knowing when—or if—they will return. *Boundary ambiguity* arises when a person feels unsure who is still part of the family and who is not. Most people will deal with boundary ambiguity at some point in life as family members move away, leave for college, return from deployment, marry, divorce, lose spouses, relocate, or suffer dementia.[12] Confusion about who counts as an active part of the family or other group based on circumstances can cause stress, anxiety, or uncertainty about the group itself among those who are still in it. When a person goes missing, that person is absent physically, psychologically, and socially, and yet others carry the knowledge and commonly the hope that the missing person could return and be a part of the group or family once again. Uncertainty is stressful. Uncertainty can make it hard for family and friends of that person to move forward.[13] They do not want to treat the missing member as someone who is gone because they do not know for sure that they are, but they also need to keep living and moving forward. The family exists in a sort of limbo state.[14]

When Will goes missing, boundary ambiguity emerges among members of both his family and his close friend group. While they are hopeful and (mostly) believe Will to be alive, they do not know for sure. He is both gone and not really gone. Will's friends Mike, Lucas, and Dustin go to school, but they do not return to fun activities such as *Dungeons & Dragons* without him. Joyce and Jonathan go back and forth between working and actively searching for Will. This resembles how real-life family and friends feel. They try to go about their daily lives and follow a routine, yet there is this missing piece. Loved ones of missing people find it difficult to exist while their loved one is absent. As Will tries to get in touch with his mother and friends, this creates more boundary ambiguity. He is not physically there, but he is talking with them, albeit not in a familiar way. As Joyce creates her alphabet Christmas light display to communicate with Will, she is furthering that ambiguity because she believes she is talking to Will and that he is alive, but he is not part of the family unit physically or in any way she or anyone can understand.[15] She cannot see or hear him or reach him through conventional means. Hearing from him gives her both hope and anguish. This type of stress can be seen in real-life missing children's cases as well, if some limited contact exists between the missing person and the loved ones (such as random letters home or ransom messages). As a result, there can be greater distress for loved ones as the person knows they are out there. The "not knowing" or ambiguity surrounding the place of a missing person in the family is often one of the most challenging things for loved ones to endure.[16]

Rumination and Counterfactual Thinking

In addition to the boundary ambiguity that can be felt when a person goes missing, one of the other psychological issues that arises within loved ones is often a result of *pervasive rumination*, a.k.a. *ruminative thinking*, when a person goes over thoughts in their mind repeatedly.[17] They are thinking about something on a loop. It is often uncontrollable and persistent, and the individual may focus on negative thoughts or events on repeat. Loved ones of missing persons also deal with *counterfactual thinking*, when a person dwells on all the things that could have happened instead of what happened.[18] It is a sort of fantasy regarding how they wish the past could be different, even though it cannot. This includes wishing that they had done things differently before, and that their outcomes could be different now.

In families of missing persons, pervasive rumination and counterfactual thinking can become all-consuming and thus cause extreme emotional distress. During the initial crisis phase, when an active search and investigation occur (usually within the first month), pervasive rumination occurs frequently when loved ones fall into states of perpetual fear. The search and the wait stress people.[19] They believe that their child's life is in immediate danger, and they may constantly agonize about the suffering and harm possibly befalling the child. Repetitive negative thinking can manifest itself physically into gastrointestinal distress, nausea, shaking, headaches, or sleep disturbances. Depending on how long the person is gone, negative thinking can be pervasive and long-term, and can result in both psychological and physical effects.

In the case of Will Byers, he goes missing on Sunday, November 6, 1983. His disappearance is not discovered until the next morning, when Joyce gets angry with her older son, Jonathan, for not being home to watch over Will. She also feels angry with herself for not being home.[20] Rumination and counterfactual thinking each seem likely to become a focus for Joyce, based on her reaction to Will's disappearance. She grows visibly shaken and upset during the earlier part of the investigation and search for Will. Though she tries briefly to resume regular life, she does not succeed. Until Will is discovered, Joyce behaves in a way that is detrimental to her psychological and physical health as a result of ruminative thinking. The clearest example of this arises when she creates what she believes is a system to communicate with Will through Christmas lights. While the viewers know that this is accurate and that she actually is communicating with her son, people in her life would think that she has been overwhelmed with the stress of her child's being missing and has suffered some sort of breakdown. Joyce appears strained and shaken by her own effort. She herself realizes that her behavior may be seen as strange and may even be harmful to herself when she says, "Maybe I am a mess, maybe I'm crazy, maybe I'm out of my mind! But God help me, I will keep these lights up until the day I die, if I think there's a chance that Will's still out there!"[21]

Individuals who dwell on negative thoughts often suffer emotional distress, anxiety, or depression, sometimes with aforementioned physical symptoms such as headaches or vomiting.[22] Ruminative thoughts can also lead to changes in behavior that many would not understand. Parents of missing children may find themselves consumed with these thoughts and may turn to things that many would deem "crazy," such as working with a detective, psychic, mercenary, or con artist to find their child. Will's friends, desperate to find him, turn to Eleven. Joyce asks Eleven to use her psychic gifts to help them find Will in the Upside Down, and this ultimately leads his friends and family to rescue him. This behavior, if viewed by others, may be seen as harmful to themselves and as a result of endured stress from a friend going missing.

Barbara Holland's loved ones also experience ruminative thinking, aching to know what happened to her. Jonathan and Nancy look for Barb extensively and fixate on what happened to her and where she could be. This takes them into the Upside Down, where they discover Barb's lifeless body. Later, they learn that Barb's parents have expended their funds and are selling their house to pay for an investigator to search for Barb, despite Nancy and Jonathan's knowing the truth that Barb will never come back or even be found.[23] Barb's parents have thought of little else other than finding their daughter and learning what could be happening to her. They cling to hope for her return.

Eleven's mother, Terry Ives, shows the most extreme example of ruminative thinking. After her daughter Jane gets stolen by Dr. Brenner,

Terry is told the baby died at birth. Terry never believes this, though, and insists her child has been kidnapped. This already causes much rumination as Terry dwells on what has happened to her daughter and imagines the worst. Terry tries to get her daughter back legally but is unsuccessful. The loss of the legal battle arguably would cause further rumination, as she would be focused on the pain her daughter may be experiencing while feeling helpless to help her. The ruminative thinking may then be what pushes Terry to then try to take her daughter back by force by going into Hawkins Lab with a gun, shooting a guard in the process.[24] After Jane's captors cause Terry's brain damage and induce a vegetative, catatonic-like state of *unresponsive wakefulness*,[25] the functioning part of Terry does little but ruminate.

Coping

Different coping strategies emerge. For many, the means they pursue is clinging to the idea or hope that the loved one will return. At first, hope flares strongly in all of Will's friends, his mother, brother, and Chief Hopper, who oversees the investigation. They believe the boy to be alive because they want him to be. Barb's loved ones also employ the coping strategy of hope. In each case, the adults take action. Joyce puts up Christmas lights, whereas the Hollands take the normally more-reasonable action of hiring an investigator to find their daughter. Families of missing children often remain hopeful of their child's return to cope with their feelings. For example, some families keep a child's room just as they left it even though decades pass as they cling to any hope that loved one will come home. Others set a place setting each night at dinner in case they return. This effort to manage stress may paradoxically distress members of the group or family as there is no closure or ending to their pain. Some missing persons cases are never solved, and the loved ones spend years or decades waiting. This is often why after a period if a missing person is not found, the family may hold a memorial service or funeral for them. It allows the loved ones to have closure and know that the person is gone. Barb's parents finally hold a funeral for her after a report is released that she has been killed, supposedly by toxins released by the Hawkins Lab.

Missing persons' families can also catastrophize and imagine the worst. Depending on how long their loved ones are gone, this could take a heavy emotional toll. Individuals experiencing loss may need to work with a professional therapist or counselor who understands the complexities of missing persons. This can help families cope through the process and prepare for the possibility they must let go. When Joyce and Chief Hopper eventually find Will, he is in the Upside Down. Even the worst fears that they may have ruminated on have not prepared them for what they see or for how near he may still be to death. Will is found unconscious in a strange world with a tendril from a monster down his throat. Real-life families of missing children are often unprepared for the reality of what happens to their children if recovered. Despite imagining the horrible things that could have happened, facing the reality is often hard to deal with.

The Return of Missing Children

Loved ones normally feel overjoyed when a missing person returns. However, there can be obstacles to smooth reunification. Reuniting can cause emotional distress and psychological consequences. During a readjustment period, one reacclimates to life before the trauma. Though Will is later back home in Hawkins, he experiences flashes of seeing the Upside Down.[26] This parallels how missing children who return home may feel. They can have flashbacks and otherwise relive the trauma, even though they are safe now. The visions Will experiences mirror experiences of those who suffer posttraumatic stress disorder (PTSD). They can be okay and living their lives one moment, but then experience a trigger that reminds them of their trauma and the time when they were gone. Joyce, too, exhibits symptoms of PTSD in the second season with her own trigger. Each time the phone rings, for example, she freezes with fear. This likely brings back memories of when, during Will's absence, the phone would ring. The sound of the phone elicits all those turbulent feelings she had while hoping he would call yet fretting over how to help him.

After Will returns, family and friends are elated, but he is not the same child anymore. Joyce notices this and assures him, "I will never,

ever let anything bad happen to you ever again. Whatever's going on in you, we're gonna fix it." This is a common reaction from family members. They want to fix or restore their child to who they were before, and they try to protect them from future danger. A typical response from loved ones, especially parents, is a desire for things to go back to "normal." Joyce does seek the help of doctors who work in the lab, but the doctors are unable to help Will in any meaningful way. In Will's case, it is because of his connection to the monster and is paranormal in nature. Loved ones who want to move forward and "let it go" may feel frustrated if those who have returned need or seek treatment, as if some the loved ones feel that treatment may prolong the issue. Children may have issues communicating what happened and how they feel about it. Trauma does not get an easy fix. Though unable to verbalize completely what he has experienced and how he is feeling, Will is able to communicate through art, by painting pictures and coloring with crayons. *Art therapy* is a powerful and useful tool for children who have experienced traumatic events. It is often used with children as part of a *treatment plan* for those who have been missing.

Finally, in terms of coping, sometimes people who experience trauma find that value in making new start or removing themselves from places or items that hold traumatic memories. In the case of the Byers family, they and Eleven do exactly that after Hopper's disappearance and apparent death: They move out of Indiana. Relocating can sometimes be helpful because it gives individuals physical distance from sources of trauma in addition to removing physical reminders that can be triggering. While you may take the internal trauma with you, leaving the daily reminders of it behind can, up to a point, help ease the pain.

The Path Forward for Loved Ones of Missing Children

The stories of Will and Barb as missing youths, as well as the experiences of their loved ones, give audiences a glimpse into what it would be like to have a child go missing. In a different way, Eleven's story does this too. While there is a supernatural or science-fiction twist on their disappearances, the feelings their friends and families experience are a good representation of the pain and desperation people feel in real life.

Having a loved one go missing is traumatic and can cause a host of enduring psychological consequences. Families should work with professionals who specialize in the reunification process, the process of reuniting families and loved ones of those who are missing. Loved ones, too, should work with professionals as they need to understand this specific kind of trauma and respond in a helpful way, as well as needing to deal with their own trauma.

The focus in the 1980s on missing children and stranger danger does not change the fact that the issue of missing children remains important today.[27] We no longer have children on milk cartons, but we do have mechanisms to alert us of missing children such as AMBER Alerts and organizations actively dedicated to bringing missing children home.[28] Awareness about the circumstance of missing children can be helpful in recovering those who are missing. The Center for Missing and Exploited Children provides a wealth of knowledge for parents, guardians, friends, family, and every interested person to better educate themselves on how they can help in the fight to help missing children.

Shelly Clevenger, PhD, chairs the nation's first department of victim studies at Sam Houston State University. She has authored peer-reviewed journal publications and books on victimization. Her research and teaching include looks at violence and victimization in comic books and popular culture. She volunteers with survivors to create their own comic books to cope with their victimization. Her teaching and survivor activism have been recognized with several national awards.

8

Missing You
An Exploration into Missing Persons, Ambiguous Loss, and the Journey to Acceptance

Brittani Oliver Sillas-Navarro & Travis Adams

"Sometimes, when one person is missing, the whole world seems depopulated."
—author/poet Alphonse de Lamartine[1]

"You're talking about grief. This is different."
—Joyce Byers[2]

Bad things can happen to good people. The world we live in can at times feel full of peril and terror. Nevertheless, we try to prevail. In the Upside Down, all our true fears emerge.[3] The Upside Down presents a dark and distorted reflection of anxieties we lock away in hidden rooms while monsters lurk just beneath the surface. *Stranger Things* depicts a heroic tale of people who choose to believe in the extraordinary possibility of their missing person's return. *Stranger Things* also introduces grief and loss as it relates to the experience of missing or unidentified persons. Community members experience loss in which people who are found do not all return unscathed, and for some families the missing never come home. The characters are tasked with building their own resilience through the ebb and flow of the re-traumatizations that occur when an individual goes missing. It is in these stories that we find mothers, brothers, community members, and even strangers who summon courage and strive to perform a rescue that may seem impossible, and sometimes we see those lost souls find a new way home and endeavor to restore the possibility of life after loss.

Grief and Ambiguous Loss for the Missing

The experience of losing a loved one can be profound. The complexities of grief and bereavement can become daunting and unrelenting. Conceptualizing the loss and expressing painful emotions in the grief process are critical elements in the grief experience.[4] Although commonly expected to diminish over time, the throes of grief and loss can span a lifetime. The inability to process one's responses or inclination to live in denial can complicate the grief process.[5] Cultural expectations can also negatively influence the grief experience, as when grieving persons are mourning beyond the culturally acceptable timeframe. The bereaved are more susceptible to shame and being labeled as those unable to grieve in adaptive and functional ways.[6]

Joyce Byers feels driven to solve the problem of her missing child even if that effort gets dismissed by others. Joyce holds hope for her son's safe return despite feeling minimized by authorities. Her suffering is mislabeled as a desperate and unnecessary response to her child's disappearance, thus culturally negating her concerns.[7] Complex and persistent grief expressions are displayed in long-term periods (*chronic grief* beyond a year). These include but are not limited to yearning, longing, intense pain and sorrow, preoccupation about the deceased or missing person, shock, emotional numbness, anger, bitterness, social disruption, difficulty trusting others, meaninglessness, detachment from others, and role confusion. Although grief after a loss can be inevitable, people demonstrate different styles of grieving we may go through, styles that vary from person to person and by the type of loss we each experience.[8]

When we repress or suppress our grief, it can become harmful and form into *distorted grief*, a type displayed through an intense sadness that becomes disabling to the individual along with an intense anger.[9] When ex-husband Lonnie arrives at Joyce's home, he shows little emotion about the fact that their son Will is missing, focusing instead on the state of the house (including, admittedly, huge holes in the walls).[10] Lonnie may be struggling with *delayed grief*, which may present through denial of grief and lack of emotion.[11]

Ambiguous loss occurs when an individual experiences unresolved grief that yields no closure due to not knowing an individual's whereabouts or state.[12] Ambiguous loss also creates an endless cycle of unanswered questions and is significant in the survivors of a missing person. Joyce Byers has lost a child in a flash of a moment and must cope with the complications.[13] She's depicted as an overly stressed and worried mother who amplifies her urgency and concerns about her missing child to others while simultaneously experiencing the incessant dread that her son Will may be dead or never found. This ambiguity leads her to have a heightened fixation on the fact that her son is missing and an uncontrollable urge to continue searching for him relentlessly. Here lies the motivation of so many family members who have a missing loved one in the world: They yearn for answers. Ambiguous loss for the missing is exemplified through holding onto the hope that the person will be found whether alive or dead, or having to exist in a world in which neither outcome is substantiated.[14] Due to this sort of frozen-grief state and constant contemplation of possibilities, families of the missing can experience immobilizing trauma and difficulty coping.[15] The Byers family members present various versions of their grief present while searching for answers. Survivors of the missing may experience emotional attacks, denial, intrusive images, guilt, searching, emotional need,[16] searching for justice, and complicated grief.[17] The lack of proof and emotional ambiguity for presumed death of missing persons can induce psychological distress and preoccupation with the missing.[18]

The Anatomy of a Missing Person

In the United States, approximately 2,300 people are reported missing daily, with more than 90,000 missing person cases remaining active at any given time, around half a million throughout the year.[19] Although many of these individuals are found alive, still others are found dead or are still considered missing. In fact, up to 4,400 human bodies go unidentified each year in the United States. Officially, a *missing person* is someone whose location is currently unknown and thus causes concern for their current state and safety.[20] Missing persons have diverse backgrounds with various cultural factors and a wide range of outcomes.[21] They include abductees, runaways, and people who are lost, missing, or injured.[22] Their cases can be determined as *missing intentionally* (family stressors, mental illness, dementia) or *missing unintentionally* (illegal activities, foul play).[23] Some risk factors for missing persons include mental health issues, substance use, limited supervision, risky behavior, rural areas, poverty, history of abuse, sexual exploitation, dysfunctional family dynamics, youth (especially among women), and limited parental advisement.[24] The community's quiet, rural setting may increase susceptibility for persons gone missing. In addition, Will becomes a prime target for becoming a missing person not only due to his age and biological sex, but also because adult supervision is limited.[25] A concurrent theme in *Stranger Things* is adults are often absent in situations where terror is likely, and this potentially invites the younger characters into harm's way.[26] Additional negative consequences for anyone who has been a missing person include the possibility—or fear—of becoming a missing person again, reexperiencing the negative event as *secondary victimization*.[27] As we see in the case development of Will Byers, he is unable to escape the trauma of the Upside Down brought on by suffering flashbacks,[28] having his personal souvenir arrive in the form of the slug he throws up,[29] plus his lingering link to the Mind Flayer.[30] For Will, the initial missing event produces additional retraumatization and increases the likelihood of revictimization leading to more risky behaviors, with children being the most susceptible.[31]

Eleven also goes missing when abducted by a government-controlled conspiracy during her infancy[32] and then again after destroying the

Demogorgon as she approaches adolescence.[33] These repeated experiences demonstrate the high-risk population that often finds itself prone to additional risky and potentially life-threatening events. Protective factors that can reduce the likelihood of becoming a missing person include positive social support, age, and higher cognitive ability.[34] In her initial descent to the Upside Down, Nancy finds that she can evade threats due to her size, agility, and cognitive functioning, and knowledge gained there later prepares her and helps protect against subsequent danger.[35]

Loving a Missing Person

Individuals who love a missing person undergo unique challenges. Those who have a missing person in their lives may face occupational and financial difficulties, lack social support, suffer blame and emotional distress, and have continued ambiguity over the loss. Coping with ambiguous loss is complicated if no resolution for the missing ever comes. Families whose missing persons are found, whether dead or alive, are allotted *closure* in their experience, whereas those whose loved one remains missing perpetually reexperience the loss and longing for the missing and thus struggle to cope.[36]

Joyce's struggle in facing a disappearance leads to additional difficulty regaining stability in the home.[37] Jonathan, who initially blames himself for the disappearance, experiences his own set of unique grief provocations. The family spirals as each member and their concurrent supportive persons must tackle the challenges of wishing Will to be found alive and well. Some families of the missing actively search and do everything within their power to find their missing loved ones, while others passively search and some wearily wait. When Hopper first learns about Will's disappearance, he attempts to dissuade Joyce in searching for her son, mentioning statistics that nine out of ten missing persons are with relatives.[38] Grieving rituals are common for those who have missing persons, including memorials and dedication services as well as finding additional strength and insight since the disappearance.[39] These life-changing circumstances can dramatically affect mental and emotional functioning as well. Those with loved ones who are missing may experience increased persistent complex grief,[40] relational and interpersonal issues, and increased detachment. "Living in limbo" while experiencing ambiguity "between grief and loss" becomes a common theme for those who have loved someone who is missing.[41]

Due to the volatile nature of Jane's abduction to the Hawkins Lab so she may be indoctrinated as Eleven, it is evident from her mother's attempt to rescue her—and the violent aftereffects of her attempt—the experience of loss is psychologically profound and persistent.[42] This experience can lead to higher rates of psychopathology, including depression, PTSD, and regression.[43] Examples of increased symptomology for survivors of the missing include higher rumination, painful thoughts, and elevated psychiatric symptoms and inflexibility.[44] Ambiguous grief for missing persons has been seen as vacillating grief[45] or chronic distress and agony due to lack of closure.

The Holland family displays this anguish when Barbara's parents continue to struggle with the absence of closure over their missing daughter.[46] The push to live normally can be complicated for those with a missing person unrecovered.[47] Family functioning and boundaries can be negatively impaired due to having to adapt to life without the presence of the missing person.[48] Risk factors that perpetuate continued complex bereavement for survivors include external stressors, conflict, ambiguity, relational issues, social disenfranchisement, isolation, stigmatization, political and public silencing, and cultural and spiritual stressors.

A family's struggle while processing their loved one's vanishing can reduce their receptiveness to help. Communities tend to gather in aid and support. Chief Hopper and his deputies search for Will begrudgingly. Upon locating his bike along the roadside, Hopper finally accepts that this is a legitimate missing person's case. He and his deputies bring the bike home while organizing a search party with the residents of Hawkins to help.[49] With the aid of the community, police are often given more resources such as additional law enforcement officers from nearby towns. These increased efforts generate more information from the community, a decrease in discretion from police and community leaders, and additional supplies donated to aid the search party.[50] Once the chief believes Will has gone missing, he stays out all night with volunteers looking for the young boy while community members surround him and the other officers.[51]

While many members of the community offer their assistance in searching, these individuals are receiving something for their time and efforts, an *intrinsic* (internalized) reward for providing long-term empathy.[52] Through an understanding of others' emotions, empathy allows for a deeper and more altruistic motivator for helping others.[53] Other factors that impact a community's response are the inclusion of individuals within an in- or outgroup. Communities associate positive emotions for those within the *ingroup*, those who are members of any specific group (as opposed to *outgroup*, those not in the group). When a community relates to a member of the ingroup who has gone missing, they tend to be more empathetic to the missing individual and provide greater helping behaviors with longer-lasting aid.[54] When a person from the outgroup goes missing, the levels of empathy appear lower, and expressions of judgment and prejudice toward the missing persons are higher.[55] During a school assembly to discuss Will, two bullies laugh and joke about the boy's disappearance, infuriating Mike, who is Will's closest friend and the leader of their D&D group. Mike pushes one of the bullies to the ground, challenging the inappropriate behavior.[56] Through this interaction, we see examples of both compassion and disdain from teachers and students within the school.[57]

Resilience and Recovery

When a person has gone missing but then returns or is found, they and their family members and close friends may have significant long-term effects personally and within their support networks. Left-behind members and the returning individuals learn to readjust, making social changes while they reunite. The left-behind often must try to ease the previously missing person back into their own life.[58] Characteristics that could impact one's ability to reintegrate can include how long the individual was missing and the severity of any traumatic events experienced. The shift in returning for the individual can add to their sense of guilt and shame.

Will finds himself met with positive messages from many community members but name-calling by others. He receives messages of

"Zombie Boy" written on a newspaper article about "the boy who came back to life" shoved in his locker, and school bullies call him this name as they pass him in the hallway.[59] Too often, unfortunately, the voice of the young person is ignored.[60] Though Will attempts to ignore these comments, they do not go unnoticed by him or those closest to him.

When a missing person has returned home, they are sometimes encouraged to reintegrate back into their routine at a pace dictated by friends and family instead of at their pace, a pace more comfortable to themselves. By expediting their reintegration, persons who have returned can exacerbate trauma symptoms, increasing the confusion while reentering their own lives. Those who may have experienced additional trauma such as sexual assault, physical or emotional distress, or mental abuse while missing may find it difficult to assimilate in a healthy manner even when they control the pace. These changes are impacted with the connection they have to their ingroup. The closer they feel they are connected and supported by others, the greater the reduction in symptoms they may exhibit. Conversely, if they feel disconnected from their ingroup, they may amplify symptoms. Other factors that may have an effect on their reintegration is how they handle levels of stress and any traumatic reminders they experience.[61]

During Will's routine medical tests, Dr. Owens describes how victims of traumatic experiences may undergo personality changes as the anniversary of their trauma nears,[62] the so-called *anniversary effect* or *anniversary reaction*.[63] Individuals experiencing trauma or who have developed posttraumatic stress disorder often find a spike in symptoms as they near the anniversary date of their trauma despite work previously done on their recovery.[64] Common symptoms associated with PTSD include nightmares, flashbacks, hypervigilance, emotional numbing, or isolating and avoiding. Flashbacks and other *reexperiencing* symptoms can happen at any time without intent or directly associated thoughts, whether due to a memory, movie, scent, taste, or other trigger. These can be overwhelming, causing physical reactions of anxiety, shortness of breath, and, in some cases, panic attacks. Will Byers struggles to tell his friends and family about the things he still sees after returning from the Upside Down. Unable to share, he internalizes his pain and attempts to handle it alone.[65] As Will struggles after his return, he attempts to hide his thoughts and feelings that remind him of his trauma, which adds to the symptoms of isolation and avoidance.[66]

Although not the norm in missing persons cases, those found deceased[67] leave behind family and loved ones struggling to accept the reality of their loss.[68] Nancy worries when she doesn't see Barb the day after Steve's party. She searches for Barb, rejecting the idea that she has run away. Nancy struggles to accept this, and blames herself for not being with her and choosing to spend time with Steve. She feels alone in her grieving, and isolates herself from her family and friends.[69] The ambiguity Nancy feels causes her to struggle, denying her the ability to process the loss and guilt. She suffers self-blame and lacks trust in others. Nancy finds only a little closure when she learns that Barb has been killed in the Upside Down, but she finds more later when she is able to confirm Barb's death and provide Barb's parents with some answers.[70] Helping them find closure helps her find some too. Memory of the guilt lingers, of course, which may be why she later keeps less-experienced adventurer Robin close while they hunt for Vecna.[71]

Living in ambiguity, friends and family of missing persons who never return may act in ways that others cannot comprehend.[72] There is no manual for how to feel, and yet others will scrutinize reactions that defy their expectations. If a person or body cannot be recovered, the families' process of unresolved grief may cause them to freeze in decision-making, set unclear or unhealthy boundaries for a meaningful life, or focus on the missing person to the exclusion of anything else.[73] Through ambiguous mourning, families left behind who are unsure of their loved one's status may hang on to hope to avoid grieving the loss or may accept that the person is truly gone in order to feel some closure.[74] Nancy and Steve visit Barb's parents for dinner on a regular basis. Barb's mother discusses how she knew the dinner was this night but time "got away" from her and she finds she lost track, so she went to get takeout. Her focus and thoughts distract her from her day-to-day living. Steve and Nancy ask about the for-sale sign in the front yard, and the parents share how they are selling their house to help pay for an investigator to help find Barb.[75] Often, family members who have remained behind ruminate on their desire to change the past and begin to practice negative self-talk with a focus of self-blame and shame. They will criticize their own previous behavior from before the individual went missing and may begin to make any sacrifice to help find the missing loved ones.[76]

My Missing Story

"You act like you're all alone out there in the world, but you're not. You're not alone."
        —Joyce Byers[77]

When a person has gone missing, the primary focus is on locating them, preferably alive and well. This should not be the only focus for law enforcement or community search parties, though. Searchers' reactions to those found need to be expressed in ways that do not create feelings of guilt and shame.[78] When Will returns from the Upside Down, he is placed in a hospital to be checked over physically. When Mike, Dustin, and Lucas can see him, they overwhelm Will with the retelling of the adventures they experienced in their efforts to find and save him.[79] If a person returns and is immediately brought into questioning without care and compassion for what they have experienced, this can add to their already-growing sense of shame and distress. Returned persons find that coming back into a community can be extremely stressful and would benefit from occurring slowly over a few days.[80]

Stranger Things allows its audience to experience the emotions and heartbreak that happen when those who went missing are found, lost, or mourned. Ambiguous loss engulfs those who remain behind, waiting an unknown amount of time for news about whether their loved one is still living or will be found deceased. Those who struggle with ambiguous loss report feeling alone, detached, angry, and struggle with role confusion. Upon return, those who have gone missing may struggle with an inability to trust others, may be filled with guilt or shame, or may feel overwhelmed integrating back into their community. When accepting someone back into your life after their absence, it is normal to be met with difficulties. It is important to understand that those who return often suffer lasting psychological effects. For their support network, it is important that compassion and empathy will play a role in their reintegration.

"Nothing is going to go back to the way that it was. Not really.
But it'll get better. In time."
—Chief Jim Hopper[81]

Brittani Oliver Sillas-Navarro obtained her master's degree and is currently ABD for her PsyD in couples and family therapy. She has presented nationally and internationally on topics such as culture and sexuality, and she specializes in grief and bereavement. Mrs. Oliver Sillas-Navarro has been a contributing author on *Black Panther Psychology: Hidden Kingdom*. She has paneled at Comic-Con and on podcasts discussing the topics of superhero therapy, popular culture psychology, and sports psychology.

Travis Adams received his MSW from the University of Southern California and is currently a readjustment counselor working with United States active-duty military and veterans. A Marine Corps veteran who specializes in helping service members diagnosed with PTSD, anxiety, depression, struggle with substance-use disorder and other diagnosas, he utilizes various types of therapy to aid service members in their recovery. He has incorporated the use of popular culture in conjunction with standardized treatment models. Find Travis on Twitter: @themarine_peer.

Lonely Things
Surviving Trauma and Loneliness with Some Help from Our Friends

Janina Scarlet & Jenna Busch

"Yet we do deny our loneliness . . . as if feeling lonely means there's something wrong with us. We feel shame around being lonely even when it's caused by grief, loss, or heartbreak."
—social work researcher Brené Brown[1]

"Society left them behind. Hurt them. Discarded them."
—Kali (Eight)[2]

When people experience any traumatic experience such as a breakup, abandonment, kidnapping, torture, or emotional or physical abuse, they are also likely to feel disconnected from other people in their lives. Think about how Hopper shuts himself away from the world after his young daughter, Sara, dies and his marriage ends.[3] Similarly, Eleven's mother, Terry Ives, retreats into her own world after her daughter is stolen from her even before a toxic assault leaves Ives broadly unresponsive;[4] Max distances herself from everyone else when burdened by guilt over Billy's death;[5]

and imprisoned Hopper comes to think Joyce would be better off with-out him.[6]

Even trauma survivors who have friends and loved ones around them might still feel emotionally disconnected from other people. This kind of perceived emotional disconnection fosters the feeling of loneliness.[7] For example, Mike's mom, Karen Wheeler, feels lonely much of the time, like her life is empty even though her husband lives with her. His physical presence alone is insufficient. The two barely talk and hardly spend time together. As a result, Karen feels disconnected from him, causing her to feel sexually tempted by Billy Hargrove, Max's stepbrother.[8]

Many people feel emotionally disconnected from others after expe-riencing trauma. In fact, feeling distant and cut off from others appears to be one of the most central symptoms in many trauma survivors.[9] Will later feels like his friends don't understand him, especially when he believes that they are moving on with their lives and their girlfriends while he remains stuck in his trauma.[10] And even though his friends are physically there with him, they can't reach him emotionally.

Feeling disconnected from others leads to loneliness, which nega-tively affects people's mental and physical health. It can even be respon-sible for their continued suffering and premature death.[11] On the other hand, supportive communities can help improve people's mental and physical health and expand their lifespan.[12] Both Eleven and Dustin struggle with feelings of loneliness, and both benefit from their connec-tions to others. As Eleven gets closer to Mike and his friends, and later establishes her friendship with Max, she grows visibly less lonely and more comfortable with herself.[13] Similarly, when Nancy dances with Dustin at the Snow Ball dance after she sees him crying, Dustin visibly attains a newfound level of confidence, knowing that someone cares about him.[14]

Perceived Social Isolation

"The most common ailment I saw as a doctor was not heart dis-ease or diabetes. It was loneliness."
—former U.S. surgeon general Vivek Murthy[15]

Many people assume loneliness implies the absence of social interaction. However, loneliness is the *perceived* emotional disconnection, whether someone is actually in the presence of other people or not.[16] Even though Hopper is married during the illness and eventual death of his daughter, he feels isolated. He cries alone in a stairwell after reading Sara a story, despite his wife being at the hospital too.[17] Similarly, Nancy publicly acts like she is all right around her friends after the disappearance of her friend Barb but, knowing Barb is dead and feeling guilty over that fact, she cries alone in the bathroom without letting anyone know what she is going through.[18] (Though Nancy grows stronger and finds some closure after achieving a measure of justice for Barb, enough guilt lingers that Vecna later attempts to use those feelings against her as she crosses between worlds.[19])

For the past several decades, researchers who observe detrimental effects of loneliness on people's physical or mental health have suggested that the rates of loneliness have reached epidemic levels.[20] One of the main concerns doctors warn about regarding perceived loneliness is that its long-term effects can severely damage people's health. Prolonged effects of perceived loneliness have also been associated with an increased risk of heart disease, Alzheimer's disease, obesity, and certain types of cancer.[21] Along those lines, Will's mother, Joyce, seems to be going down this path through the first season, before her friends (and her children's friends) rally around her. Similarly, Murray Bauman, a conspiracy theorist and former journalist, lives alone and possibly in poor health. He seems to blossom as he connects to other characters such as Nancy and the Russian scientist Alexei (although losing any of his few known connections may also predict subsequent misery).[22]

Loneliness can significantly impede people's ability to sleep well, which, in turn, can reduce their ability to think clearly.[23] Joyce can barely sleep during Will's absence. Similarly, loneliness can also impair people's ability to regulate their attention, impair their ability to complete tasks (*executive function*), and it can reduce their ability to solve logical reasoning tasks such as solving work or numerical problems.[24] Joyce shows this as well throughout Will's disappearance. She's full of anxiety and has no friends that we are aware of. She forgets her keys, can't manage breakfast, and can't remember other simple things.

Because loneliness is so painful, people who feel lonely are more likely to become *hypervigilant* (excessively guarded) to being rejected. To avoid the hurt of rejection, they may isolate themselves in a vicious cycle.[25] Ever since Joyce's marriage fell apart, she keeps herself isolated and trapped within a cycle of working, coming home, sleeping, and repeating when we first meet her. Her older son, Jonathan, has been ostracized at school, so he turns to a solitary task, photography. Instead of trying to go out and make friends, he spends his time alone, as the observer, photographing people without their knowledge.[26]

Continued cycles of loneliness, hypervigilance, and social withdrawal can increase risk of illness (such as a common cold), physical pain, irritability, substance abuse, or interpersonal conflict.[27] These are evidenced in several characters on the show. Hopper regularly escapes through pills, alcohol, and sex before he makes meaningful connections to Eleven and Joyce.[28] Nancy initially tries to cope with the death of Barb by excessively drinking at a party and fighting with her boyfriend, Steve.[29] After several years of repeated crises and traumas that start with his brother's disappearance and presumed death, after the cycle of an otherworldly ordeal keeps whirling and coming back around like a spinning top, Jonathan may prefer to relieve ongoing tension by staying stoned with his friend Argyle.[30]

Many researchers now say loneliness poses as high of a risk for premature death as chronic smoking or alcohol abuse.[31] Were Joyce, Hopper, or Nancy to continue down the paths they follow before forming meaningful connections with others, they could potentially get ill or die prematurely. Similarly, older people who experience significant life stressors such as loss, abuse, divorce, or illness have a higher risk of dying over the next several years following the stressor if they are also experiencing loneliness, but hardly any additional risk factors if they perceive themselves as having adequate social support.[32]

Many people report the emotional pain of chronic loneliness to be so overwhelming that loneliness is considered a major risk factors for suicide.[33] Loneliness is associated with an increased risk of both suicidal thoughts and suicidal behaviors, regardless of the presence of mental health disorders such as depression.[34] For instance, Eleven's mother grows trapped in her loneliness and trauma after she is separated from her daughter and discovers that she cannot do anything about it. She has retreated into her own mind, constantly repeating the terrible memories of her loss over and over.[35] Whereas Eleven's mother experiences these symptoms because of electroshock treatment, many people experience similar symptoms after struggling with trauma and loneliness.[36]

Perceived Social Connection

The pain of loneliness and rejection may rank among the most painful experiences human beings can go through. Loneliness produces not only psychological pain but also physiological pain. In fact, researchers have found that taking Tylenol can reduce not only physical but also emotional pain because the two affect the brain in a similar way.[37] Throughout the first season, Hopper is clearly having physical issues in addition to his already-existing substance use problems.

This does not mean everyone should resort to taking pain medication when experiencing loneliness. Instead, researchers suggest that the presence of meaningful social connection can often help to soothe both physical and emotional pain. For example, when people who are experiencing mild-to-moderate pain have a compassionate stranger such as a nurse holding their hand, they often experience lower physical pain and lower emotional distress compared to people who do not receive any support. When a loved one, especially someone who has a good relationship with the person in pain, holds their hand, the pain sufferer is likely to experience a reduction in physical and emotional pain, more so than when a stranger holds their hand.[38] When Hopper comforts Eleven, he also shares his own story about losing his daughter, Sara. As he shares this with her, he holds Eleven's hand and comforts her, allowing her to feel better and reduce her emotional pain.[39] Similarly, when Will is struggling at school, his older brother, Jonathan, helps Will to feel better by relaying how being a "freak" is cool, and how they are both similar in that way.[40]

In fact, the presence of meaningful social connection can significantly improve the individual's physical and mental health altogether, creating inverse effects to perceived loneliness. Meaningful social connections (both in-person and long-distance) have been shown to reduce inflammation, improve quality of sleep, reduce depression, and improve people's connection with others.[41]

Physical exercise such as riding a bicycle and meaningful social interaction such as group therapy or playing *Dungeons & Dragons* with friends can increase the length of telomeres by as much as 10 percent, potentially giving us several extra years of life.[42] Throughout the series, the boys play *Dungeons & Dragons* together, bonding over their shared love of the game and the lore. When his friends seem to move on from *Dungeons & Dragons*, Will feels great loss and loneliness.[43] We see this as well when Steve and Dustin bond over girls and hair products. It might seem like a small thing, but Dustin gains confidence and happiness because of the meaningful social interaction of mentoring.[44]

Facing Demogorgon and the Loneliness Monsters Together

Overall, facing loneliness can be as dangerous as consuming harmful substances[45] or maybe fighting monsters from the Upside Down. And it seems that by working together and facilitating deeper emotional connections, people are likely to save each other's lives in more ways than one.[46] It doesn't have to be as grand as saving a child from the Upside Down by working together. It can happen every day.[47]

Janina Scarlet, PhD, is a licensed clinical psychologist, author, and full-time geek. The United Nations Association bestowed upon her the Eleanor Roosevelt Human Rights Award for her work on *Superhero Therapy*. She also authored *Super-Women, Dark Agents, Harry Potter Therapy*, and chapters in all books in this Popular Culture Psychology series. She regularly consults on books and television shows, including HBO's *Young Justice*. Reach Dr. Scarlet via her website super-hero-therapy.com or on Twitter: @shadowquill.

Jenna Busch is a writer, host, and founder of Legion of Leia, a website to promote and support women in fandom. She currently writes for /Film (Slash-Film.com) and Vital Thrills. She cohosted *Cocktails with Stan* with comic legend Stan Lee and hosted the *Most Craved* weekly entertainment show. NPR, Al Jazeera America, *Nightline*, *Attack of the Show*, the documentary *She Makes Comics*, and many other outlets have interviewed her as a popular culture expert. Busch has coauthored chapters in most books in the Popular Culture Psychology series. Her work has appeared all over the web. Twitter: @JennaBusch.

10

The Now-Memories
The Nostalgic Appeal of *Stranger Things*

Dawn R. Weatherford &
William Blake Erickson

*"The nostalgic is looking for a spiritual addressee.
Encountering silence, he looks for memorable signs,
desperately misreading them."*
   —social critic Svetlana Boym[1]

"They're now-memories, happening all at once. Now."
                                          —Will Byers[2]

Memories build the self. Sometimes these memories swirl around us to form a shield against the present moment, leaving us feeling listless and longing for something familiar. This shield's name is *nostalgia*.[3] Nostalgia may draw upon something personal, or it may hearken to shared historical experiences permeating an entire culture. From modern reboots of decades-old movie franchises to political campaign appeals harkening back to bygone eras, people are bombarded with the question, "Remember when?"

However, nostalgia is more than just a collection of memories. It is a complex interaction of cognitive processes, biases, emotions, and social mechanisms integral to a person's identity.[4] *Stranger Things* embodies nostalgia itself with its immersive recreation of 1980s middle-American youth culture with a period-accurate soundtrack. More importantly, it weaves nostalgia, its causes, and its functions throughout its narrative and characters.

It's All in Your Head

Although nostalgia has undergone several makeovers throughout time, researchers generally characterize it as a bittersweet emotional state brought about by memory cues for a specific person, place, or time.[5] Subsequently, nostalgic experiences activate both positive and negative feelings. We may simultaneously long to reconnect with and recoil from our past. Nostalgia plays a major part in *autobiographical memory*, memory for personally lived events. For the most part, memories for which we feel nostalgic are largely positive.[6] They can be distinguished from the recurring, intrusive negative memories that might foreshadow depression[7] and share some similarities with *flashbulb memories*: vivid memories for unexpected, emotionally charged events, such as the attacks on September 11, 2001.[8] Although the body discovered in the Sattler Quarry is not really Will's, Jonathan will no doubt carry a flashbulb memory for its reveal at the morgue, continuing to "see" his brother's face on the false corpse,[9] its clarity bolstered by the emotion of that moment.

Like flashbulb memories, nostalgic memories are fueled by intense emotions. This intensity makes memories more durable and long-lasting at both *encoding*, the state in which memories are made, and *retrieval*, the state in which memories are called back to consciousness. Despite television's stylistic embellishments to the brain scans, Dr. Owens and his team at the Hawkins Lab are correct in characterizing Will's memories of hiding in the Upside Down as showing heightened activity in the paralimbic and limbic systems.[10] Specifically, nostalgia recruits the brain's *hippocampus*, a region central to forming memory, and *amygdala*, a region central to regulating emotions.[11] In combination with the *prefrontal cortex*, these structures allow us to call upon the richness of our memories as if we are traveling back in time, albeit not quite as vividly or magically as Eleven can.

I Am on a Nostalgia Voyage, and I Need my Memories to Travel

Experiencing mixed emotions when we recall aspects of our pasts may serve an adaptive function. Nostalgia benefits physical health, protects psychological well-being, and slows age-related cognitive decline.[12] Why might that be? Mentally reexperiencing our personal history facilitates an accurate and constantly updating sense of identity.[13] Building a candid self-representation allows us to be pragmatic about our past as we calibrate our expectations for the future. You must know who you are and where you came from if you want to know where you're going. Nevertheless, this evolving identity does not really begin to take shape until we can grasp a sense of self. People generally forget most direct experiences from infancy, a phenomenon called *infantile amnesia*, and become accustomed to constructing their early life story from descriptions and pictures.[14] However, adolescence marks a time when individuals grapple with establishing identity and avoiding *role confusion*, a feeling of just not fitting in.[15] Developing language skills coupled with the *storm-and-stress* of puberty[16] produce nuanced, intense emotions that allow viewers to relate with the show's young protagonists on a personal level. Perspective-taking is made possible by recalling strongly held memories made during the *reminiscence bump*, the time between ten and thirty years of age that dominates characterizations of self well into late adulthood.[17] Still reeling from the violent death of Bob, Joyce and Hopper share a cigarette in the parking lot outside the school dance and reminisce about doing that very thing when they were in high school.[18] Memories from the bump protect us from the present.

The pivotal life transitions depicted in each episode create a sense of watching a personal biopic for many viewers. Despite having different personalities, each character's plot unfolds around a stereotypical sequence of life events referred to as a *life script*.[19] Life scripts reflect shared cultural experiences involving major developmental milestones on the road from childhood to adulthood. The audience and characters share experiences that serve as memory landmarks for reminiscence. We get to relive our past as we watch the characters grow up and struggle to find themselves. Season one centers around the D&D party's coming of age. Mike, the game's Dungeon Master and the group's de facto leader, guides the group of intelligent and curious boys as they discover who they are and how they fit.[20] The party goes from being bullied as social outcasts in season one, to managing embarrassment for wearing movie-quality Ghostbusters costumes to school in season two,[21] to leaning into the nerd label repeatedly flung at them by Lucas's sister, Erica.[22]

In addition to showcasing characters' identity development, *Stranger Things* also prompts us to reminisce with the characters as they explore an important crossroads of adolescent development: *intimacy versus isolation*.[23] In this psychosocial stage, young people seek intimate, perhaps romantic relationships as further establishment of independence. Viewers are there when Mike and Eleven first kiss,[24] when Dustin swallows his pride and belts out *The NeverEnding Story* theme for Suzie over his behemoth ham radio,[25] and when Lucas works up the courage to ask Max to dance.[26] Will's lack of romance represents the divergent path: Unable to find the sort of intimate connection his friends have found elsewhere, he instead retains his childhood enthusiasm for D&D, wearing wizard costumes and obsessing over campaigns while his friends slowly grow apart in different ways.[27]

Older teens Nancy and Steve also experience shifts while walking the fine line between childhood and adulthood. Early on, Nancy cannot resist Steve's popularity, charm, and Farrah Fawcett hair. She breaks character to explore this new romance. Barb notices how the attraction signals Nancy's growing autonomy and independence at the expense of Nancy's previous identity by remarking, "This isn't you," at the pool party.[28] After their flame fizzles, they need to find themselves again. Both pursue jobs that reflect their character traits: Nancy asserts herself while trying to break the glass ceiling at the local newspaper while Steve flounders in a part-time job not of his choosing: "I couldn't even get into Tech, and my douchebag dad's trying to teach me a lesson."[29] Perhaps Steve's father is as cold and unsympathetic as Steve thinks, or perhaps he believes these experiences will provide Steve a sense of meaning and skills that he failed to develop in high school.

Can't Fight This Feeling

Nostalgia is not only experienced by individuals. It may determine the course of entire cultures. Does a culture consciously decide whether something is classic or cliché? If something is too recent, it's passé and dated. If it's too old, it's divorced from an intimate connection to any living person. Music industry experts have long identified a ten-year cycle that drives what is popular and when, and it interacts with events and trends in the broader culture.[30] The cycle begins with the "pop" phase, abounding with familiar, traditional style and optimistic themes. As the familiar becomes boring, a desire for something fresh or different spurs the "extremes" phase, where experimental and exotic cultural products dominate. Many of a decade's unique and iconic cultural events take place during the extremes phase. People begin to tire of this as well, entering the final "doldrums" phase, where cultures become melancholic and reflective (in other words, nostalgic) after a crisis. This yearning for the familiar heralds the cycle to begin again, and it does so about midway through each decade. Therefore, *Stranger Things*, premiering in 2016, is the nostalgia of the early 2010s incarnate, allaying American anxieties such as political uncertainty and existential threats such as climate change and terrorism.

Memory's Upside Down

As with any beneficial aspect of a person's psychological makeup, nostalgia can have its own Upside Down: the dark territory where the unwary may be imprisoned and consumed. The word *nostalgia* itself was developed by seventeenth-century Swiss physician Johannes Hofer, who used it as a clinical term to describe "the sad mood originating from the desire to return to one's native land."[31] Ironically, he constructed the word from two Greek roots, *nostos* (homecoming) and *algos* (ache), appealing to the sentimental connection Western cultures feel toward their own ancient heritage.[32] Nostalgia's dark side produces not merely a feeling most people today might call "homesickness" but also a serious disorder preventing people from adapting to the uncertainties of the present moment. Chief Hopper returns to Hawkins, his hometown, to get away from the trauma of his daughter's death and failed marriage. The familiarity and positive associations he had made with the people and place were like a weighted blanket keeping out the Indiana winter. But blankets cannot keep out the cold forever. "Feelings," Hopper concedes in his letter to Eleven. "The truth is, for so long, I'd forgotten what those even were. I've been stuck in one place. In a cave, you might say. A deep, dark cave."[33]

For early psychoanalysts focused on deep symbols driving thoughts and behaviors from the murky chambers of the unconscious, nostalgia hearkens to the "lost paradise" archetype found throughout world mythology.[34] Instead of a parable of Atlantis or Eden, nostalgia creates an idealized version of a person's past that never existed, and the lack of overlap between the real and ideal builds resentment over having lost something never possessed. Eleven's personal journey throughout the second season illustrates this: Her true memories are horrifying, being subjected to uncountable tortures at the hands of Dr. Brenner.[35] They intrude on the present, disrupting her ability to function. To cope, she seeks the mother she never knew, to gain a sense of normalcy.[36] Unfortunately, this journey would end with its own set of horrible discoveries, driving her to seek further dysfunctional relationships with Kali's party.[37] The only way for Eleven to purge these conflicting feelings is to embrace her new party, her present, and therefore her future.[38]

Mid-twentieth-century psychologist Willis McCann took a scientific approach, studying nostalgia in homesick undergraduates (a rare instance where sampling solely from this population is completely appropriate). From survey and interview responses, he grouped nostalgia's various symptoms into four major types: adverse physiological sensations, depression, unsatisfied longing, and the inability to mitigate these feelings any other way than by returning home.[39] Students succeeding in their coursework and/or having formed strong peer bonds through extracurricular activities felt immunized from this malady, leaving the socially isolated and personally unfulfilled at risk. He classified these feelings as an autonomic, *fight-or-flight* nervous system response found in those with an unhealthy emotional attachment to any previous situation. In other words, nostalgia can turn our memories into a kind of drug. That the Mind Flayer easily possesses Billy, Doris

Driscoll, and other emotionally isolated citizens of Hawkins[40] is no coincidence: They are most susceptible to being imprisoned in the comforting realms of pasts where love and personal fulfillment still exist for them. Separation from the source of these feelings causes extreme withdrawal, as it does with Doris, who screams at the paramedics to let her go back to the false embrace of the Mind Flayer's psychic powers.[41] So, too, a person can satisfy nostalgic cravings by returning to the object of longing, but doing so risks strengthening the addiction even more.

Longing to Belonging

Does nostalgia always represent the dark side of our memory and emotional processes? As Greek hedonist philosopher Epicurus insisted, all that brings pleasure is best taken in moderation.[42] Modern researchers emphasize nostalgia's clinical significance in treating *anxiety*, the disordered worrying about lack of control over the present and future, and *dementia*, the global impairment of cognitive functioning and loss of memory that can accompany advanced age.[43] Clinical psychologists call the therapeutic technique *nostalgic reminiscence*, and it involves patients suffering from dementia focusing on highly personal, cherished memories to tighten the grasp on their identities. Despite the Mind Flayer's control over Billy in the real world, his most cherished memories nonetheless persist underneath the beast's influence. Eleven, gifted with psychic abilities, summons one of Billy's most precious memories—a day surfing with his mother—to disrupt the Mind Flayer's influence by showing Billy some of the good within himself.[44]

Fortunately, most people are not under the influence of a Mind Flayer, whether it be an extradimensional creature from the Upside Down or devastating neurological deterioration. In fact, flights of nostalgic fancy benefit everyone who sometimes finds themselves in an existential funk, so why not draw upon our best experiences and feelings to get out of that slump? The average person experiences a nostalgic episode three times a week, and its restorative properties range from bolstering the sense of self after a difficult period[45] to tightening the social bonds we share with others.[46] These functions no doubt serve Will and Eleven as they embark on a new chapter away from

Hawkins.[47] The interplay of emotion and autobiographical memories will reinforce their own senses of self as well as their bond to each other. They have both been uniquely touched by powers beyond their comprehension, so only they can understand how each other feels. This will help them stick together no matter what the future holds, and disclosing these stories to trusted new friends will enhance the intimacy of those new relationships.[48]

I Cast Nostalgia Missile!

Nostalgia isn't just a powerful influence on personal or cultural well-being (for good or bad). Nostalgia means big money for corporations eager to bank on the sentimental feelings of would-be customers. Marketing researchers use the term *enchantment* to describe making ordinary products or services seem extraordinary, and employ such slogans as "Just like Mom used to make!" to exploit our most personal memories and make us hand over money.[49] In a culture wallowing in doldrums, nostalgia is an easy spell to cast. It's no wonder a streaming service experimenting with original content would produce a series like *Stranger Things*, set in the childhood of one of its largest target demographics (the now middle-aged Generation X) and starring Winona Ryder, Sean Astin, and other actors who rose to popularity during the era it depicts. Many of these viewers now have children, who may approach the show hoping to learn something about their parents. Although younger audience members have no personal memories of the period, the show's visual and thematic tropes serve as stereotypic cues to trigger *rootless nostalgia*, transmission of cultural history invoking emotions and imparting lessons from one generation to the next.[50] Perhaps the next major wave of big-selling nostalgia content will appeal to those born around 1980 up to the time our heroes first encounter the Upside Down.

Don't Close the Gate!

Nostalgia, an ancient concept encapsulating all the ways that our personal memories create a longing for belonging, is not going anywhere.

Despite its historical conceptualization as an illness preventing personal growth, modern researchers cast it as an emergent property of our memory and emotional processes that builds our identities and social connections. Without nostalgia, we couldn't be ourselves. That's what makes *Stranger Things* so appealing. People of all ages can appreciate the call of what seems like a time when life was simpler, and a weekend's worth of adventure and companionship is just a dice roll away. *Stranger Things* joins a lineage of TV's nostalgia trips including *Happy Days*, *The Wonder Years*, and *That '70s Show*, reminding us where we have been, what we used to aspire to be, and where we might find our direction for the future.

Dawn R. Weatherford, PhD, is an associate professor of psychology at Texas A&M University at San Antonio. Her research interests include cognitive psychology, face perception, and information processing at the applied and basic theoretical levels. She is a member of the Psychonomic Society, serving on their communication board. She has published original research in *Cognitive Research: Principles & Implications*, *Applied Cognitive Psychology*, and the *Journal of Creative Behavior*.

William Blake Erickson, PhD, is an assistant professor at Texas A&M University at San Antonio. His research interests include face perception and eyewitness memory. He serves on the editorial board of the journal *Psychology, Crime, & Law*, and has published work in *Applied Cognitive Psychology*, *Science & Justice*, and the *Journal of Police and Criminal Psychology*.

11

A Strange Feeling

Investigating Murray Bauman's Grand Conspiracy

Billy San Juan

"How gullible do you think I am?"
—Max Mayfield[1]

"No amount of belief makes something a fact."
—skeptic James Randi[2]

"It is a curse to see so clearly."
—Murray Bauman[3]

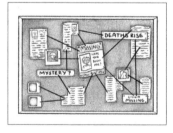

Cryptic messages. Elaborate schemes. Surveillance. Log on to the internet, they're tracking you. Turn a corner, they're watching you. They know everything you've done. Everything you've said. Everything you've *thought*. You try to tell someone. Anyone. But you're dismissed. Ignored. Even mocked! They don't see it, but you do. You know the one thing that eludes everybody else: The Truth.

Murray Bauman is an eccentric visitor to Hawkins. A journalist by day and conspiracy theorist by night, he displays an abundance of caution in case *the man* tracks him down. His home is a bunker surrounded by fence and barbed wire, and no entrance is granted unless you look into his security camera and state your full name to his satisfaction. If the person knocking at his door is perceived to be a threat, he will not hesitate to greet them with a double-barreled shotgun.[4]

Murray isn't alone in his hunt to uncover The Truth. The urge to connect dots is part of our human nature. But sometimes the conspiracy isn't a conspiracy. Sometimes the theory isn't a theory.

At least, not in Hawkins.

Human Nature

Though the concept of a conspiracy theory suggests images of shadowy organizations and agents in suits and sunglasses, the phenomenon is not a modern-day occurrence. They have been a part of society not simply throughout the most recent century but have spanned history at least as far back as the records of the Roman Empire and Greek mythology.[5] Conspiracy theories are not unique to Western civilization either, having been recorded in Eastern Europe, Asia, the Middle East, Amazonian tribes, and rural African villages.[6] Throughout the ages, people have contemplated whether manipulative, malevolent forces may exert control over aspects of their lives. The machinations of the human mind may explain why belief in an overbearing and malicious organization is a universal constant. Murray's original choice to gravitate toward journalism related to conspiracies is relatable to anyone who has sought to explain mysterious circumstances. After all, many share the same fascination with the possibility of government cover-ups.

Cognitive Factors

Wielded by brains designed to detect patterns, ready to connect the dots whether patterns relating them really exist or not, an array of cognitive (mental) processes and factors shape conspiracy beliefs.[7] One factor is the difference between reflexive open-mindedness and reflective open-mindedness.[8] *Reflexive open-mindedness* is an openness to new information or experiences. *Reflective* or *active open-mindedness* is also an openness but with the added feature of critical analysis of the new information obtained. Murray, like many who believe in conspiracy theories, is open to new information. However, instead of fully examining the information, he places it into his preexisting conception of events—*assimilating* information into his existing mental pattern (*schema*) instead of changing the schema to *accommodate* new information.[9] This may explain why his timeline of events is wrong, as Nancy Wheeler points out.[10] Any new information remotely related to his Russian invasion conspiracy has not yet been examined independently but has instead been squeezed into his preexisting paradigm of beliefs.

This reflexive open-mindedness may resemble scientific curiosity, but it prioritizes intuition over rational thinking.[11] Murray follows his intuition, both in his investigative research and in his penchant for making assumptions about other people's romantic relationships, shown when he sees sparks between Nancy and Jonathan[12] and later between Hopper and Joyce.[13] He revels in his ability to read their dynamic and states smugly that he sees more clearly than they do.[14]

Actively reflecting upon new information is one aspect of conspiracy theory beliefs, but we are also unconsciously selective in the new information we receive. Human beings have a natural tendency to pursue and retain information that fits with preexisting assumptions while ignoring or dismissing data that can challenge those assumptions—a phenomenon known as *confirmation bias*.[15] The human mind will attempt to fill in the blanks with information based on previous knowledge from prior experience when we have an idea or perception that is missing information, and with time these temporary assumptions become difficult to discard despite whatever evidence to the contrary may arise.[16] Murray has diligently sifted through "200 tips" about the events surrounding the odd occurrences in Hawkins. He attempts to connect the dots between mysterious events, including a Big Buy employee's account of a girl shattering a door "with her mind" and a report that "some Russian girl with a shaved head" was living in Ted Wheeler's basement.[18] Though this all seems accurate within his reality, Murray then connects these pieces of information to come to a conclusion about Barb's fate: that she was kidnapped or killed by Russians. He suggests that there is a Russian invasion in the town of Hawkins. Murray holds no evidence to support his conclusion, yet he still finds it convincing enough to express his concern to the local police department. Only by coincidence do Russians later show up.

Many other cognitive variables play into the beliefs of conspiracy theories. One that is salient for Murray and his setting is the *illusory control*. He lives during the Cold War, a time when Americans feared Russian subversion and invasion. Hunting a possible Russian spy and uncovering a possible Russian invasion have given Murray a perception that he wields some control or influence over a global situation beyond his influence. Some researchers believe that conspiracy theories help manage the distress of perceived helplessness over highly complex, global, and sociopolitical situations.[19] If Murray can uncover a secret Russian invasion in Hawkins, or if he can identify a Russian super-weapon that uses psionic abilities, then he is no longer prone to elements beyond his control. He would exert agency over his own situation, and thus feels he would avert his own anxieties.

Social Factors

Perceived personal benefits of believing in a conspiracy theory may outweigh social consequences. After all, the townspeople of Hawkins mock Murray for his beliefs. One police officer scoffs at him and asks, "Got any proof on your butt-probing aliens yet, Murray?"[20] Conspiracy theories sometimes result in public mockery, and it might seem that this social backlash would result in an averseness to the phenomenon. So how do these theories propagate in a sociocultural context?

One strong social aspect to conspiracy theories is the *ingroup/out-group effect*. According to social psychologists, human beings tend to divide people into categories, those who are in your own group (the *ingroup*) and those who are not (the *outgroup*). Those in the ingroup tend to be more like us, and we tend to view them more favorably. Conversely, those in the outgroup tend to be not only different from us but also more alike amongst others in the outgroup.[21] Murray explicitly draws a line between himself and Nancy, bringing her into his ingroup and highlighting the difference between them and others. He tells her, "Those people, they're not wired like me and you, okay? They don't spend their lives trying to get a look at what's behind the curtain. They like the curtain. It provides them stability, comfort, definition."[22]

Some researchers believe that conspiracy theories arise as a defense mechanism against threats toward a group to which the person belongs. People who show the highest defensiveness about their particular ingroup may use conspiracy theories as a way to provide explanations for their ingroup's disadvantages, whether those disadvantages are real, exaggerated, or imagined.[23] This is related to the idea of *collective narcissism*, the belief that one's ingroup is not sufficiently appreciated.[24] Murray displays this belief that his own insights and talents are unappreciated, sardonically responding to Hopper's criticisms by asking if his Russian translation services aren't "good enough."[25] This lack of appreciation follows a pattern for Murray, reinforced by the mocking he receives upon entering the police station and his eventual dismissal by Hopper.[26] As people in Hawkins continue to ridicule his investigations, Murray decides society's members "like the curtain." The believer in conspiracies may try to cling to feelings of superiority and insightfulness, escalating commitment rather than allowing others' ridicule to tear down the believer's self-esteem.[27] Such feelings, though, tend to arise in overcompensation for low self-esteem.[28]

Mental Illness

If the belief in conspiracy theories is an isolated trait that does not cause Murray any significant dysfunction in his daily functioning, then the question begs no clinical examination. The visitors and residents of Hawkins are entitled to their own quirks and endearing qualities. But if living in a bunker with security cameras while monitoring radio waves for secret government transmissions causes Murray any sort of negative effect, then he may be a paranoid man experiencing the symptoms of mental illness. Murray's eccentricities may be attributable to two general types of psychological condition: He may be experiencing a psychotic disorder, or he may be living with a personality disorder.

Psychotic Disorders

Psychotic disorders, a classification of mental illness involving severe loss of contact with reality, are characterized by symptoms such as delusions, hallucinations, disorganized thought or speech, grossly disorganized motor behaviors, and *negative symptoms* (those in which something is missing from behavior, such as barely moving or not speaking coherently). Specific to Murray, *delusions* are fixed beliefs held despite contrary evidence.[29] Several subclassifications of delusion fit into the conspiracy theory narrative.

Persecutory delusions are beliefs that someone is getting harmed or harassed by an entity, whether that entity be a single person or an organization such as the government. *Grandiose delusions* are beliefs that the self is exceptional in some unrealistic way (beyond their actual skill or importance), such as in being so skilled or insightful that you have uncovered a truth nobody else understands. *Somatic delusions* are beliefs about one's body that aren't true, such as the implantation of a microchip or the removal of an organ. More extremely, *bizarre delusions* are beliefs that are completely implausible. This includes the idea of *thought insertion* (an entity is implanting thoughts into my mind) and *thought withdrawal* (an entity is removing my thoughts).[30] Murray's intense security measures at home are indicative of persecutory delusions, that he is (or will be) harassed by the government for his delving into their schemes. He also appears prone to grandiose delusions, believing that he is enlightened to the grander scheme of government and military plans, whereas the rest of society merely eschews these malicious machinations in lieu of their comfortable, ignorant lives.

With an understanding of delusions in the context of mental health, let's explore whether Murray's belief in a conspiracy theory is applicable to a mental disorder. One empirical study found a major difference between psychotic delusions and conspiracy theories: Delusions tend to be focused on the self and are typically held only by the person experiencing it.[31] Meanwhile, conspiracy theories tend to be externally focused and socially driven, with a focus on moral superiority and social support. In essence, a delusion is typically a phenomenon of the self whereas a conspiracy theory is more likely to be a phenomenon of a group. In addition to this differentiation, Murray's beliefs do not appear to impact his daily functioning directly. He is employed and does not appear to be otherwise affected in a negative manner by his convictions.

But if Murray doesn't suffer from a psychotic disorder, what else can explain his . . . Murray-ness?

Personality Disorders

"You're not clever. You're not special. You are just simply one of the many, many nimwits to call here, and the closest you will ever get to me is this prerecorded message. So at the beep, do me a favor: Hang up and never call here again. You are a parasite!"
—Murray Bauman's voicemail message[32]

Personality disorders are pervasive patterns of "inner experience and behaviors" that are consistent and lead to dysfunction in someone's life, and that begin "in adolescence or early adulthood."[33] Most other psychiatric disorders may go through time-limited episodes but, as the name suggests, personality disorders are ingrained in a person's very nature. They affect daily life, social interactions, and other areas of functioning. Murray's life is arguably affected throughout areas of social interaction. He has built an isolated bunker in the woods and lives in such a heightened state of paranoia that he has pointed a shotgun at a stranger before scanning him with a device (perhaps a Geiger counter or metal detector).[34] These behaviors deviate from the norm of the town's residents and greater society and may be indicative of a personality disorder.

A *personality disorder* may be at work when a person shows deeply ingrained, persistent, and pervasive personality traits that affect that person's whole life and interfere with functioning. Murray is characteristically *eccentric* (off-center) at the core of his personality. If he qualifies for a personality disorder, he may fit somewhere into the "Cluster A" group of personality disorders, the group collectively defined by odd, eccentric traits.[35]

Schisms Within

The root of the word *schizoid*, like in the terms *schizophrenia* and *schizophreniform*, derives from the Greek word *skhizein*, which means *to split* (as in the more common English word *schism*). Schizoid refers to a series of symptoms that resemble schizophrenia but do not meet full criteria for the disorder and are more persistent across lifetime and situations. In the case of schizoid personality disorder, most of the resemblance lies in social dysfunctions like those displayed by Murray.

Schizoid Personality Disorder

Schizoid personality disorder is characterized by a penchant for solitary activities, lack of desire for emotionally intimate relationships, lack of interest in sexual experiences with others, lack of pleasure except in limited (if any) activities, indifference to criticism or praise, and overall emotional detachment.[36] Murray does not show signs of emotional or physical intimacy prior to the events surrounding Hawkins, and his bunker in the woods indicates a shortage of interest in obtaining these relationships.

Though Murray exhibits some of these tendencies, he arguably does not meet most criteria for the disorder. He develops relationships with citizens of Hawkins throughout the course of events, even taking a mentor-type role with Alexei, which shows a close emotional bond as they mutually enjoy a carnival. This bond is accentuated in grief when Alexei gets murdered, indicating the closeness Murray felt with his fallen comrade.

Schizotypal Personality Disorder

Perhaps a better diagnostic fit for Murray lies in *schizotypal personality disorder*. Like schizoid personality disorder, schizotypal is differentiated by "cognitive or perceptual distortions and marked eccentricity or oddness."[37] This personality disorder is identified by *ideas of reference*, wherein various incidents are incorrectly interpreted as having a meaning specific to that person. There is a presence of odd beliefs not found within subcultural norms, such as an obsession with paranormal phenomena or conspiracies. Perceptual alterations may occur, regardless of reality. Cognitive processes are characterized with odd thoughts or speech, such as sentences that lead nowhere or are incredibly vague. There may be noticeable suspiciousness or paranoia. The expression of emotion may be lacking, or inappropriate for any current situation. Behaviors or appearances may be offbeat or odd. People with schizotypal personality disorder often lack close relationships beyond first-degree relatives, and they experience an ever-present social anxiety.

Murray certainly meets the criteria for several of these measures. He exhibits odd beliefs, including an obsession with aliens to the point that his hunt for them has garnered mockery from Hawkins residents. He is obviously prone to diving into conspiracy theories and shows high levels of paranoia. However, though his expression of emotion is quirky, it is not quite inappropriate for the situations at hand. Likewise, his unkempt appearance is offbeat, but not to the point where anyone else mentions it. Maybe another personality disorder, one more paranoid than schizotypal or schizoid, would better describe Murray's eccentricities.

Paranoid Personality Disorder

Like the term *schizo*, the word *paranoid* is often used as a derogatory term to denote a person's odd behaviors or beliefs. Colloquially, many people use the word to indicate somebody who is hypervigilant or scared about something insignificant, but when psychologists use this term, it refers to a strong distrust or suspicion with no basis in evidence or reality. If extreme paranoia is present in several diagnostic criteria and is persistent throughout life despite having no other psychotic-seeming symptoms, a diagnosis of paranoid personality disorder may be fitting.

Paranoid personality disorder is characterized by various symptoms.[38] Suspicions of exploitation, intent to harm, or deception without evidence endure as part of the individual's core personality. Unjustified doubts of loyalty or trustworthiness can ruin friendships, if those friendships even form despite the pervasive reluctance to confide in others. Benign statements warp and are perceived as threats. Because of these distortions, grudges are formed and held. Perceived attacks on a person's character are met with that person quickly reacting, oftentimes counterattacking.

At first glance, Murray's *modus operandi* fits into this disorder. The word *paranoia* is right there in the name of the disorder. However, upon closely looking at the criteria, they do not fit, based on his actions throughout the course of the events in Hawkins. He begins to develop strong, trusting relationships with his peers. Moreover, personality disorders are pervasive patterns that occur throughout life unless significant clinical intervention occurs. Though Murray's life has been marked with strong suspiciousness, he begins to trust in his friends with his very life. He follows Hopper into the lair of the enemy, an underground military base, to help their mission, and he later accompanies Joyce into icy enemy territory, a Soviet prison, to help rescue Hopper.[39] A person with paranoid personality disorder would not go this far and would doubt his companions' loyalties.

The Truth

Conspiracy theories share many features with mental illness symptoms, specifically delusions. It is indeed tempting to dismiss Murray's yarn-lined corkboards and isolated shelter-bunker as the dwelling of a man with severe, untreated psychosis or a pervasive personality disorder. However, there may be something else at play to explain Murray's Murray-ness. He may find meaning in knowing The Truth. He becomes part of an elite social circle, communicating with hidden messages through ham radios. He finds meaning as an important member of a resistance. It fills a need for belonging, one that is replaced as he begins to build and foster relationships with his fellow Hawkins citizens.

At the end of it all, Murray's pursuit of conspiracy theories is explainable by one key factor about him: Murray is human.

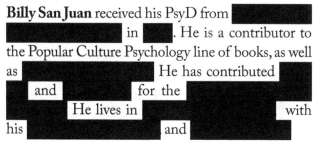

Billy San Juan received his PsyD from ███████. He is a contributor to the Popular Culture Psychology line of books, as well as ███████ He has contributed ███ and ███ for the ███████ He lives in ███████ with his ███████ and ███

12

Shame, Survival, and Trauma Processing in the State We Call Fear

Benjamin A. Stover & Travis Langley

"Whereas we'd once believed that the symptoms and behavior exhibited by our clients primarily reflected their psychological defenses . . . now we better understood the symptoms as manifestations of instinctive brain and bodily survival responses."
—therapist/author Janina Fisher[1]

"Fireball him!"
—Lucas Sinclair[2]

Hero stories, comic books, tabletop role-playing games (RPGs), childhood make-believe, and other adventurous fantasy can provide people with the opportunity to audition their survival skills mentally while experiencing safety physically.[3] The ability to rehearse responses to danger from relative safety is an important part of survival play for both children and adults. It helps develop *resource memories*, recollections that become psychological resources people find helpful or emotionally boosting in later circumstances—in this case, memories of what they can do to be like favorite characters and how they hope to feel when facing danger. Heroism researchers consider *mental rehearsal* one of the most important factors in preparing people to take action when the time comes and crises call. *Heroic imagination* prepares heroes-in-waiting.[4] Stories, games, and sports provide controlled situations for people to experience the body engaging automatic responses to fear. This creates opportunities to develop familiarity and trust in the spontaneous solutions that emerge instinctively when facing a threat. Children across cultures learn about their own capabilities while imitating the actions of their favorite heroes during sports and pretend play.[5]

When you're dreaming, daydreaming, watching movies, or reading fiction, much of the brain is activated as if you were doing the imagined activities. To parts of the brain, *imagination is actuation*.[6] Research shows that actively processing fiction promotes gains in empathy, honesty, perspective-taking, and social skills. Envisioning oneself in the hero's role and mentally rehearsing what to do in a similar or symbolically related situation creates a sense of comfort and empowerment over the unknown. The downside of seeing the hero being able to do this in a carefully crafted story is that it may interact with a youthful *illusion of invulnerability*[7] to create an expectation in children that they should be able to respond optimally and lead their party to victory, regardless of their own experience level, the difficulty of the quest, or the level of threat. That type of belief leads the "party members," as the kids consider themselves, into a campaign against wide-ranging forces—local bullies, their parents, two governments' shadow operatives, interdimensional beasts, Vecna, and more—with the expectation that they will prevail like their *Dungeons & Dragons* (D&D) characters do in their games.

This expectation that they will be able to respond like their favorite characters do, however, ignores the facts that our brains are hard-wired with a prime directive to survive and that, when we enter a dangerous situation, we tend to respond instinctively much more than we respond logically. When the brain determines that a situation is dangerous, a switch is figuratively flipped and the brain switches power from the rational processing center (*prefrontal cortex*) to give more power to reactionary processes (areas devoted to basic motivation and emotions in the primitive *limbic system*, such as the *amygdala*). Similarly, in a science fiction starship, one would have to switch power off of the navigation in order to divert "power to shields!" Mentally preparing to respond in the moment like favorite heroic characters do may also prepare the individual to set aside the situation's terrifying nature, and the version of oneself that emerges in order to survive can itself be terrifying. Stories of loss and survival are not always accounts that people feel proud to tell. Such experiences can produce unresolved feelings from what they experienced, feelings that later events or reminders may reactivate, including feelings of shame and guilt over what they had to do—or feel they failed to do—in order to survive.

The entity called Vecna preys upon characters who feel burdened by those monsters of shame and guilt, upon individuals haunted by *survivor guilt* (feeling wrong for having survived when others did not, regardless of whether self-blame has any logical basis) and mired in *counterfactual thinking* (dwelling over thinking "if only" unchangeable facts such as past events could be different—see chapter 7).[8] Speaking to her stepbrother Billy's grave and hoping he can hear her somehow, Max acknowledges that she has been repeatedly replaying his death, ruminating, wishing she could have altered the outcome: "I play that moment back in my head all the time, and sometimes I imagine myself running to you, pulling you away." Even though she knows the wish is unrealistic, she nevertheless keeps picturing a life in which they could have become friends, "good friends, like a real brother and sister." Such thoughts immediately precede Vecna's first attempt to slay her the way he has killed others, as if the guilt and reality-distorting wish feed the magic that the villain uses to alter reality his own way.[9]

Guilt over surviving can creak open doors into terrible corridors long and dark. Isolating herself from friends while wishing she could have developed a better relationship with Billy may seem paradoxical, but Max feels she no longer deserves the connections she wants. She worries that having her in their lives may somehow harm those she cares about. Isolation has become a defensive reaction because she has learned to associate independence with strength. Sometimes a cue as simple as a story, game, reflection in the mirror, or song may help break a cycle of self-imposed shame, remind them of their priorities and who they are, and give them the extra push to run through darkness back to the party of friends. Because survivor guilt can make it harder to want to survive, new experiences of surviving with no direct harm to others can help break through guilt's chains.

Survival

Early in their adventures, the party members learn quickly that battling real monsters is not a game with a guidebook and that doing what they must to survive can change people forever.

> **Scott Clarke:** All living things, from complex mammals to single-celled organisms, instinctively respond to danger. Expose a bacterium to a toxic chemical, and it will flee or deploy some other defense mechanism. We're very much the same. When we encounter danger, our hearts start pounding. Our palms start to sweat. These are the signs of the physical and emotional state we call fear.[10]

The human brain is tasked with a prime directive: Survive. Even reproduction arguably serves survival of the species. Due to this neurological imperative, human beings come equipped with a threat response system that can engage automatically, the *sympathetic nervous system*, which is responsible for priming and deploying the physiological changes the body utilizes to respond to any perceived or actual danger.[11] When a monster lurches out of the night to seize them, characters such as Will and Barb do not pause to decide how they feel about that.[12] No, the nervous system evokes the emotional first response. Adrenal glands unleash hormones that trigger responses all over the body, both external and internal: Pupils dilate, heartrate elevates, reflexes sharpen, blood flow increases to muscles and vital organs, breathing quickens possibly to hyperventilation, and more. The hormones also inhibit override distractions such as digestion and hunger.[13]

Stepping into danger ahead of everyone else time and time again, Steve gets hurt so often because he takes on the fighter role and therefore takes the hits so others won't. His junkyard fight with the

Demodogs[14] illustrates the changes in core ability due to sympathetic activation. To protect the kids and survive an attack by four Demodogs when he was only expecting one, he rapidly switches from sarcastic mentor into brave fighter mode. Steve demonstrates increased sensory awareness and reflexes that allow him to utilize his athletic talents to connect his bat blows, before diving over cars and back into the bus using levels of strength, dexterity, and athletics beyond anything he normally shows.[15]

Once a situation is perceived to be life or death, the brain will auto-select the best action for responding to the presenting threat and enter *fight-or-flight*. *Polyvagal theory* holds that this is done automatically rather than cognitively, through a process called *neuroception*. As the nervous system assesses a threat in the environment,[16] neuroception results in our human brain turning off and our more primal "lizard" brain turning on. Upon recognition of a threat, the brain seeks confirmation of the threat and elevated physical response from the prefrontal cortex, which tries to verify whether real danger is present. If confirmed, the sympathetic nervous system engages and dumps adrenaline into the body and enters fight-or-flight until the threat is over.[17]

Despite the traditional name *fight-or-flight*, there appear to be four main responses to danger: *fight, flight, freeze, or fawn*.[18]

- *Fight*, the brain's equivalent of a barbarian's rage, prepares the person to charge into danger, deliver attacks, and perceive less pain. Examples include Eleven fighting her first Demogorgon, Hopper fighting a Terminator-like Russian and later another Demogorgon, and Billy trying to fight everyone.[19]
- *Flight* (as in fleeing, not airborne travel) is the real-life version of taking a *disengage* action, running away from danger as fast as possible. The individual in flight tends to ignore that action's consequences, perhaps leaving allies behind or opening oneself to attack while trying to escape. When the Demogorgon attacks Barb, she naturally and desperately tries to get away.[20]
- The *freeze* response means that one cannot act, whether struck immobile, playing dead, hoping not to be noticed, accepting death as inevitable, or disconnecting from consciousness. A

growing number of researchers refer to the range of reactions as *fight-flight-freeze* now.[21] During the chaos of Demogorgon attacks against soldiers in Hawkins Lab or prisoners and soldiers in the Soviet prison, some people attack and some try to run away, but there are also those who stand shaking, unable to act.[22]

- Some researchers now add one more.[23] The *fawn* response aims to please or appease. Its actions attempt to charm, seduce, humanize oneself, or otherwise demonstrate feigned or actual compliance with the tormentor in order to make the attack stop—e.g., Max trying to placate her hostile stepbrother, Billy,[24] or Alexei bonding with Murray, Hopper, and Joyce.[25]

We cannot always anticipate which reaction we will manifest or how we will face danger until it arrives. "Outside of D&D, I am no hero," Hellfire Club leader Eddie Munson decides, assessing his own threat response based on his recent reactions to otherworldly threats. "I see danger and I just turn heel and run—or at least that's what I've learned about myself this week."[26] Eddie also points out that mild-mannered Nancy Wheeler charges into danger to save others without wasting one second. Even Lucas Sinclair's brash and brave sister, Erica, who boldly asserts that they might encounter booby traps before the room they're in abruptly turns out to be an elevator, turns stock-still in fear when that particular danger turns real. Her eyes widen, her bravado fades, and she whispers it again: "Booby traps. . . ."[27] These characters, however, also show that a single pattern does not define anyone because all three of them each show a range of reactions from the fight-flight-freeze-fawn spectra. Though Erica may freeze at the thought of booby traps, she will run from a direct attacker and, when she must, she fights back.[28] Roles change.

To engage these functions, the brain may disengage aspects of morality, empathy, doubt, or any other mental function that might trigger inhibition. Joyce has to set aside her healing and nurturing ways at times in order to take aggressive actions that she would normally never perform. Normally, she would never risk Will's life by making him overheat, and so she must dissociate away from her role as his nurturing mother, separating that part of herself in order to face the monster inside him and drive the Mind Flayer out. Joyce's face and body language harden as she turns off mom mode to switch on exorcist mode. This also happens when she ends the Battle of Starcourt by pulling the switch to shut down the Key even though Hopper seems certain to die if she does.[29] Having to sacrifice Hopper requires her to dissociate away from certain core values to do what is necessary to end a threat. This is also the kind of situation that generates shame and *survivor guilt* (feeling guilty for having survived when others did not) that can complicate the processing of the event long afterward.[30]

Dissociation

In order to do what is necessary to survive, the brain has the ability to *dissociate* ("dis-associate"), temporarily disable access to aspects of consciousness that are not relevant to the immediate needs of the situation.[31] This includes disconnection from sense of self, time, reality, memories, as well as thoughts and feelings. Doing so allows the person in danger to detach internal inhibitors such as doubt, guilt, and shame that would otherwise govern behaviors. Some practitioners and researchers divide these core functions of personality even further and use language identifying these functions as "inner parts" or simply "parts" in order to help clients identify the different functions taken on by different aspects of their consciousness.[32] These parts describe the divide between (1) the non-traumatized parts of the personality that goes to work, plays softball, makes dinner, and performs other mundane functions and (2) the survival parts that represent the functions of our personality that can step in and take over when we need them to perform actions that our core self is not capable of doing.

In D&D terms, dissociation and other selective manifestations of oneself allow for our consciousness to split into a full raiding party that takes advantage of the unique skills of each class in whatever combinations are called for. This includes being able to ignore warnings from our internal Dungeon Master (DM) that the chosen course of action will likely end poorly. This allows our back-line characters to enter combat situations outside of their normal roles. By his own admission, Bob Newby has never been a risk-taker and seems averse to danger. He is a sage, certainly not a fighter like Hopper, a trained soldier and war veteran who has been trained to manage the body during combat. Bob has not had experience with dangerous situations like Hopper, Eleven, and Kali have or even as much as the show's other kids, and so he cannot rely on muscle memory and unconscious reactions to run mental "scripts" on what to do to survive. He has no reference for applying what worked in the past to handling the present situation.

The most epic fight tale Bob has to share involves standing up to a clown in a nightmare when he was a child.[33] Bob is what some gamers affectionately call "squishy," a specialized support character who has valuable skills but is neither good with weapons nor able to fare well in the center of a battle.[34] However, when he realizes he is the only one who can get the doors open in the lab, Bob is able to dissociate away from his core self, the part of him that would never run back alone into that building full of monsters. Engaging his "superhero" part, he pushes the near certainty that he will not survive away from his train of thought in order to use his knowledge of BASIC computer language to open the doors and save everyone else.[35]

Wizardly Eleven's rapid shifts from a vulnerable child wanting to play with her friends to a hardened warrior with no fear shows how "parts" of a person's psyche can engage in drastically different behavior, depending on the needs of a situation. People who have been exposed to chronic trauma, as she has, are far more likely to dissociate than people who have not.[36] Eleven's history gives her rapid and spontaneous access to her defense systems much faster than Mike or the other party members due to their previously privileged existences. Eleven knows this is not a game. She switches rapidly from her vulnerable core self to her hardened protector mode when she needs to eradicate threats immediately, often while other party members are still deciding what to do. Sometimes her fighter part is grandiose, moving trains and snapping the necks of enemies telekinetically. However, her fight response can also look like a rebellious preteen not cooperating with a punishment, jealously pushing over another girl flirting with a crush, or shutting down the boyfriend who violated the sacred rule, "Friends don't lie."[37]

Other characters also activate different parts in response to the intense situations they encounter. When Will confronts the Mind Flayer, he engages his fight response, screaming for the monster to go away but, once it starts to possess him, he switches into a freeze response unable to move as the monster takes him over.[38] Dustin often relies on a fawning response to manipulate, inspire, and charm others into doing what he needs when he is in trouble: convincing his mother to leave him home alone by using charm and false information, forming a brotherly relationship with Steve along the railroad tracks, charming a grown Dart with a Three Musketeers candy bar into not eating them in the tunnels.[39] Once their desperate situation drives him to override shame or concern that everyone from the party can overhear, Dustin goes into fawning compliance as his bard part proceeds with the epic duet of *The Never-Ending Story*[40] theme so he can get Planck's constant from Suzie.[41]

Shame

Shame, a state that causes humiliation and intense negative feelings when a person feels or is made to feel they have done something wrong, can be such a powerful negative state that many people try to avoid it at all costs. Shame-avoidance efforts can take a variety of forms collectively known as the *compass of shame* for the four directions a person might take: two in attack (against others or against oneself), and two in escape (withdrawing or avoiding).[42]

Nancy and Steve demonstrate all of these during their dinner with Barb's parents and at the house party they attend afterward. As Nancy reckons with her guilt and the weight of keeping Barb's death secret, Steve encourages her to avoid the feelings entirely, to follow his lead by pretending to know nothing, and to enjoy KFC while the Hollands discuss selling their house to pay conspiracy investigator Murray Bauman.[43] Steve suppresses his shame that telling them the truth about Barb's death would prevent them from losing their home. During dinner, Nancy excuses herself to the bathroom, where she punishes herself mentally by miring in her guilt and shame over her last conversation with Barb.[44] Steve later admits that fear of what the Department of Energy agents will do to them if they fail to stay silent keeps him from telling the truth. Because of this fear, he outright encourages Nancy to "pretend to be stupid teenagers" and forget it all.[45] Seeking escape by dissociation, she goes to the party, where she unsuccessfully attempts to pretend to be the stupid teenager. Unable to have fun as herself, she blends the *avoid* and *attack* strategies: After she gets drunk (avoid mode), Steve correctly identifies this and tries to get her to stop, but she switches into attack mode against him.[46]

The social aspects of shame are learned early in life.[47] Children learn that behaviors have consequences that can last beyond the immediate interaction, that these consequences may determine how they are perceived and whether they are accepted by their peers and family. Shame is a powerful negative emotion that serves to keep our behavior in line with the established social norms of our tribe.[48] Unfortunately for the kids in *Stranger Things*, bullying was an accepted social norm among many in the mid-1980s,[49] and so the bullies who pick on them do not get shamed by others in order to correct poor behavior but instead are often get reinforced by active or passive encouragement of the bullying behaviors, which allows them to continue. Human beings are pack animals that rely on cooperation to survive. Getting ostracized, cast out of the tribe, bodes poorly for survival in nature. Behaving in a manner acceptable to the tribe, therefore, may grow out of survival instinct.[50]

The party members have created their own tribe with its own code in order to gain inclusion and protection from the town bullies. This could be why inducting Eleven into the safety of the party is done in such a ritualistic way and why the party members adhere to the group rules so strongly.[51]

Joyce engages her parts to overcome her response to social shame. When she first appears, Joyce has a meekness about her. She demonstrates submissiveness and social withdrawal consistent with shame and low self-esteem. When she learns her child is in danger, Joyce's fight part activates and she no longer shows concern for people's perception of her. She becomes an unstoppable juggernaut of determination when her mama bear mode activates to do whatever is necessary to compel an initially dismissive Chief Hopper to take Will's disappearance seriously.[52] Pain exists to communicate danger. By sharing functional aspects of both drives and emotion, it causes an immediate shift in the body in response to aversive stimuli called a state alteration. Joyce is in immense pain when Will goes missing and in response she changes from gentle and passive to stern and assertive to get her needs met from others regardless of her circumstances. Demanding advance pay and a new phone from her boss and chastising Hopper for not seeming to take Will's disappearance seriously are also examples of state alteration.[53]

Shame commonly manifests with "eyes down, head down and averted, blush, accompanied by mental confusion and at higher levels by disorientation" as affectual responses.[54] Jonathan demonstrates all of these when confronted by Steve about taking voyeuristic pictures of Steve, Nancy, and Barb from the bushes during a party at Steve's house. Feeling both shamed and surrounded by bullies who threaten to destroy his most valued possession is a significant enough threat to cause a change in consciousness and enter a survival mode. Rather than activating his fight part, shame activates his freeze response causing Jonathan to freeze up with head down and gaze averted, barely able to utter an intelligible word to explain himself.[55]

Trauma Processing

Trauma, diagnostically considered a situation that creates intense fear when directly or indirectly threatened with bodily harm, sexual violence, or death,[56] takes on more forms than commonly understood. As distinguished by one researcher, "Big T" Traumas are caused by such life-threatening events, whereas "little t" traumas are caused by other distressing events that don't rise to the level of mortal danger. Either can foster shame and have a lasting impact on quality of life by changing the way a person sees themselves or the world.[57] Examples include breakups, firings, and public embarrassments such as getting belittled at work or made to pee your pants in front of the whole school.[58] Trauma is relative. What traumatizes one person may not traumatize another. *Stranger Things* characters face dangers involving both "Big T" and "little t" stressors. The important component to consider in evaluating if an event was traumatic is how an event made someone feel at the time and how they still feel about it even years after the fact. Traumatized people may feel chronically unsafe.[59] A person does not need to encounter mortal danger to feel so unsafe that a trauma response is stored in their nervous system. Emotional bullying, loss of social standing or support, and public embarrassment are more than enough to cause trauma, especially in children.

The people of Hawkins encounter dangerous situations throughout the course of the story. Battling monsters both human and otherworldly requires characters to set aside who they thought they were and become different versions of themselves who can do whatever is necessary to survive. But what happens to them when the monsters are defeated and they return to their core selves? Therapist Janina Fisher writes that "the brain's innate physical structure and two separate, specialized hemispheres facilitate left brain/right brain disconnection under conditions of threat"[60] and emphasizes that the prefrontal cortex is connected to the analytical left brain, but not the reactionary and survival-based right brain.[61] This means that in order to activate survival parts, the brain separates processing from an integrated whole to two separated but simultaneously operating halves that experience the event differently. Once the danger is over, information stored by both the rational and reactionary parts must be reintegrated through processing.

During a survival situation in which interdimensional monsters, Russian soldiers, or shopping malls invade our small town, we may have no time or need to process every decision. We need to be able to react on instinct in a pinch. In order to do that, our brains need immediate and uninhibited access to any bit of information we have ever stored in our memory that can help survive the presenting threat. To combine useful information from similar situations known to us already (whether from firsthand experience, secondhand accounts, or fictional stories), the brain may use dissociation to disconnect the inhibitions that the rational core self might impose as well as activate the reactionary survival parts of the brain that can do things the core self cannot. Thinking about what will happen to Hopper when she turns the key makes Joyce pause, and so she must separate herself from that long enough to do what must be done.[62]

What Comes Next

Hero stories often focus on the glory of victory and leave out the reality that defeating a monster often requires doing monstrous things. Characters in *Stranger Things* face this repeatedly throughout their journey. When the monsters are all defeated and life returns to normal, they will each have a lot of work to do to process the horrors they have faced.

They could benefit from professional guidance to help process the losses and permanent changes to their lives. They will also need to overcome their shame and make peace with the differences between what they could have done and what happened.

Unprocessed memories sometimes result in people getting stuck replaying the terrifying experiences they've had and all the information they possess after the fact. Mentally reexperiencing past events, trying to find the perfect move that would have kept everyone safe, happy, or alive can wear a person down. Counterfactual "if only that hadn't happened" fantasies may feed depression because the past will not change.[63] While Max's favorite song about an impossible wish helps to save her life, the reminder of its importance for her sense of self also helps her move away from the consuming monster of guilt, to reconnect with those who care about her and better tether herself to life among the living.[64] Life is not like a hero story that has been carefully crafted to lead to a happy ending with minimal damage to the main characters, but that reality makes life's victories all the more precious.

Real life-or-death scenarios are chaotic, and survival often depends on a split-second instinctual reaction that there is no time to think through. Therapy exists to help survivors of trauma heal from the impact of those decisions and cope with the impact of any shame felt over the automatic response their body took to keep them alive in their darkest moments.

Benjamin A. Stover, MA, LCPC, is clinical director at Ardent Counseling Center in Chicago, Illinois, and a clinical therapist for the Chicago Police Department. His clinical work focuses on trauma, grief, and mood disorders. He created and cohosts the psychology-and-film podcast *Popcorn Psychology*. He has been a participant on several convention panels as well as a guest contributor to popular culture podcasts and blogs.

Travis Langley, PhD, edited this volume. His biography appears on the last page of this book.

13

Stranger Things in the First Episodes

Lessons from the Start

William Sharp & Kevin Lu
with Greta Kaluzeviciute

"I love to train writers to be analysts. They seem to know intuitively how to build a relationship."
—psychoanalyst Phyllis Meadow[1]

"I am on a curiosity voyage and I need my paddles to travel."
—Dustin Henderson[2]

Growing up, you might have been told not to judge a book by its cover. The fact that there is such a prohibition alerts us to the fact that this is a common deed, but it includes no reason why we should not do it. "Don't judge a book only by its cover or you may miss out" may prove more effective. Psychoanalysts gather data about patients from first contact. Evelyn Liegner, a modern psychoanalyst in New York City, detailed many ways that our patients' subpersonalities "show up," so to speak, in their behaviors, chains of thought, and movements toward and away from certain feelings.[3] The data that therapists gather about clients will provide an outline of whom we are meeting in the way a police chalk outline initially sets the stage of a crime scene. This is paralleled in good fiction as well and may help us understand why some shows like *Stranger Things* almost instantaneously draw us into the narrative.

First sessions and first episodes help us to decide if this is something to which we want to devote our energy and time. In therapy, patient and clinician are trying to see if there is a fit. In television, viewer and creative team are trying to make a match. Looking at both first episodes and first sessions at the beginning of therapy or a TV series, we see that there were many clues to the major themes that bring patients and therapists—and audiences and creative teams—together in a relationship. Sometimes a stronger understanding of this emerges only achieved in hindsight. Between start and finish, curiosity helps us stay with both treatment and viewership. If we lose that, the treatment falters and we stop watching.

What follows is an attempt to highlight the importance of first encounters. Clinically, the first session has been hypothesized to contain everything the therapist needs to know about the patient's issues, but the therapist does not yet have the ability to understand. They have not yet learned the unique language of the patient's unconscious. It is a situation where hindsight is 20/20. Things really must get "stranger" (vis-à-vis enactments, projections, and transferences—all things patients do in treatment) before we can hope to grasp what was presented at the outset. The first episodes of *Stranger Things* in each season provide good examples in both the content and process of things therapists see in treatment progression. From a deep read of this, we see how psychoanalysis has something to say about *Stranger Things*, and how *Stranger Things* has something to say about psychoanalysis.

Season 1, Episode 1, "The Vanishing of Will Byers"[4]

The opening of *Stranger Things* frames a steel door. We do not at first know if it is to keep something in or to keep something out. A man in a lab coat is running from something. He attempts to escape on the elevator but gets attacked from above. The tone has been set: Danger in this series will be extreme. The next scene flips to Mike, Will, Dustin, and Lucas playing the iconic game *Dungeons & Dragons*. Mike, as the Dungeon Master, indicates something is coming. Dustin comments, "We are so screwed if it's the Demogorgon." At first, the party is relieved it is not the Demogorgon, only to find—surprise—that it is. Will's character in the game has a choice: Is he going to use a protection spell to save himself, or cast a fireball at the threat? Will chooses the fireball even though he needs to roll a 13 or higher on a 20-sided die. His attempt fails and he confesses to Dungeon Master Mike that "the Demogorgon got me." Shortly thereafter in their world, the Demogorgon really does.

Likewise, we learn what is to come from the patient from the first contact, even before we meet in the first session.[5] Does the patient have availability and flexibility or is their schedule so tight (a symptom of something) that an intake cannot even be scheduled? Does that also say something about their willingness (or ambivalence) to engage in treatment? In other words, is the therapist met with a steel door? Much like that of Will Byers, the patient's first choice is whether to jump headfirst into the conflict of exploring their own troubles in treatment or to retreat and protect themselves. This comes out in other early-treatment destructive behaviors. To get into an office, you need a code at the door. Patients are instructed on the phone and via email to press # (pound sign, hashtag) and then the four-digit code. There is anticipation, however, on the part of the waiting therapist to answer a frantic or frustrated call at the new patient's hour when they "can't get in" nine times out of ten because they forget to hit #. These enactments all begin to tell something of the character of the patient. Often, the first choices that patients make—their proverbial attempt to get through the door—say a lot about their character.

The starting point for the therapist is to ask, "What else could that mean?" Posing that question is, arguably, one of the greatest and most enduring contributions both psychoanalysts Sigmund Freud and Carl Jung have made to psychotherapy specifically and mental health more generally.

A patient reported offhandedly in the first session that her art instructor as a youth had said, "You are technically proficient, but

passionless." Little did the therapist know then this statement's importance. This offhanded comment aptly summed up the patient's issues in
life. Her work was technically good, with accurate scale and proportion
in art and sculpting, but people who viewed her art never felt connected
to her pieces. They never felt any feeling in it. As a result, finding jobs
and promotions always proved challenging. This core conflict was
expressed in other aspects of her life. She struggled to get second or
third dates from romantic interests for the same reason. After a series
of fruitless first dates, the patient decided to call a former one-date
interest and ask why there was no second date. The response echoed the
very remark made by her instructor and was relayed in the first session:
"I didn't know you were interested in going on another date."

Everything happened on the date like a checklist. The patient
arrived on time, engaged in small talk, agreed to split the bill. Check,
check, check. But there was a lack of connection that only comes with
feelings and passions. There was a steel door at the meeting, which the
patient used to protect herself, but which the date perceived as disinter-
est. Old familiar and repetitive thoughts came down from above to
attack the girl, saying that "you should have been more charming" or
"you shouldn't make an advance or show interest this early." Listening
for these repeating conflicts and issues is central to much work in the
therapies of depth, insight, and relationships like psychoanalysis. Freud
found that the "talking cure" often led people to tell stories in sessions
about scenes from their lives that had similar themes and conflicts.
Freud called this tendency in our personalities the *repetition compulsion*.[6]
The episodes a patient retells often have different characters and scenes
but, at the core, the same conflict keeps arising throughout them. This
was eventually studied, even systematized, by other researchers in the
core conflictual relationship method[7] and the briefer *relationship anecdotes
paradigm*. Both involve learning to listen for themes to emerge and have
been invaluable in training future therapists. This attentive listening to
a story can often tell the listener all they need to know about future
episodes.

Hopper's question in *Stranger Things* resembles something most
patients who engage in depth work eventually come to ask: "What if
this whole time that I have been looking for Will, I have been chasing

STRANGER THINGS IN THE FIRST EPISODES   137

something else?"[8] Patients may often find that they are trying to run from something or to something that they perceive on the outside—an object, so to speak, that is the aim of their drive—but we find that when confronted with the data that they themselves have relayed in treatment, it turns out that the "it" is something completely different, much like Hopper's realization in the first season.

Parents of a child patient reported he was struggling to pay attention at school or get work done, and that he was motor-restless and, apparently, always overstimulated. When the therapist met with the child at the first session, he was caught off guard as the child launched into a barrage of personal questions like "Do you live in a house or an apartment? Do you live alone or are you married? Do you have kids? Do you ever sleep on this couch in your office? Do you date men or women?" Eventually regaining some composure, the therapist was able to say, "What's your guess to all that?" The child responded by relaying a chaotic fantasy image of an overstimulating home. With a little time and distance, the therapist was able to realize that the overstimulation was not experienced during the school day, but rather in the child's homelife. Helping the parents recognize that they had a sensitive child who needed more structure and clearer boundaries helped settle things down for the child in both home and school settings.

The opening of *Stranger Things* season one tells us there is a lot more going on than meets the eye. But the viewer, like the therapist, must stay curious and keep exploring to understand. All behaviors may attempt to communicate something.

Season 2, Episode 1, "MADMAX"[9]

The second season starts with a lot of fun details. "To slay the dragon, you must use the magic sword," Princess Daphne advises players of the arcade game *Dragon's Lair*.[10] Viewers are exposed to a game within a game here in the same way the viewer is introduced to a Russian plot, which eventually becomes the hallmark of the season after that. This is akin to a game of politics being introduced during a game where life and death hang in the balance. Billy arrives on the scene with his stepsister, Max. Viewers meet Bob, Joyce's short-lived boyfriend who is destined to be mauled by the Demodogs. Relationships and connections are developing and dwindling. In first sessions with patients, there are many games within games, and the psychoanalytic practitioner must study the drive to increase tensions through connection and the drive to decrease tension through disconnecting.

"If, during the early phase of treatment, I am successful in staying with the patient, neither over nor understimulating him," wrote one therapist, "the patient may become a person who can engage successfully in emotional communication."[11] We see that when "boundaries" are crossed and defenses overtaxed, we do not feel emotionally alive and ready. Instead, we are in fight-or-flight, searching for connection in strange ways in an even stranger inner landscape. We are reminded of the pain inherent in connecting with others through the Duffer Brothers' evocation of nostalgia. In the show, Mike is charged by his mother with collecting two boxes of toys to give away. This is, symbolically, a request to disidentify with an aspect of himself of which he may not be ready to let go. It has been 352 days since El fought the Demogorgon, and the group continues to mourn and yearn for her return. They desire to relate with her once more. Will is bullied, now being called "Zombie Boy" since he came back from the dead, and we can infer that Will has identified with that *toxic introject* (that is, he has allowed that description to become a part of his own personality) as seen in his drawing himself as the Zombie Boy character. By accepting what others think of him, Will is unable to relate, in a more integral manner, to the traumas shaping who he is becoming. The importance of inner and outer relationships to psychological health gets played out before our eyes.

The strangest and most bizarre discovery in the first episode of season two is that Hopper has kept El in his own home, "for her protection," but which we quickly see is reminiscent of her experience in the lab facility from which she escaped in season one. The theme being presented here—of locking someone or something away—brings us back to the image of the steel door in season one, episode one. We witness here again the problem of the repetition compulsion. The dangers of not becoming more aware of these patterns is described, by Jung, as a tension of opposites. He writes:

The psychological rule says that when an inner situation is not made conscious, it happens outside, as fate. That is to say, when the individual remains undivided and does not become conscious of his inner opposite, the world must perforce act out the conflict and be torn into opposing halves.[12]

Hopper's action tells the viewer—in the same way a patient's complex or repetition tells the therapist—that something is afoot and not being explored. This time, Hopper performs the role of imprisoning El, the replacement for his own lost daughter (and perhaps a sign of pathological narcissism). El is arguably undergoing her own process of individuation or *becoming*. She leaves the infancy of season one where she struggles to come to know the new world outside of the lab, and now struggles to become her own person. Princess Daphne's advice in the *Dragon Lair* arcade game—to use the sword—conjures up the important role aggression can play in serving the character's growth and development. El and most of the other characters must assert their own free will to alter the damaging repetitions that have gripped their lives. Both in first episodes and first therapy sessions, it becomes evident how the characters before us are currently using relationships as a way of figuring out who they are and who they want to become. Getting to the bottom of how relationships are being used is a springboard to understanding the surface issues and underlying themes that will come to grip both audiences and individual therapy.

Many patients arrive in therapy hoping for magic to happen. This is not only a wish of their own making, but a consequence of the fantasy sold by manualized/short-term treatments and the self-help industry, promising a quick fix. There is no magic wand or sword. Personality is shaped from early on and reinforced over time. To change core aspects of self requires time and effort, and comes at a price. As a result, we tend to get stuck in old patterns that simply do not work. Freud asserted that the repetition compulsion is a byproduct of the destructive drive, which is interested in returning the organism to a tensionless state.[13]

An education officer at the Freud Museum aptly captures our resistances to progressing in what he calls one of the greatest Freudian findings: "We strive to be unhappy, but the trauma of happiness intervenes."[14] Even when given a chance to do things differently, we will not bite. We get stuck in repetitive patterns.

In treatment, the attentive therapist can see a patient trying variations on a theme that lead, not surprisingly, to the same outcome they are trying to avoid. A patient once noted that he hated his father and found him impossible to live with, yet he did not move out of his parental home. He had a well-paying job, so money was not the issue. He used his mother as an excuse, saying, "I have to protect her from him," but gave no data to show that she was in any way in danger or that he was doing anything to protect her. In fact, over time, the opposite came to light. In many ways, the men of the house all felt castrated by successful mothers, wives, and sisters. There was a rigidity and resistance to even thinking about a life outside of living with his father, even though that seemed like the obvious answer to the patient's stated woes. A game was afoot. Like Hopper "protecting" El, this patient was creating the prison from which he could escape but chose not to. What the patient needed to do was assert himself and his identity outside of his relationship to his parents. Trying to beat this game and solve this patient's problems for him, a clinical error on the therapist's part, led to the treatment becoming as stuck as the patient—a dead-end in a game within a game.

Season 3, Episode 1, "Suzie, Do You Copy?"[15]

The opening of season three presents us with the image of the Upside Down trying to reach through to our own world with tentacle-like roots, flashing lights, and flakes of that world drifting into our own. At the same time, in the (arguably) Rightside Up, we see scientists drilling into the Upside Down. In place of tentacles, we have machine wires, electrical currents zapping, and pieces of our own world drifting into the Upside Down. The image should make you question: Who is invading whom? Who are the good guys and bad guys in this situation? Jung's notion of archetypal *Shadow* is instructive to framing this scene. Shadow can be defined as that which we often project onto others, but really is just a cast-off part of our own character. Who is aggressively trying to get into whose world? And for what nefarious purposes?

The tension within and desperation of our protagonists is palpable as they are grouped into smaller search parties, with each group seeking something different. In the end, of course, they all come together each time, but they keep taking an entire season to make it happen in much the same way a therapy group has to struggle with the vicissitudes of coming together and moving apart. As evidenced in practice-based data, we need to come to the idea that, although we may not really know where the Upside Down is, we do know that we must accept that there is no enemy "Other" besides ourselves.[16] We are all both villain and hero, good and bad. We all have our own Upside Down—our Shadow—with which to contend and accept if we hope to make choices that lead us to the connection and personal growth we so desperately seek.

In season three, everyone is looking for something. El and Max are looking for Billy. Mike and Lucas are looking for Will as he is breaking down his hideout and sanctuary, Castle Byers. Hopper and Joyce are looking for "him" at the installation. Billy and Heather are looking for the next meal for the Demogorgon. Nancy and Jonathan are looking for rats and Ms. Driscoll. Dustin, Steve, and Robin are looking for the "evil Russians." The search is significant, and all these searches are symbolically connected.

The characters of *Stranger Things* are developing deeper intimate connections—moving out of Freud's latency into a more genital stage. With that comes vulnerability, questions about who is with me and who is against me. Fears of merger and invasion abound. At least unconsciously, we must face the inevitable loss and ending of any connection. While convincing a patient that, according to Tennyson, "'Tis better to have loved and lost/Than never to have loved at all"[17] falls outside the purview of the therapist, the possibility may still be brought up. In group therapy, for example, a therapist might invite a patient to make an emotional communication about a feeling they are having toward another patient in the room, but these instructions are often ignored because the risk of making a bridge between oneself and another seems too great a risk for many. Although there is an intention to connect, there is a stronger wish to remain safe, alone, and isolated. It is, we suggest, this desire to find a balance between being alone and together that defines the feeling tone as the series progresses.

In both group and individual therapy, patients are given a chance to better understand themselves, but when given that chance to "put feelings into words," many often struggle. The enemy is the other: "You are treating me like I am your mother;" "I am not sure if I should say how I really feel;" "I don't want to hurt anyone's feelings or be misunderstood." Keeping up a mask or false self in the group, and in life, comes at the expense of real connection. It is a resistance to the stated goal of many therapeutic groups, which is to just "talk."

Many patients in our groups will say that they are searching for something but will express unconscious conflicts either through withholding behaviors or statements. These lead to disconnection by taking the group away from feelings and, in a way, "out of the room." In many instances, a participant in a therapeutic group will address one of us as if in a one-on-one session, while "thinking" aloud about how to interact with someone else, mainly the person who is presently sitting in the circle that the group has created. This is a clear demonstration that the patient has left the "here and now" of present feelings to escape into the more familiar, intellectualized thoughts of a "there and then" world of their own isolation—in other words, their own private Upside Down.

Similarly, in season three of *Stranger Things*, the characters are all searching for something on their own or in subgroups. Participants are convinced that their search is theirs alone and unique. But in the end, the realization comes that there is a universality to their search, and, if shared, that search can bring them together to surmount most odds. That is a message of hope that a group might instill therapeutically, if the risks and dangers of connection are undertaken, and if group members are brave enough to expose the parts of themselves that are often hidden.

Season 4 Episode 1, "The Hellfire Club"[18]

The opening of season 4 immediately evokes the interconnected themes of membership and belonging. Who is included? Who is not? Who knows something and who is in the dark? Based on the three opening episodes already discussed, we could guess that the season will be about people who are "in" and people who are "out." The parallel in therapy may revolve around what is being said now (in session) and what is being kept hidden (out of session), and the distinction between the two is particularly important if progress is to be made.

The first episode starts with Dr. Brenner in a flashback to 1979. The day begins as many others often do: a newspaper, some tea, a crossword puzzle, and then lessons to telekinetic kids being held in the Hawkins lab. But the day quickly goes "wrong" when Dr. Brenner asks the boy called Ten to "see" into the room where another scientist is working with another child, Six. "Something's wrong. They're screaming. Six and Dr. Ellis are dead. They're both dead." From here, the "ordinary" and what is considered "routine" are gone. We, as an audience, are forced to confront the "truths" and "lies" that may be hidden beneath the "routine." In other words, we are compelled to dig deeper and to uncover what lies beneath the surface.

When a patient comes to therapy for help, telling their emotional truth is difficult. It might seem counterproductive that someone comes for help and immediately resists it, but that is one of the biggest contributions Freud made to our understanding of the human psyche. When a patient comes to the consulting room, there is a conflict between protecting themselves on the one hand (preserving the *Persona* they have built to hide their vulnerability) and showing their deepest darkest hidden parts (acknowledging their *Shadow* as a pathway to self development). Those dark parts are often shameful and guilty ideas which will be hinted at in the upside down. We also find expression of how these hidden elements may be integrated into consciousness in service of expanding the personality. As a case-in-point, Eddie Munson, by confronting his (inner) demons in the Upside Down, faces his cowardice from his first episodes to become a real leader through his self-sacrifice. "I didn't run this time, right?" he says to Dustin with his last breath.[19]

Eleven's letter to Mike is full of "fake news." She claims to be doing better in California and says she made friends. She brings others into this web of deceit as well. She claims Will is painting, nothing that "maybe it is for a girl." She knows he likes someone but does not bother to ask. It is unlikely that Will would tell the truth regardless. Jonathan is smoking "safe plants from the earth but don't tell Mom anyway." Eleven's name, Jane, is not even really her name, not as she thinks of herself, and only those outside of the gang call her by it. Steve Harrington is searching for love and what it means beyond sex, while attempting to hide his enduring feelings for Nancy. Robin has fixated her affections on someone whom—at least on the surface—she thinks she cannot have. Nancy and Jonathan are trying to define, leave, and lie about their relationship to anyone who will ask. The tension between "truth" and "lies" abounds.

What makes the season's first episode out even more is that there is actually "counseling" included, and the first episode is a prelude to what is the most therapeutically oriented season thus far. Max is going to a counselor (and no surprise, lying about how she is doing outside of the consulting room). All Vecna's victims—Chrissy, Fred, Patrick, and Max—have experienced death-related trauma and are suffering symptoms of PTSD. From a psychological perspective, Vecna becomes a manifestation of the trauma each victim has chosen to ignore. Rather than engaging their respective traumas and finding ways to live with them, our "victims" choose to ignore and repress their emotions. Stated another way, what should find an outlet and expression "outside" is hidden away "inside." As a result, the trauma that grows in the unconscious (or Upside Down) becomes all-powerful, dangerous, and autonomous. Fault lines in the fabric of personality (and the town of Hawkins) are thus created. Season four explores what happens when the "inner demons" we keep hidden find the "gates," cracks, and ruptures in consciousness that will allow them to 'escape' and wreak havoc on our everyday, 'normal' lives. Vecna is the perfect image of unresolved traumas and complexes coagulating around the most terrifying aspect of the Shadow.

Max emerges amongst the victims as someone who may yet be able to save her "soul" from the unrelenting clutches of Vecna. By later writing those letters to loved ones,[20] reconnecting with her friends (especially Lucas), and making her peace with Billy, she literally (and metaphorically) makes a "deal with God": She rekindles that connection with her inner God or archetypal *Self* that may yet save her from the clutches of inner despair and an overly harsh superego.[21]

The Nina project (like the consulting room of a therapist) is an isolation tank built to help El (and patients) access repressed memories and feelings unfelt. When El needs to recover her powers, it becomes her metaphor for overcoming the blocks, gaps, and barriers we erect to save us from facing the "truths" about ourselves. It is fitting that El is reunited with her "Papa," a father figure from her past, in the torturous process of rekindling her powers. The explanation as to why El has lost her powers and how she can get them back is couched in psychoanalytic language. She has to (a) remember her past trauma, the massacre at Hawkins lab, and the emotional connotations triggered by the bullying; (b) retrieve her memories surrounding this event, with the help of her father figure/therapist and his vast "library" of knowledge; (c) not just "see" the past but to "fully re-experience" it;[22] and (d) fight her resistance and desire to forget, all of which are "held" and "contained" within the (therapeutic) vessel that is Nina. Brenner states that El's wish to forget is, in fact, "a defense mechanism in place to protect it [our brains] from bad memories, from trauma. [She] buried these memories long ago." El's fragmentary vision of blood is, according to Brenner, "tied to another memory, a more powerful one invading from your [El's] sub-conscious." He continues, "You have demons, Eleven. Demons from your past. That is why we must proceed carefully. One step at a time. One memory at a time. If we go too fast, I'm afraid you could become lost in the darkness."[23] The process Brenner and Dr. Sam Owens have devised to restore El's powers is essentially a therapeutic one. The therapeutic vessel that is Nina provides the safety necessary for El to regress, relive and, with the help of her therapist-father, to reintegrate the past into the present in service of a more hopeful future.

The real key to understanding the season's first episode lies in how the two scenes before Chrissy's death are woven together. The basketball team is in the championship and the captain wants the ball, but Lucas Sinclair makes the last shot before the buzzer. His sister, Erica, likewise, is making the final roll after Dustin's failed attack with the 20-sided die. Things in the show and in a session are going to be tense and fraught while questions abound regarding what is "true" and what is "false." Who are the enemies, and who are the allies? Is the therapist on my side or not? Can the enemies (for instance, Dmitri and Yuri) also become allies given the right circumstances or when seen from a different light? In therapy, there is a lot to be said for going slow, staying curious, and always questioning our inclination towards certainty and concrete "final" answers.

Conclusions on Beginnings

Beginnings, then, do indeed contain all we may need to know, either about a patient in treatment or a character in a show. The story arcs can be predicted and our understanding deepened if we listen. The therapist, however, lacks what is necessary to decode it all, and the viewer of a show does not initially understand how it all fits together. A successful treatment and popular show require the participants to be open and curious about what is to come. The dynamics at work in our unconscious are not unique to us. They operate at individual, group, and societal levels. It is not that we are under attack by others—Russians, Demogorgons, etc.—but rather that we are in a prison of our own design and the enemy we thought was out there has a home in us that we must integrate to function as a whole. We can play lots of games within ourselves to avoid that realization, but if we are to "individuate" in the Jungian sense, we must integrate unknown aspects of ourselves to increase self-awareness and be more aware of what makes us tick—both conscious and unconscious things. The way these elements are portrayed in *Stranger Things* speaks to why it has become such a phenomenon in the present day. The way it resonates with us can also help the clinician further appreciate that much is often presented in the first session that will only be understood in time and with exploration. But keeping these in mind throughout the therapy may be beneficial for both patients and therapists alike.

William Sharp, PsyD, is an associate teaching professor at Northeastern University and director of the master's in clinical mental health counseling program at the Boston Graduate School of Psychoanalysis. He is a training and supervising analyst with a private practice in Brookline, Massachusetts. Follow him on Twitter: @DrWilliamSharp.

Kevin Lu, PhD, is a senior lecturer and director of the Jungian and Post-Jungian Studies MA at the University of Essex. His publications include articles and chapters on Jung's relationship to the discipline of history, Toynbee's analytical psychology, critical assessments of the theory of cultural complexes, sibling relationships in the Chinese/Vietnamese Diaspora, and Jungian perspectives on graphic novels and their adaptation to film. His paper on racial hybridity was awarded the prize for best article published in the *International Journal of Jungian Studies* in 2019.

Greta Kaluzeviciute, PhD, is an academic at the intersection of psychoanalysis, psychotherapy, epistemology and mental health, working in the United Kingdom and Lithuania. She is an associate professor (senior lecturer) of psychology at Vilnius University, Institute of Psychology.

14

The Strangest Things
Choices, Chances, and the
Dungeons & Dragons of Life

J. Scott Jordan & Victor Dandridge, Jr.

"If we started out just playing games, at what point did we forget that we were playing?"
—anthropologists David Graeber & David Wengrow[1]

"The play's the thing."
—Hamlet[2]

I magine, if you will, the Midwestern United States, Hawkins, Indiana, 1983. The settling dusk fills quaint suburban streets with feelings of suspense and dread as water sprinklers and barking dogs stand guard against the Upside Down. In a dimly lit basement, four preteen boys play *Dungeons & Dragons*. Mike as Dungeon Master (DM), creator, and moderator of this evening's campaign, peers wickedly over the top of his Dungeon Master screen.

"Something is coming," he says in hushed tones while shifting his gaze from player to player. "Something hungry for blood." The room seems to fill with shadows. What if it's the Demogorgon? Anxiety creeps across the faces of the players, then turns to dread as the DM slams a figurine onto the table and shouts, "The Demogorgon!"

Emotions fly, and the players scramble to react.

In the game world of D&D, as in the ebb and flow of daily life, players pursue constellations of goals, either cooperatively or competitively, within an imagined or live-action yet largely unpredictable space. Within daily life, the unpredictability stems from the fact that reality is an *open* system.[3] This means that while we can work to control certain aspects of it, it is simply too large and complex for anyone or anything to control completely. Such unpredictability snaps them back into the mundane world when Mike's mother hollers downstairs that it is time to stop playing. Although Mike is the DM in that night's D&D game world and controls quite a number of the other players' options in that space, the game world is always vulnerable to unpredictable interruptions from forces outside of it—for example, one's mother. (Sometimes he will also adventure under other DMs such as Will and Eddie, subject to their whims and worlds.)[4]

Unpredictability gets introduced into the D&D game by using dice to randomize certain outcomes, such as when Mike announces the arrival of the Demogorgon. Because Mike has not predetermined the outcome of this encounter, Will must roll a 20-sided die to determine whether or not his fireball attack succeeds against the monster. If he rolls a 13 or higher (a 40 percent probability), his attack will have been successful and then he will roll another die to determine how many points of damage his attack inflicts upon the Demogorgon.

Players in the game world of D&D make choices, as in daily life, and the impacts of those choices play themselves out in unpredictable ways. As a result, stranger things are bound to emerge. In other words, we play and live out our lives at the intersection of choice and chance. And while such pronouncements might read more as poetry than truth, exciting discoveries in psychological science increasingly indicate that this contextually inescapable intersection is what forces us to become a "someone." In short, we each *become* our journey.

"Choose Your Character!" How Choices and Chance Constrain Our Possibilities

In *Dungeons & Dragons*, players each create a character by choosing a *class*, an adventurer type such as warrior, wizard, cleric, or thief. Players then rely on chance to determine the character's ability scores for strength, dexterity, constitution, intelligence, wisdom, and charisma, plus maybe a few more traits depending on which game edition they play.[5] While the D&D method for creating who you are in the game world by rolling combinations of die might seem far removed from how we become who we are in life, rolling the dice in D&D is meant to model all the uncontrollable, unpredictable factors that influence you all the time, at many different levels: genetically, neurologically, psychologically, and culturally, to name a few. For example, in *Stranger Things*, Mike and Lucas get into an argument about El.[6] Terrified by the aggressiveness, El tries to stop the fight with her powers but unintentionally hurls Lucas off Mike, through the air, and into the side of a bus. Later, Dustin tries to explain to Mike why he needs to make up with Lucas:

Dustin: He's your best friend, right?

Mike: Yeah. I mean, I don't know.

Dustin: It's fine. I get it. I didn't get here until the fourth grade. He had the advantage of living next door. But none of that matters. What matters is that he is your best friend.

Dustin is clearly aware that although he and Mike are *good* friends, Mike and Lucas are *best* friends due to a chance factor over which Dustin had absolutely no control—specifically, the points in their lives each first met Mike. If "being best friends" fell among characteristics players must determine in *Dungeons & Dragons*, they would roll dice to simulate these uncontrollable chance factors.

Given the lasting impact that unpredictable events have on who we become, it is sometimes difficult to be clear about what a choice is. As a matter of fact, some psychologists claim this *feeling* we have, that our choices cause things to happen, what is referred to as *conscious will*, is an illusion.[7] For example, remember what it felt like when you decided to buy this book, and you did. Imagine what it feels like for El when she decides to say to Mike, "I love you, too," and she does.[8] According to the *theory of apparent mental causation*,[9] although we feel that our thoughts and decisions cause things to happen, they don't. Instead, these psychologists believe that even our choices are caused by a host of factors that exist outside of our conscious control. In short, we are all zombies who live in the hellish Upside Down of believing we can make choices that cause things to happen.

The reason some psychologists believe conscious will is an illusion is because they think of choices as being like balls on a pool table. When one ball rolls into another, we say it *caused* the other ball to move. The problem is that choices don't work that way. In life, they play their part in determining who we become by *constraining* the constellation of unpredictable chance factors we encounter.[10] Choosing to read a book means choosing not to rewatch an episode of *Stranger Things*, at least not without dividing your attention. Choices don't *cause*, according to this line of reasoning. They *constrain*.

In *Stranger Things*, choices made in season one constrain the unpredictable events that play out over subsequent seasons. Mike's initial decision to hide El in his basement[11] creates the future possibility of the two of them experiencing the magic of falling in love, the heartache of breaking up, the forgiving thrill of getting back together, and the terrible sense of loss of later being separated. Again, choices don't *cause*. They *constrain*, restrict the range of subsequent possibilities. As a result, in *D&D*, as in life, there isn't a single moment that does not play itself out at this intersection of choices and chance.

To be sure, sometimes chance has such a constant, imposing impact on who we can be, it robs us of our ability to believe we can make effective choices. In extreme cases, uncontrollable events can make us experience *learned helplessness*, a state in which we believe our choices don't matter at all.[12] Research reveals strong connections between learned helplessness and depression,[13] child abuse,[14] and poverty.[15] Research also reveals that preadolescents diagnosed as having certain learning disorders exhibit more learned helplessness, as well as anxiety and depression, than non-diagnosed peers.[16]

Clearly, all choices are not created equal. In *Stranger Things*, choices and chance lead to the moment in the season three finale when Joyce Byers has to decide whether to explode the reactor and apparently kill Hopper.[17] There is no thrill in this choice, no sense of freedom. There is a strong sense of agency, for sure, but one filled with dread, regret, and remorse, no matter the choice. When we come to understand this about ourselves, that the unpredictable, open reality we live in (1) has the power to influence the nature of our choices, (2) can lead us to choices that have nothing but dreadful outcomes, and (3) can result in learned helplessness in ourselves and others, then we become able to experience and make our choices differently. All choices constrain the possibilities of ourselves and others. Everything we do in this open reality constrains the future for everyone and everything.[18] While we can each choose to become someone who experiences life as a lone actor, making decisions based on one's own first-person perspective, we can also choose to be someone who experiences choices for what they truly are: necessarily complicated, often cruel, constraints we put on ourselves and therefore others in a wildly open reality full of billions of other people learning and struggling to do the exact same thing.

"Create a Fellowship!"
How Choices and Chance Constrain Social Groups

Although our choices might feel like individual, personal events when we make them, the fact that they also constrain the future possibilities of others means they are also social. Even selfish choices are social. For example, couple Steve Harrington and Nancy Wheeler have an argument after Nancy tells him she went to his house looking for her missing friend Barb.[19] Instead of empathizing, Steve's first reaction is defensive and self-centered. He immediately becomes concerned the police will want to question everyone who was at the party at his house, where Barb was last seen, and will discover they were drinking alcohol. Nancy is incensed. "Barb is missing, and you're worried about your dad?" Even though Steve asks Nancy to lie to the police about the beer, his seemingly selfish choice is still social: It's about what his dad will do if he finds out about the party.

A dominant theme of *Stranger Things* is the tension of determining who is and isn't a member of a group. In season one, Mike begins to include El in more and more of the "party's" activities. Lucas does not trust El and feels his best friend status with Mike is at risk. Mike wants El to become a member of their party, whereas Lucas doesn't. This tension comes to a head in the above-mentioned scene when Mike and Lucas end up in a fistfight. Later, it's Lucas who wants to bring a new member into the party—specifically, Mad Max. Ironically, Mike is the one most clearly opposed to the change: "We don't need another party member. I'm our paladin, Will's our cleric, Dustin's our bard, Lucas is our ranger, and El is our mage!"[20]

These relationship dynamics are prominent in adolescent life, as teens begin to form couples around developing issues such as sexual cognitions and desires[21] along with a variety of strong emotional connections.[22] And while we might *feel* these factors influencing our choices, the factors themselves would not be something we would refer to as a "choice." In addition to culture and socialization, changes in brain chemistry that occur during puberty strongly influence the types of stimuli that attract individuals sexually or emotionally.[23] Because emotional and sexual attractions are regulated by different brain systems,[24] we can fall in love with people to whom we are not sexually attracted or feel sexually attracted to people with whom we are not in love. And what is more, none of these motivational systems in the brain feel as if they are under our control. As a result, they seem to fall more on the *chance* side of the "choices and chance" intersection.

This idea is given beautiful expression during season three in a relationship that develops between Steve Harrington and his code-cracking, ice cream shop coworker Robin. Having been captured, drugged, and interrogated by Soviet soldiers, the two, still under the influence of truth serum, become ill after exiting a showing of the then-new movie *Back to the Future*[25] and stare up at the mall's dizzying dome ceiling. After vomiting, the two sit on the bathroom floor next to separate toilets where Steve both admits to his earlier, selfish ways and declares the feelings he has developed for Robin. The two then have a conversation in which Robin shares not only her surprise that she actually likes Steve as a person but also her fear he will reject her if he learns her truth, that her classroom infatuation during high school was not with him but instead concerned a girl in the class.[26]

After spending one long moment silently contemplating the implication that Robin's sexual orientation has for their relationship, Steve quips, "I mean, yeah, Tammy Thompson, you know, she's cute and all, but, I mean, she's a total dud!"[27] At this point, the background music becomes dramatically happy, slowly increasing in amplitude, filling the scene with a sense of positive growth. The lighthearted manner in which Steve talks to her about her interest in Tammy is that of a friend. The effect on the viewer is to signal that Steve has grown, that he is now able to distinguish sexual desires from emotional attachments and *chooses* to be in a type of relationship he has never experienced before. He has developed a new appreciation of Robin's vulnerabilities, and instead of becoming serious and asking her to speak more about her feelings, he *chooses* to lean into the fun-loving nature of their relationship and finds a roundabout way of letting her know that he values her and is there for her. At the same time, Robin's willingness to laugh along with Steve's jabs at Tammy's voice—and ultimately to agree with him—signals her delight at forming this new, trusting relationship with Steve.

Clearly, this scene has been crafted as a normalization and celebration of this type of relationship. And while Steve and Robin's friendship is depicted as emerging unexpectedly at the juncture of choices and chance, it turns out the decision to write the scene this way had more to do with choice. In an interview with *Vulture* magazine, Maya Hawke, who plays Robin, reported that the writers initially planned for Steve and Robin to end up in a romantic relationship. However, roughly midway through production, the actors suggested the alternate result that we saw in the show.[28] Interestingly, this outcome also reflects the influence of chance. The writers and actors clearly understood changing norms around gender, sexuality, and love—a cultural context they simply found themselves living in while creating the show—and then *chose* to reflect these changes in their creation. And the dance between choices and chance continues.

"Travel the Realms!" Developing Your Own Choices

Observing relationships such as that of Robin and Steve can change the types of choices we make. When we watch the two of them interact, we can feel immediate, rewarding emotions such as fun, thrill, and empathic sadness.[29] These emotions can lead us to form *parasocial relationships* with the characters, "socioemotional bonds that audiences develop with fictional characters and celebrities similar to real-life friendships."[30] Developing these types of emotional bonds with characters outside of our *ingroup* (any group we are in) can decrease prejudice against and increase empathy toward members of an *outgroup* (any group we are not in, including but certainly not limited to those whose sexual orientations differ from our own).[31] In order to achieve this positive social effect, however, we watch many episodes of a show because parasocial relationships develop over time,[32] and watching only one episode involving an outgroup character can activate outgroup prejudices and lead to more negativity.[33] In other words, repeated exposure can improve perception of outgroup members as individual human beings, while a single example may help but also may last only long enough to reinforce existing biases. In *belief confirmation* bias, especially likely during isolated exposures to people or information, we focus on any details that can reinforce beliefs we already have and discount details that might challenge those beliefs. Change tends to take time. Just as Steve bypasses that by learning to think of Robin as a special individual and to value her friendship before he learns information that could predispose some people against viewing her more fairly, viewers also learned to like Robin first without the bias that might have tinged some points of view.

One of the strangest things about these types of changes in our choices is that they can happen without our knowing it. This is possible because we develop and experience parasocial relationships *automatically*, outside of conscious awareness. Specifically, when we observe others, whether in daily life or on our phone, computer, or television, we experience their emotions with similar areas of the brain we use to experience our own.[34] However, as we do so, the brain continually tracks the changes in our experiences that are due to *our* choices, versus something else. As a result, when we watch Robin struggling to tell Steve, we feel her fear, but she is the one who *chooses* to tell him. We are not. We simply choose to watch her. Our brain knows this. As a result, it assigns the emotions to Robin even though we feel them as well.

But this takes us back to the zombie problem! If watching others can change our choices without our knowing it, aren't we really just couch-potato zombies having choices pumped into us by faces on screens? The answer may be, to some extent, yes. When choices are being tracked by the brain, they can change because the brain also creates associations between the events that followed the choice and the choice itself.[35]

Once viewers develop their own parasocial relationships with Steve and Robin, then experience the positive resolution of their friendship during the bathroom scene, memories of that positivity can later be activated during real-life situations involving sexual orientation or any other differences between people. Such remembrances may influence one's choice in those moments. In short, the consequences of the choices we see others (even fictional others) make can influence the natures of choices we make in the future, and this can happen completely outside our conscious awareness.

This ability of the brain to associate choices with chance and therefore change our choices is the zombie part. The association work is automatic, beyond conscious control. As a result, even though our choices *feel* as though they are solely ours to make[36] and we can feel extremely alone when we make them, they are never solely about the moment of choice. They are *always* about the journey we have lived up until that point, memories of how choices and chance have played out over our entire life. When Joyce realizes the horrid decision she has to make, when she chooses to destroy the portal-creating reactor even though she knows Hopper can't get away from it soon enough and looks certain to die, she looks at him.[37] He nods yes for her to do it. She is the one who must choose whether to destroy the reactor. Hopper knows this, knows he will probably die, and assures her it is all right. For both characters, as well as the viewer, this moment feels like the end of Hopper's journey. The moment, however, is not experienced as being just about the death. It's experienced in terms of all the choices and chances that have brought them to this place. The scene has such rich depth because of the parasocial relationships we have created with both characters over three seasons and, in that moment, we feel the full depth of Joyce and Hopper's journey.

Similarly deep emotions can be experienced when a player's character dies in a game of D&D.[38] Players comment that character death in D&D is more meaningful than in digital games that have an automatic "resurrection" rule because the death "was the consequence of collective and individual human actions, rather than those of machines or artificial intelligence."[39] Players also assert that "death in D&D was heightened by the inherent physical proximity and social realities they shared with other players."[40] These reports are consistent with the idea that parasocial relationships are formed automatically as we observe others. When players sit together in a common space, collectively making decisions for characters—as Mike, Will, Lucas, and Dustin are doing during the beginning and end of season one—they experience the unintended consequences of those choices, including the laughter, frustration, and fear of the other players. They also experience the formation of emotional bonds that include parasocial relationships with the characters. In a real sense, game world and real world become emotionally fused. And while players can clearly distinguish the two, because their individual brains are constantly tracking their individual choices, the emotions and grief become a part of both worlds. One player interviewed by researchers noted that the death of his first character left him in a state of denial, wishing his character had not died in the first place. He experienced the death as unfulfilling and he "grew a habit of creating characters that were similar to his first."[41] Another player stated that "as with death in the real world, grief is a complicated emotion that comes hand in hand with a flood of reminiscences. It reminds us of all the other fond memories of a person/character and challenges us to move forward without them."[42]

Clearly, in D&D as in *Stranger Things*, the moment of character death isn't just about that moment. Rather, it is experienced as an absolute end of the possibility of future interactions with that character. While the players can, of course, continue to have relationships beyond the game death, that particular character was the parasocial medium through which the player journeyed the realms of choices and chance with other players. Emotion-filled memories are generated as players made choices and dealt with the consequences, together. The death of the character can simultaneously mean the death of a certain social group, even if it is, at its core, a parasocial group.

Because of the brain's ability to automatically associate choices with outcomes, choices made in the game world can change future choices made in both the game world and real world. One player interviewed about the game reported that the death of his first character became the moment when he "first wanted to be a DM."[43] Another player commented on how a character death in the game world influenced his real world in profound ways:

> I was so grieved by this death that I went on this three-week streak of 'I'm not going to talk to anyone'—a grief coma. When I woke up from this grief coma, I changed my values. It was actually . . . really strong for me to go through, not just in character but as a player. I went on a day vacation, visited a park, had a nap in the forest. I had a lovely day.[44]

Given that our choices can be changed by their consequences in such profound ways, despite the fact that we aren't aware such changes are being made, it seems that choices aren't so much the opposite of chance as they are the collection of remembered choice-chance episodes we've experienced over the course of our lives. When we make a choice, the issue isn't whether we've achieved what we intended. Rather, the simple act of choosing allows us to distinguish changes that are due ourselves, versus everything else. In the midst of this distinction, we become an "I." As that "I" will make progressively more choices that become associated with progressively more unintended chance consequences, it changes. It ends up in different places, meeting new people, traveling to many realms never imagined when previous choices were being made. As we said at the beginning, we become our journey.

"Roll the Dice!"
Accepting a World of Choices and Chance

"To be or not to be. That is the question."
—Hamlet[45]

In the end, *Stranger Things* opens a portal into the shared truth that we all live at the inescapable intersection of choices and chance, where things, as in D&D, rarely, if ever, go as planned. We all occasionally close off our emotions, our grief, our anxiety, our trauma, because the moment demands we make a choice. Perhaps the strangest thing of all is that despite the truth of never-ending change, we nonetheless continue to choose, to act, to be. And occasionally, if we're fortunate enough to have someone to guide us, family to hold us, and friends to carry us, things can be good . . . for a while. We can learn to manage our own portal, our own way, and appreciate the moments of love, belonging, and contentedness that occasionally emerge amidst the chaos, while simultaneously knowing deep down, regardless of how much we want things to stay the same, they will eventually change.

This idea of accepting the beautifully ugly reality of choices and chance is given exceptional expression in the letter Hopper crafts for El and Mike when he feels they have been spending too much time together. Joyce finds the letter while preparing to move, after Hopper has supposedly died in the reactor chamber. She gives the letter to El, who reads it in a scene voiced over by Hopper:

Hopper: I don't want things to change. So I think maybe that's why I came in here, to try to maybe stop that change. To turn back the clock. To make things go back to how they were. But I know that's naive. It's just not how life works. It's moving. Always moving, whether you like it or not.[46]

After El finishes reading this letter and begins to cry, the background music becomes Peter Gabriel's mournful cover of the David Bowie song "Heroes," which suggests that anyone can become a hero, even briefly. The words reveal an understanding of the never-ending dance of choices and chance, along with what it means to choose to make our choices more about others. Just as Steve becomes a hero for Robin by providing a space of trust and respect in her most vulnerable moment, as Robin becomes one of Steve's heroes rushing to defend him against winged monsters,[47] as Hopper becomes a hero for the kids, as the kids become heroes for Hawkins, and as El and Joyce each become heroes for the entire world, we, too, can choose to be heroes for others. Will we know when? Probably not. As all things, such moments will emerge spontaneously, as our choices merge with the world of chance. What should we do until then? Simple. *Roll for initiative!*

Post-Script:
The Stranger Things You Find . . .
by Victor Dandridge

When we were creating my first roleplaying game character, my Dungeon Master rolled dice totals that made my character weak overall, too low for the tabletop gaming bug to bite. And though my name travels well in circles of geekery, the world of gaming has so often been one I didn't indulge or understand. Or so I thought . . .

As a creative voice in the world of comics and popular culture, my first canvas was always me. Overlaying the stories I consumed, whether that be in film or the colorful periodicals tucked into the newsstand, I became the characters I most aligned with. Note, I said characters and not specifically *heroes*. And everyone I know has done the same by invoking the personification of their favorites as their own.

Scour a neighborhood or playground and see it play in real time. Whether using living-room furniture or backyard play sets, you'll hear the resounding chorus of selection and choice as, rigorously and sometimes competitively, playmates sing the hymn of "I am . . ." But when the bounds of make-believe are seen as childish, quick to be outgrown for more mature social engagements, that doesn't mean that the urge to recast yourself goes away. And to those who embark on its exploration, there's a nifty little community for you, built around hours-long campaigns of mystery and adventure, monsters and suspense, victory and oblivion— the world of *roleplay*.

While tabletop gaming has definitely ventured into other genres, as all good literature can (let's never forget that even these games are vehicles for telling stories), there's a ubiquitous correlation with the genre of fantasy. Worlds of magic, with goblins and orcs, kingdoms and bogs, wait for you to find treasures of bounty and fellowship. You could surely levy the same genre expectation to superheroes and comic books. But, despite its conjoined appearance, there's something about that word "fantasy" that works so well in this space.

Fantasy involves the act of imagining things, especially things that are impossible or improbable. The importance of the persistent voice of influence we experience throughout our formative years cannot be overstated. In our earliest years, what we like (or don't) is largely comparable to the other family unit members' preferences, so they hardly stand out as true definitions of our character or interest. But as we align our favorite things in association with other people, an indelible mark begins to form, classifying our affiliations and activities. Sure, some of these classifications are stereotypical misnomers that only serve to generalize negative traits—but even to challenge those overcast ideas, one has to know where they stand in relation to others in their sphere. And that's what makes this timeframe of influence so impactful: As susceptible to suggestion and influence as one tends to be, we are increasingly more fluid to our defined self, able to shift on a whim to meet the hierarchy of our interests and wants.

Even from my neophyte perspective, the game of *Dungeons & Dragons* breeds and builds on this sense of self-determination. As our natural tendency is to first project our true selves before concocting a fictional version, player sheets for beginners tend to stack real-world assumptions and expectations against the fantastic representations. Are you more athletic and physical in your everyday life? Then the appeal of action-centric characters like barbarians, paladins, or fighters may be alluring. Got a higher aptitude for scholarly pursuits? Consider the thoughtfulness and knowledge it takes to be a dazzling cleric, wizard, or artificer.

These character classes become self-reflecting in their earliest use. As you see yourself, so does your character communicate, advance, and react with the members of your party. Aspects of alignment—your character's motivational traits (lawful good, true neutral, chaotic evil, etc.)—coincide with your actual perception of self. These expectations of your personage could almost be charted in a straight, consistent line, never straying too far from comfort, by design. To this end, early players yield most of their agency to the power of the dice—as fickle and unpredictable as the voice of influence. They play the game as though the outcomes are predetermined, like an "if/then" diagram.

With time, experience, and familiarity comes freedom, in the game as in life. Acknowledgment and acceptance of who you are in lived life gives permission to explore and build in a counterintuitive sense of self. Naturally good-natured and kind-hearted people can exercise their more vindictive or destructive interest through characters who don't encapsulate their personal ideologies. It's through this demonstration that the true power of roleplaying is unleashed! As seen throughout popular culture—such as when Spider-Man is far more type A, assertive, and at times aggressive than his Peter Parker alter ego—the character you *choose* to play and to be within the game has more power and flexibility in their presentation and voice.

The D&D experience is cyclical, bringing as much out from the game as brought into it. Where gamers first infer their vision of self to the board, they take away their best selves, developing critical thinking skills, problem-solving tactics, and merits that can boost their *actual* perception and coping mechanisms in the real world. Their dance with choice and chance becomes a critical dice roll in their development as a successful, functioning member of society and the world at large—a roll for their role.

Post-Post-Script:
The Puppets and Masters of Fantasy
Scott Jordan

When metal-loving Dungeon Master Eddie Munson enters the world of *Stranger Things*, our middle-school heroes of previous seasons find themselves thrust into the "Satanic panic" of the 1980s. The nature of this cultural movement is described quite well during a meeting of the Hellfire Club in the high-school cafeteria, when Eddie reads aloud from *Newsweek* magazine, in his best anchor-man imitation, "The Devil has come to America. *Dungeons and Dragons*, at first regarded as a harmless game of make-believe, now has both parents and psychologists concerned. Studies have linked violent behavior to the game, saying it promotes satanic worship, ritual sacrifice, sodomy, suicide, and even *murder*." One of his friends says, "Society has to blame something. We're an easy target."[48]

The actual *Newsweek* article appeared in its September 9, 1985 issue, and was titled, "Kids: The Deadliest Game?"[49] As paraphrased by Eddie, the article describes both religious and secular movements that blamed the game for over 50 teenage deaths. On the religious front, an organization known as BADD (Bothered About D&D) was founded by Ms. Patricia Pulling, whose son, a D&D fan, supposedly committed suicide because another player sent him a curse that he interpreted literally. Pulling believed the game was a form a sacrilegious brainwashing. On the secular front, psychiatrist Thomas Radecki, chair of the National Coalition on Television Violence asserted that kids start living in their fantasy and can't find their way out of the dungeon. As a result, "The game causes young men to kill themselves and others."[50]

Together, these religious and secular movements attempted to ban students from playing D&D in schools. There were many forms of resistance to them, though. The school board of Putnam, Connecticut refused to ban the game. TSR Hobbies, the game's manufacturer, included a warning in the instructions that players should not identify too strongly with their characters, and that "the more the two are kept apart, the better your games will be."[51] Media psychologist Joyce Brothers asserted, "Games are just games if you have fun." The Association for Gifted-Creative Children suggested that playing the game leads children to read authors such as Tolkien, Shakespeare, and Asimov.

In the midst of these cultural struggles, Joseph Laycock, professor of religious studies, proposed that what made *Dungeons & Dragons* such a threat to religious groups was that the two have much in common, for both are actually socially-constructed systems of shared meaning. As a result, certain religious groups that feel the need to control culture's fantasies saw the game as a direct challenge to the authority they had historically held over the types of socially-constructed meanings people believe. Ironically, as they waged their war on the imagined worlds created in D&D, they did so with levels of vigor and conviction found in the imagined heroes of that realm, engaged in a battle against a deep, dark conspiracy.

Thinking of Eddie Munson in this light, when he thrashes Metallica's "Puppets and Masters" as a strategy to draw demons away from his friends and toward himself,[52] he becomes what D&D players refers to as a bard: a master of music, language, and the magic of their merging.[53] He also becomes a fictional embodiment of the never-ending struggle to own your fantasies, to have the power and ability to try on different identities, different systems of values, different fantasies.

For me, being a guy who played D&D in his friend's basement in the game's early days, just like the characters Dustin and Mike, Eddie is a hero, and his fate pains us. The parasocial relationships with fictional characters (mentioned in this chapter) occur in D&D, too. When a character dies in the game, players can feel the grief and loss. The point is, whether I'm sitting in a basement with friends, trying to save a character's life with a healing spell, or sitting in a pew, reading scripture in unison with the congregation, I am socially co-creating the world I am in. I am being empathetic, I am being social, and the people I am with are trying to help each other. Having the ability and power to try out these different possibilities of belief is a cultural value worth fighting for. Thank you, Eddie Munson.

J. Scott Jordan, PhD, chairs the department of psychology at Illinois State University. His research examines the neuroscience, psychology, and philosophy of cooperative behavior. With over 150 publications, he regularly contributes to the Popular Culture Psychology series. He is a co-organizer of ReggieCon, a virtual comic con panel series that celebrates diversity and heritage months during the academic year. He produces the Dark Loops Productions channel on YouTube, and he is extremely proud of his international comic book collection.

Victor Dandridge, Jr., writer, publisher, graphic designer, and educator, is a leading new voice for innovation and production within the self-publishing market. He has found acclaim with his own imprint, Vantage: Inhouse Production; the weekly internet review series *Black, White & Read All Over*; and the popular culture podcast *Hall of Justice*. Victor launched Cre-8 Comics, a unique bridge between comics and classroom fundamentals.

15

It's All in the Game

How Fighting Fake Foes Teaches Us to Face Our Fears

Justine Mastin & Larisa A. Garski

"We are never more fully alive, more completely ourselves, or more deeply engrossed in anything than when we are playing."
—psychologist Charles Schaefer, the "father" of play therapy[1]

"This isn't D&D. This is real life."
—Mike Wheeler[2]

Play is a vital part of human life,[3] and it is powerfully healing. Though once relegated by psychologists and psychotherapists to the realm of children, play is currently embraced as both a necessary part of life and a key component of many types of therapy for humans of all ages.[4] Hopper and Eleven engage in a variety of play—including dancing, reading together, and playing tabletop games[5]—demonstrating how play can build generational bridges,[6] helping children and adults to process their pain and connect over time. For children, play acts as the lens through which they begin to understand the often-overwhelming stimuli and expectations of the adult world. Play enables kids to focus on parts of what often feels like a chaotic world, learning cognitive flexibility in the process.[7] In their gameplay and invocation of game analogies, both the children and the adults of *Stranger Things* learn strategy, improvisation, morality, empathy, and creativity. Through the innately therapeutic world of *Dungeons & Dragons* (D&D), they train to face a real-live Demogorgon, puberty, and the Upside Down experience of processing their feelings.

Healing Domain

The use of play in a therapeutic context offers an experiential way for children, adolescents, and adults to process overwhelming emotions without having to give words to traumatic experiences. This enables children to express feelings and sensations around experiences for which they do not yet have language.[8] Though humans tend to equate emotional vocabulary struggles with childhood, adults and adolescents can also find themselves at a proverbial loss for words when faced with intense feelings. The ability to act things out with dolls or puppets, or to draw or paint, helps people to get their message heard by the therapist or trusted other, creating a shared language and meaning. Creative expression enables children and adults to both express the lived experience of events and process their corresponding feelings without getting overwhelmed. Aided by the power of play, Eleven uses D&D miniatures and the game board as representations to explain where Will is hiding and the concept of the Upside Down.[9]

As both a coping skill and a method to teach coping skills, play promotes emotion regulation and connection. It also provides a safe structure for learning skills and strategies to function in reality.[10] *Play therapy*, the purposeful incorporation of play into therapy, includes but is not limited to engaging clients with toys, storytelling, and expressive art. Will and his mother, Joyce, mimic the therapeutic dynamic as they engage with Will's drawings. Joyce regularly questions Will about his drawings, searching for the underlying emotional meaning in the art he gives to her. Joyce lets Will know his drawings are important to her and shows this by encouraging him to draw and buying him a 120-color box of crayons.[11] Building this rapport around Will's drawings proves important when he is unable to express the image he is seeing in his mind while "spying" on the Shadow Monster. He draws it in the familiar medium of crayons and paper and invites his mother to interpret the drawings. Ultimate they discover a map of Hawkins where vines are growing beneath the town.[12]

Therapeutic play also allows for a therapist and the client, or for those in a family, to engage in play together to learn how to simply be with one another while engaging in a shared activity—a form of rapport-building also known as *joining*. Joining is a vital part of the therapeutic process for therapist and client and can sometimes be difficult for children and adolescents, as well as for adults who have experienced trauma, in other words an event or series of events that put a person in mortal peril, activating the nervous system's fight/flight/freeze response.[13] After moving into the cabin together, Eleven and Hopper play games on many evenings, and this becomes a bonding time for them, a meaningful time for the pair to solidify their new relationship as father and daughter. Hopper recalls these times in his written heart-to-heart speech[14] and admits that discussing feelings—or even experiencing them—is difficult for him. But in a game, Hopper gets to engage in something concrete, where he knows the rules and can safely engage with his new daughter, Eleven.

Asking for a trusted other to engage in gameplay is a bid for connection. Gameplay offers an opportunity for focus on a single project and the other players. When Hopper feels Eleven is growing distant from him, this feels distressing for him because Eleven has ceased accepting his bids for connection.

This dynamic proves particularly painful for Will. As the other boys in the D&D party each grow invested in flirtatious and romantic play (dating), they start rejecting Will's bids for connection through D&D gameplay. Because the gameplay was a vital part of their relationship and shared language, rejected bids for this engagement have the impact of an attachment injury.

> **Mike:** We're not kids anymore. I mean, what did you think, really? That we were never going to get girlfriends? We were just

going to sit in my basement and play games for the rest of our lives?

Will: Yeah, I guess I did.[15]

Dungeons & Dragons & Therapy

All play can have therapeutic application, and the structures of roleplaying games (RPGs) create ideal opportunities to practice social skills, build cognitive flexibility, and co-create meaning. RPGs are games in which players enact the roles of fictional characters in a fictional world, and *Dungeons & Dragons* is arguably the most popular RPG of all time.[16] Considered dangerous by some during the so-called "Satanic panic" early in the game's history (as represented by Hawkins citizens' reactions to Eddie Munson and the high school's *Dungeons & Dragons* club),[17] D&D's therapeutic properties are so ubiquitous that there are now many therapeutic D&D groups and training programs. The rise of D&D play during the COVID-19 pandemic has helped to stave off loneliness for many who were in isolation.[18] Often identified as a game for those lacking in or struggling with social connection, the game has been shown to help fulfill real-world needs and promote relationships with others.[19]

Mike, Lucas, Dustin, and Will bond while playing D&D and craft a shared language with which to create meaning and understand the world around them. When presented with something they don't understand—a terrifying monster—they are able to conceptualize this as a Demogorgon, a monster they have fought in the game before and one they know something about. While still frightening, they're able to put this new entity into a context with which they're familiar. They can continue using language borrowed from gameplay to discuss the additional threats they face. This expanded analogy serves the D&D party as they grow in number and provides a shortcut to understanding when new members join the party.

Dustin: The Mind Flayer.

Hopper: What the hell is that?

Dustin: It's a monster from an unknown dimension. It's so ancient that it doesn't even know its true home. Okay, it enslaves races of other dimensions by taking over their brains using its highly developed psionic powers.

Hopper: Oh my god. None of this is real. This is a kid's game.

Dustin: No, it's a manual. And it's not for kids. And unless you know something we don't, this is the best metaphor—

Lucas: Analogy.

Dustin: Analogy? That's what you're worried about? Fine! An *analogy* for understanding whatever the hell this is.[20]

Party Rules

So much of what governs human existence is created, becoming intricate systems of rules, roles, and boundaries that control the way human beings move in the world. Known as *social constructionism*, this theory argues that much of human existence is a series of codified social games.[21] *Narrative therapy* takes social constructionism one step further by inviting both clients and therapists to notice the created human constructs that govern our reality and to make changes to these inventions if they no longer serve them.[22] A similar interaction occurs in gameplay.

To play any game, the players must decide on the rules of the game. It is through the gameplay that players decide what is fair and unfair. If instructions are included in a game, there is still room for players to decide what they consider appropriate within the game space. In this way, play helps people identify morals and ethics and invites co-creation of meaning.[23] For Mike and his friends, their D&D party establishes rules, roles, and boundaries that the teammates carry out into the real world. Play helps young people imagine the world the way they believe it should be, rather than how it is. In the self-focused era of the 1980s, the party imagines a world where "he who spills first blood" must be the one to initiate the repair in the relationship.[24] The D&D party members agree that if this is not done, then the party member who caused the pain must be banished from the party. These rules are explicitly stated and reiterated, showing not just morality but also the ability to communicate with one another and use direct communication.

By creating the rules of their game, they are creating the rules of its magical world. These rules follow them out into the real world, and so, as they create the rules of the game, they create the rules of their lives.

Empowerment Spell

Play can be empowering, especially for children. Choice, for children and adolescents, is limited. But in the game space, options are much vaster, especially in a game such as D&D. While the Dungeon Master (DM) has a plan for the game, players' choices and the element of chance (the rolling of dice) all work together to determine outcomes. Depending on what happens during gameplay, new choices reveal themselves, requiring players (and often the DM) to improvise.

Play offers opportunities for imagination and considerations of what could be. Through play, new ideas emerge that would not have been previously considered.[25] Thus, play helps players learn cognitive flexibility, the ability to adapt both thinking and behavior to their environment and circumstances. Play invites people to open their curiosity doors and not keep them locked. In play, people ask the question "What if?" and allow a variety of possible answers to arise, such as "What if the Upside Down has similar mechanics to the Vale of Shadows in D&D?" If that outside-of-the-box hypothesis is correct, then the D&D party could use their D&D manual to form more potential solutions.[26]

Choices presented can pit the individual against the collective. In the D&D party's interaction with the game's Demogorgon, Will must decide which spell to cast: protection or fireball?[27] To cast a protection would shield himself, while unleashing fireball could potentially (based on dice roll) defeat the monster and save the whole party. Other members of the party express their wishes for Will, but ultimately it is his decision. He is learning how to solve complex problems in a time-limited environment. This serves Will well out in the external world.

When the Demogorgon first comes after him, Will is able to think quickly and use the skills he gained via the campaign to try to improvise: He gets inside his home and locks the door, then tries the phone. When the phone is unavailable, he yells for help, then finally heads to the shed to grab the shotgun. At each turn he makes a choice and, depending on the metaphorical roll of the dice, he moves on to what's next.

Roll for Initiative

In the early years of their D&D play, the boys practice communication skills, learn ways to resolve conflict, and practice both patience and listening—even when it is challenging. Following their fight, Lucas hesitates to accept Mike's apology. The two come back together to express feelings that came up for them, authentically listen to each other, and make amends. As is the case with social skills–based gameplay in therapy, the boys may then transfer these skills out into the external world, albeit with varying degrees of success. Dustin, often the group peacemaker, uses the conflict resolution skills gleaned in D&D to bridge differences in the group, such as when Mike and Lucas are fighting and Dustin reminds Mike it's the "law" that Mike be the one to shake hands because "he spilled first blood."[28] Though Mike initially struggles to use communication skills with Eleven, he eventually succeeds in connecting with her through the playful act of letting her try out his father's recliner.[29]

How people play changes over time, and different play helps in different kinds of social skill formation. For Dustin, he has the help of Steve, who guides him from the play of his youth to his next stage of play.[30] This is also transformative for Steve, forced to think outside of himself and thereby begin to understand compassion for another, even if the advice he offers about girls is not the most useful. Play can be comforting and empowering for an adolescent to pass along this knowledge to the next generation. It allows them the opportunity to feel both competent and masterful, especially when it's something meaningful to themselves. When Will decides to donate his D&D guide before his move, Dustin and Lucas take the opportunity to pass the knowledge of D&D along to Lucas's younger sister, Erica, so that the tradition can continue.[31]

Natural 20

Play is the work of childhood, the challenge of adolescence, and the meaning-making of adulthood. Regardless of age, play helps people learn, heal, and connect. With the help of play, people harness the power to bridge generational gaps, create shared meaning, and gain new skills in improvisation, creativity, and social engagement. Through play, Eleven communicates with her new friends using the D&D game pieces, a language they understand.[32] Play becomes a source of bonding between Eleven and her adoptive father, Hopper, as they engage in dance, story, and games together.[33] Play is a serious business.

For *Stranger Things'* young party members, their gameplay prepares them to face literal monsters from the Upside Down, as well as the arguably more complicated monsters of puberty and intergenerational conflict. The bond they create via their fellowship transcends gameplay and enters the physical world. When the party wins, they win together, and when they lose, they support one another. Whether on the game board or in the real world, they pull together as a team. Through their gameplay, the party gains skills of creativity, improvisation, and language. Without the practiced power of play, they would lack the tools necessary to fight the literal monsters in their midst. Play is the true hero of the story, and it wins the game.

Justine Mastin, MA, LMFT, is a therapist, writer, podcaster, and educator. Justine cowrote *Starship Therapise: Using Therapeutic Fanfiction to Rewrite Your Life* and has contributed to numerous books in the Popular Culture Psychology series. Justine is a TEDx speaker, an instructor at Saint Mary's University of Minnesota, and the cohost of the *Starship Therapise* and the *Dark Side of the Mat* podcasts. Justine takes a holistic approach to healing: mind, body, and fandom.

Larisa A. Garski, MA, LMFT, is a psychotherapist, AAMFT-approved supervisor, and the chief of clinical staff at Empowered Therapy in Chicago, Illinois. She specializes in working with folks who identify as outside the mainstream—such as those in the geek and LGBTQIA+ communities. Larisa cowrote *Starship Therapise: Using Therapeutic Fanfiction to Rewrite Your Life* and has contributed to numerous books in the Popular Culture Psychology series. She cohosts the *Starship Therapise* podcast.

Final Word: Finding

Travis Langley

"I'm not ashamed to say I'm a survivor. To me, survivor implies strength, implies that I have been through something and I made it out the other side."
—survivor and advocate Elizabeth Smart[1]

"Remember the hurt. Hurt is good, because it means you're out of that cave."
—Jim Hopper's message to El[2]

Baby Jane Ives vanishes, is raised as weapon 011, escapes, and finds a new life as "El." Will Byers vanishes, then hides from monsters until his mother and Hopper find him. Chief Jim Hopper vanishes, labors in the ice and snow, and has to find his way back. At different times, each gets presumed dead and yet survives.[3] Not everyone makes it, though, and this fact raises the stakes when we wait and hope for others such as Max Mayfield to make their way home.[4] Central to *Stranger Things*, characters go missing or get exploited by others both human and nonhuman. Behind the veneer of everyday small-town life, beyond the protagonists' fantastic adventures, the series taps into disturbing, primal fears of being taken, used, abused, dehumanized, and discarded.

Before we started working on *Stranger Things Psychology: Life Upside Down*, all of us writing this book agreed that we're doing this without pay. We're donating its proceeds to a nonprofit organization that helps missing and exploited children. This is something we've wanted to do for some time. Given the nature of *Stranger Things'* human, inhuman, and inhumane horrors, after creating other Popular Culture Psychology anthologies together,[5] we knew this book had to be the one. This book about characters who get lost but sometimes also found should do something for the missing and misused, along with those recovered and recovering, in our world.

Our driving hope is that missing children will be found, that exploited children will be freed, that they all will be safe—if not safe upon recovery, then that they may reach points of safety in their lives. Not everyone returns, and not everyone overcomes mistreatment, but we know that many can. Many who do return and overcome, whether they free themselves or get liberated by others, need great patience, empathy, and support.[6] Their loved ones need support, too, whether the people who have lost them or those to whom they return. They all face great challenges and risks in terms of mental and physical well-being.[7] When we empathize for the fictional Will Byers, abducted by other-worldly monsters, or for Jane "Eleven" Ives Hopper, taken by earthly conspirators, the act of feeling for them in their fantastic circumstances exercises the empathy we need to show people in this world. When we hope for them to overcome their challenges and discover new strengths in the aftermath, we foster our own ability to hope each individual may thrive despite pasts of any kind.

You are not your nightmares. You are not the things that haunt you. You do not have to let the dark things that go bump in the memory define you. Whatever doesn't kill you does *not* necessarily make you stronger, despite clichés, but whether it strengthens you or not, it does not get to own you. If it colors your perspectives on life and on yourself, maybe you can pick new colors. You might draw strength from that in time, or maybe you can turn it around to shine light on the future that you intend to find.

Rather than "getting over it," some use misfortune as a springboard to grow as people—*making meaning* out of trauma and tragedy. Finding value in aversive experiences or forging our own means to make them have beneficial repercussions helps many people cope and plays an important part in *posttraumatic growth*.[8] Shaking up your worldview, though it may bring aspects of your previous perspective to an end, can mark the starting point for growth.[9] Empowered by past pain, those who experience such growth and make meaning out of trauma draw upon it to find purpose as they move forward.[10] Instead of forgetting the bad things, they dwell upon them in constructive ways. Those who have been lost may help us find our way. Like the protagonists of *Stranger Things*, they really can be heroes—and not just for one day.

Stranger Things is about finding so much more, to be sure. It's about finding friendship, love, support, hope, humanity, answers to great mysteries, and especially oneself. Over the course of their adventures, the characters discover strengths previously untapped or underutilized. Priorities change. Perspectives grow. Scenery changes. In El's case, it may take a trip to the mall to find herself, to think about how she'd rather look and maybe who she wants to be when independent of Dr. Brenner, Chief Hopper, or Mike Wheeler, albeit with Max's encouragement and support (and fashion advice). Sometimes we have trouble finding our way because someone else, however well meaning, blocks the view, but sometimes we find our way—and even ourselves—more easily with help from our friends.

Over time, most people recover from trauma. When life flips upside down, it is entirely possible to make your way through the darkness and come out the other side with new strengths or new directions in life. Stranger things have happened.

"To file a missing persons report, please contact your local law enforcement agency as soon as possible. Contrary to what is seen in most television shows and movies, most states do not require a specific period of time to pass before reporting someone missing."[11] If a child is missing or being exploited, please call your local law enforcement agency, followed by the National Center for Missing & Exploited Children, **800-THE-LOST (800-843-5678)***. Learn more at* **missingkids.org** *and* **familiesofthemissing.org***.*

Notes

Note: Episode titles appear on screen with chapter numbers (e.g., "Chapter One: The Vanishing of Will Byers"). Because the chapter numbers are redundant to episode numbers, they do not appear here.

1. "Friends Don't Lie": Friendship Theory and Components

1. Episode 1-2, "The Weirdo on Maple Street" (July 15, 2016). Editor's note: Captioning omits "that" from the quote, but listen carefully.
2. Keller, as quoted by Lash (1997).
3. Denworth (2020); Hojat & Moyer (2016).
4. Collins & Laursen (2000).
5. Larson et al. (1996).
6. Christakis & Fowler (2009).
7. Episode 1-6, "The Monster" (July 15, 2016).
8. Berndt & Perry (1983).
9. Bukowski et al. (1994).
10. Bukowski et al. (1994).
11. Episode 2-1, "MADMAX" (October 27, 2017).
12. Episode 1-2, "The Weirdo on Maple Street" (July 15, 2016).
13. Episode 1-3, "Holly, Jolly" (July 15, 2016).
14. Episode 1-4, "The Body" (July 15, 2016).
15. Episode 2-3, "The Pollywog" (October 27, 2017).
16. Episodes 1-5, "The Flea and the Acrobat" (July 15, 2016); 2-9, "The Gate" (October 27, 2017).
17. Episodes 3-3, "The Case of the Missing Lifeguard" (July 4, 2019); 4-1, "The Hellfire Club" (May 7, 2022).
18. Bukowski et al. (1994).
19. Episode 1-3, "Holly, Jolly" (July 15, 2016).
20. Respectively, episodes 4-5, "The Nina Project," and 4-1, "The Hellfire Club" (May 27, 2022).
21. Episode 1-7, "The Bathtub" (July 15, 2016).
22. Episode 1-6, "The Monster" (July 15, 2016).
23. Episode 2-7, "The Lost Sister" (October 27, 2017).
24. Episode 2-1, "MADMAX" (October 27, 2017).
25. Episode 2-6, "The Spy" (October 27, 2017).
26. Episode 3-5, "Dig Dug" (July 4, 2019).
27. Bukowski et al. (1994), p. 476.
28. Episode 1-5, "The Flea and the Acrobat" (July 15, 2016).
29. Episode 2-5, "Dig Dug" (October 27, 2017).

30. Episode 1-2, "The Weirdo on Maple Street" (July 15, 2016).
31. Episode 1-6, "The Monster" (July 15, 2016).
32. Episode 2-5, "Dig Dug" (October 27, 2017).
33. Bukowski et al. (1994).
34. Episode 1-1, "The Vanishing of Will Byers" (July 15, 2016).
35. Episode 1-4, "The Body" (July 15, 2016).
36. Episode 1-6, "The Monster" (July 15, 2016).
37. Shantz & Hobart (1989).
38. Episode 1-2, "The Weirdo on Maple Street" (July 15, 2016).
39. Episode 2-2, "Trick or Treat, Freak" (October 27, 2017), regarding *Ghostbusters* (1984 motion picture).
40. Buhrmester & Furman (1986).
41. Buhrmester & Furman (1986).
42. Episode 3-3, "The Case of the Missing Lifeguard" (July 4, 2019); 4-3, "The Monster and the Superhero" (May 27, 2022).
43. Episode 3-3, "The Case of the Missing Lifeguard" (July 4, 2019).
44. Episodes 1-4, "The Body" (July 15, 2016); 3-3, "The Case of the Missing Lifeguard" (July 4, 2019).
45. Episode 3-7, "The Bite" (July 4, 2019).
46. Shea et al. (1988).
47. Episode 2-2, "Trick or Treat, Freak" (October 27, 2017).
48. Episode 4-7, "The Massacre at Hawkins Lab" (May 27, 2022).
49. Wrzus et al. (2013).
50. Halatsis & Christakis (2009).
51. Episode 3-8, "The Battle of Starcourt" (July 4, 2019).
52. Episode 3-2, "The Mall Rats" (July 4, 2019).
53. Episode 3-3, "The Case of the Missing Lifeguard" (July 4, 2019).
54. Episode 3-8, "The Battle of Starcourt" (July 4, 2019).
55. Episode 4-1, "The Hellfire Club" (May 27, 2022); 4-9, "The Piggyback" (July 1, 2022).
56. Episode 4-6, "The Dive" (May 27, 2022).
57. Bukowski et al. (1994).
58. Bukowski et al. (1994).
59. Episode 1-6, "The Monster" (July 15, 2016).
60. Episode 2-7, "The Lost Sister" (October 27, 2017).

2. Navigating the Upside Down: Nonnormative and Typical Adolescent Development

1. Episode 2-5, "Dig Dug" (October 27, 2017).
2. Satir (1988), quoted by Huffman et al. (2017), p. 301.
3. Hensums et al. (2022); Van Zantvliet et al. (2020).
4. Emmerlink et al. (2016); Favrid et al. (2017); Friedlander et al. (2007).
5. Somerville (2013).
6. Episode 1-1, "The Vanishing of Will Byers" (July 15, 2016).
7. Adams & Kurtis (2015); Bagwell & Schmidt (2011); Verkuyten & Masson (1996).
8. Episode 1-8, "The Upside Down" (July 15, 2016).
9. Huddleston & Ge (2003).
10. Episode 1-6, "The Monster" (July 15, 2016).
11. Kim et al. (2007).
12. Episode 1-4, "The Body" (July 15, 2016).

13. Episode 2-2, "Trick or Treat, Freak" (October 27, 2017).
14. Episode 2-2, "MADMAX" (October 27, 2017).
15. Smith et al. (2014); episode 2-2, "Trick or Treat, Freak" (October 27, 2017).
16. Glace et al. (2021).
17. Episode 2-3, "The Pollywog" (October 27, 2017).
18. Somerville (2013).
19. Episode 1-1, "The Vanishing of Will Byers" (July 15, 2016).
20. Episode 1-6, "The Monster" (July 15, 2016).
21. Kim et al. (2007).
22. Episode 1-1, "The Vanishing of Will Byers" (July 15, 2016).
23. Episode 1-7, "The Bathtub" (July 15, 2016).
24. Hyde et al. (2012).
25. Episode 3-1, "Suzie, Do you Copy?" (July 4, 2019).
26. Hyde et al. (2012).
27. Although, the term *stalker* as Max uses it was not popularized until the 1990s. Lowney & Best (1995); Mullen et al. (2001).
28. Schelfhout et al. (2021).
29. Glace et al. (2021).
30. Episode 3-3, "The Case of the Missing Lifeguard" (July 4, 2019); 4-8, "Papa" (July 1, 2022).
31. Episode 2-6, "The Spy" (October 27, 2017).
32. Cass (1979).
33. Episode 3-3, "The Case of the Missing Lifeguard" (July 4, 2019).
34. Episode 3-5, "The Source" (July 4, 2019).
35. Cass (1979).
36. Episode 3-7, "The Bite" (July 4, 2019).
37. Episode 4-9, "The Piggyback" (July 1, 2022).
38. Cass (1979); episode 4-1, "The Hellfire Club" (May 27, 2022).
39. American Psychiatric Association (2013).
40. Moules et al. (2017).
41. Guz et al. (2022); Yule et al. (2013).
42. Conley-Fonda & Leisher (2018).
43. Verhulst (1984).
44. Episode 3-2, "The Mall Rats" (July 4, 2019).
45. Stapley & Murdock (2020).
46. Episode 2-6, "The Spy" (October 27, 2017).
47. Episode 3-7, "The Bite" (July 4, 2019).
48. Vary (2022).
49. Jessica (2022).
50. Clark & Zimmerman (2022); Hille et al. (2020); Kassel (2021); Kelleher & Murphy (2022).
51. Elipe et al. (2021); Fabris et al. (2022); Hill et al. (2022); McCown & Platt (2021).
52. Episode 4-9, "The Piggyback" (July 1, 2022). See Casey et al. (2022); Catalano (2022); Rostosky & Riggle (2015).

3. The Upside (and Downside) of Being Social
1. Episode 2-9, "The Gate" (October 27, 2017).
2. Lieberman (2013), pg. 43.
3. Lieberman (2013), pg. 43.
4. Baumeister & Leary (1995).

5. Episodes 1-6, "The Monster" (July 15, 2016), 4-1, "The Hellfire Club," and 4-6, "The Dive" (May 27, 2022).
6. Baumeister & Leary (1995).
7. Breen & O'Connor (2011); Cohen & Wills (1985); Shaw et al. (2004); Smith et al. (2013); Symister & Friend (2003).
8. Burleson & MacGeorge (2002).
9. Arora (2008).
10. Episode 1-2, "The Weirdo on Maple Street" (July 15, 2016).
11. Episode 1-4, "The Body" (July 15, 2016); 2-2, "Trick or Treat, Freak" (October 27, 2017).
12. Episode 2-2, "Trick or Treat, Freak" (October 27, 2017).
13. Episode 1-3, "Holly, Jolly" (July 15, 2016); 2-9, "The Gate" (October 27, 2017).
14. Episode 1-8, "The Upside Down" (July 15, 2016).
15. Episode 1-1, "The Vanishing of Will Byers" (July 15, 2016); 1-2, "The Weirdo on Maple Street" (July 15, 2016).
16. Episode 2-9, "The Gate" (October 27, 2017).
17. Episode 1-1, "The Vanishing of Will Byers" (July 15, 2016).
18. Wesselmann et al. (2021).
19. Roberts et al. (2015); Substance Abuse Mental Health Services Administration (2014).
20. Episode 1-1, "The Vanishing of Will Byers" (July 15, 2016); 1-2, "The Weirdo on Maple Street" (July 15, 2016).
21. Episode 2-9, "The Gate" (October 27, 2017).
22. Dobkin et al. (2002); Stevens et al. (2015).
23. Episode 1-1, "The Vanishing of Will Byers" (July 15, 2016).
24. Riva & Eck (2016); Wesselmann & Parris (2021).
25. Chow et al. (2008); Leary et al. (1998); Stillman et al. (2009); Williams (2009).
26. Eisenberger et al. (2003); MacDonald & Leary (2005).
27. Abrams et al. (2011).
28. Wesselmann & Williams (2017).
29. Episodes 1-2, "The Weirdo on Maple Street" 1-3, "Holly, Jolly" (July 15, 2016); 2-2, "Trick or Treat, Freak" (October 27, 2017).
30. Ford et al. (2020); Klages & Wirth (2014).
31. Episode 2-2, "Trick or Treat, Freak" (October 27, 2017); 4-2, "Vecna's Curse" (May 27, 2022).
32. Episode 1-2, "The Weirdo on Maple Street" (July 15, 2016); 2-1, "MADMAX" (October 27, 2017).
33. Rudert et al. (2017); Williams & Nida (2009).
34. James (1890/1950), pp. 293–294.
35. Episode 1-2, "The Weirdo on Maple Street" (July 15, 2016); 2-9, "The Gate" (October 27, 2017).
36. Episode 2-9, "The Gate" (October 27, 2017).
37. Hayes et al. (2018); Smith & Williams (2004); Williams et al. (2002); Wolf et al. (2015).
38. Episode 3-1, "Suzie, Do You Copy?" (July 4, 2019).
39. Riva et al. (2017); Williams (2009).
40. Episode 2-1, "MADMAX" (October 27, 2017).
41. Episodes 1-2, "The Weirdo on Maple Street" and 1-8, "The Upside Down" (July 15, 2016). See also 4-9, "The Piggyback" (July 1, 2022).
42. Gibson et al. (2002); Jenkins (2012); McCain et al. (2015); Reysen et al. (2016); *Fanalysis* (2000 documentary); *Jedi Junkies* (2010 documentary).

43. Episode 2-9, "The Gate" (October 27, 2017).
44. Brewer (2003).
45. Reysen et al. (2016).
46. Episode 1-8, "The Upside Down" (July 15, 2016).

4. Boys' Party: How to Fail or Save vs. Toxic Masculinity

1. Quoted by C. A. S. King (1983/1987), p. 3.
2. Episode 3-1, "Suzie, Do You Copy?" (July 4, 2019).
3. Episode 3-3, "The Case of the Missing Lifeguard" (July 4, 2019).
4. Pollock (2006).
5. Kinsey et al. (1948, 1953).
6. Admittedly, Kinsey's work has its critics, too, such as Ericksen (1998), Smith (1991).
7. Originally called *sex roles*—Bem (1974, 1975); Constantinople (1973).
8. Brannon & Juni (1984); David & Brannon (1976).
9. Bliss (1995).
10. Levant & Lien (2014).
11. Preece (2017).
12. Karakis & Levant (2012); Karren (2014).
13. Episode 1-5, "The Flea and the Acrobat" (July 15, 2016).
14. Episode 3-1, "Suzie, Do You Copy?" (July 4, 2019).
15. Ribot (1896/2018).
16. Schwartz & Galperin (2002); Walton et al. (2016).
17. Weinstein et al. (2012).
18. Episode 3-8, "The Battle of Starcourt" (July 4, 2019).
19. Maki (2019); Prudom (2017); Thompson (2017).
20. Season 3.
21. Episode 4-1, "The Hellfire Club" (May 27, 2022).
22. Episode 1-4, "The Body" (July 15, 2016).
23. Devens & Loughnan (2019); Seabrook et al. (2019); Vaes et al. (2011).
24. Episode 2-2, "Trick or Treat, Freak" (October 27, 2017).
25. Episode 2-3, "The Pollywog" (October 27, 2017).
26. Renfro (2017).
27. Episodes 3-2, "The Mall Rats," and 3-3, "The Case of the Missing Lifeguard" (both July 4, 2019).
28. Berke et al. (2020); De Visser & Smith (2007); Fugitt & Ham (2018).
29. Episode 3-3, "The Case of the Missing Lifeguard" (July 4, 2019).
30. Reitman & Drabman (1997); Zhu et al. (2015).
31. Episode 2-1, "MADMAX" (October 27, 2017).
32. Fournier et al. (2007); Price et al. (1994); Szücs et al. (2020).
33. Kiselica et al. (2016).
34. Kiselica (2011); Kiselica et al. (2016); McDermott et al. (2019); Ringdahl (2020).
35. Will—episodes 1-7, "The Bathtub" (July 15, 2016); 4-8, "Papa" (July 1, 2022). Mike—episodes 1-2, "The Weirdo on Maple Street," and 1-5, "The Flea and the Acrobat" (July 15, 2016); 2-2, "Trick or Treat, Freak," and 2-6, "The Spy" (October 7, 2017).
36. Episodes 1-5, "The Flea and the Acrobat," and 1-7, "The Bathtub" (July 15, 2016); 4-4, "Dear Billy," and 4-5, "The Nina Project" (May 27, 2022).
37. Episodes 1-2, "The Weirdo on Maple Street," 1-5, "The Flea and the Acrobat," and 1-8, "The Upside Down" (July 15, 2016).

38. Clary et al. (2021); Karner (1995); McCreary (2022); Neilson et al. (2020); Sitko-Dominik & Jakubowski (2022).

39. Episodes 2-9, "The Gate" (October 27, 2017); 3-1, "Suzie, Do You Copy?" (July 4, 2019); 4-9, "The Piggyback" (July 1, 2022).

40. Gooden (2019); Sterlin (2020); Trollo (2017).

41. Episode 1-7, "The Bathtub" (July 15, 2016).

42. Respectively, episodes 1-6, "The Monster" (July 15, 2016); 2-9, "The Gate" (October 27, 2017); 4-1, "The Hellfire Club" (May 27, 2022).

43. Skalski & Pochwatko (2020); Wajsblat (2012).

44. Episode 2-6, "The Spy" (October 27, 2017).

45. Episodes 2-6, "The Spy," and 2-8, "The Mind Flayer" (both October 27, 2017); 3-5, "The Flayed" (July 4, 2019); 4-5, "The Nina Project (May 27, 2022).

46. Episode 3-7, "The Bite" (July 4, 2019).

47. Episode 4-1, "The Hellfire Club" (May 27, 2022).

48. Episode 4-6, "The Dive" (May 27, 2022).

49. Episode 2-8, "The Mind Flayer" (October 27, 2017).

50. Episode 3-2, "The Mall Rats" (July 4, 2019).

51. Buerkle (2019); Frodi (1977); Grieve et al. (2019); Matos et al. (2018).

52. *The Thing* (1982 motion picture). Episode 1-7, "The Bathtub" (July 15, 2016).

53. Well-meaning advice that spectacularly backfires, but it comes from the right place.

54. Nowhere is this contrast more stark than with Mike and his unresponsive bore of a father, a man who seems incapable of feeling an emotion or expressing a thought beyond the most tired of idioms.

55. Episode 3-8, "The Battle of Starcourt" (July 4, 2019).

56. Kahneman & Tversky (1972).

57. Elison (2003); Justman (2021); Link et al. (1977); Widiger & Crego (2021).

58. Episode 4-7, "The Massacre at Hawkins Lab" (May 27, 2022).

59. Book et al. (2016).

60. Episode 4-4, "Dear Billy" (May 27, 2022).

5. An '80s Daydream or a Comforting Nightmare?
An Examination of Black Racial Representation in Hawkins

1. Thepostarchive (2016).

2. Episode 2-4, "Will the Wise" (October 27, 2017).

3. Shamsian (2017).

4. Solsman (2019).

5. Riggio (2014).

6. OseiOpare (2020).

7. Wilhem (2017).

8. Bartlett (2017).

9. Mell-Taylor (2019).

10. Gomer & Petrella (2017).

11. Hayes (2017).

12. Lowy (1991).

13. Wiese (2004).

14. Episode 2-5, "Dig Dug" (October 27, 2017).

15. Graves (2017).

16. *Saturday Night Live*, episode 42-2, "Lin-Manuel Miranda and Twenty-One Pilots" (October 8, 2016).
17. Kumar (2019).
18. De Loera-Brust (2017).
19. Lozenski (2018).
20. Klotz &Whithaus (2015).
21. Bartlett (2017).
22. Boatright-Horowitz et al. (2012).
23. Zevnik (2017).
24. Lowy (1991).
25. McFarland (2017).
26. Wing et al. (2019).
27. Wing et al. (2019).
28. McFarland (2017).
29. Wilhelm (2017).
30. Bartlett (2017).
31. Norton & Sommers (2011).
32. DiAngelo (2018).
33. Case & Ngo (2017).
34. Episode 2-4, "Will the Wise" (October 27, 2017).
35. Though possibly only rebelling against the creature that has enslaved him—Editor.
36. Lamar (2019).
37. Loera-Brust (2017).
38. Smith (2013).
39. Episode 2-2, "Trick or Treat, Freak" (October 27, 2017).
40. Gooden (2014).
41. Ritchey (2014).
42. Episode 2-2, "Trick or Treat, Freak" (October 27, 2017).
43. Lamar (2019).
44. Gooden (2014).
45. Cross (1991).
46. Ritchey (2014).
47. Gooden (2014).
48. Lamar (2019).
49. Episode 3-4, "The Sauna Test" (July 4, 2019).
50. Mell-Taylor (2019).
51. Turner (2014).
52. Turner (2014).
53. Smith (2013).
54. Turner (2014).

6. Bullying: What It Is and What to Do about It

1. Olweus (1993), p. 1.
2. Episode 1-4, "The Body" (July 15, 2016).
3. Vidourek et al. (2016).
4. Episodes 1-6, "The Monster" (July 15, 2016); 2-1, "MADMAX" (October 27, 2017).
5. Andreou et al. (2021); Eyuboglu et al. (2021); Vidourek et al. (2016).
6. Episodes 4-1, "The Hellfire Club," and 4-2, "Vecna's Curse" (May 27, 2022).

7. Eyuboglu et al. (2021).
8. Midgett & Doumas (2019); Polanin et al. (2012).
9. Episode 4-1, "The Hellfire Club" (May 27, 2022).
10. Olweus (1993).
11. Episode 1-1, "The Vanishing of Will Byers" (July 15, 2016).
12. Episode 1-1, "The Vanishing of Will Byers" (July 15, 2016).
13. Episodes 1-1, "The Vanishing of Will Byers" (July 15, 2016); 1-4, "The Body" (July 15, 2016).
14. Eyuboglu et al. (2021).
15. Marsh et al. (2011).
16. Episode 2-8, "The Mind Flayer" (October 27, 2017); Pak (2020).
17. Patchin & Hinduja (2006); Olweus (1993).
18. Episode 1-4, "The Body" (July 15, 2016).
19. Episode 2-9, "The Gate" (October 27, 2017).
20. Episode 1-6, "The Monster" (July 15, 2016).
21. Episode 1-4, "The Body" (July 15, 2016).
22. Sue et al. (2010).
23. Episode 2-2, "Trick or Treat, Freak" (October 27, 2017).
24. Episode 3-2, "The Mall Rats" (July 4, 2019).
25. Galán et al. (2021).
26. Episode 1-1, "The Vanishing of Will Byers" (July 15, 2016).
27. Salmon et al. (2018).
28. De Vries et al. (2021).
29. Chen et al. (2020).
30. Chen et al. (2020).
31. De Vries et al. (2021).
32. Marsh et al. (2011).
33. Yao et al. (2021).
34. Chen et al. (2020); Yao et al. (2021).
35. Episodes 2-4, "Will the Wise" (October 27, 2017); 3-6, "E Pluribus Unum" (July 4, 2019).
36. Marsh et al. (2011); Parris et al. (2019).
37. Episode 1-7, "The Bathtub" (July 15, 2016).
38. Parris et al. (2019).
39. Episode 2-9, "The Gate" (October 27, 2017).
40. Tenenbaum et al. (2012).
41. Kochenderfer-Ladd & Skinner (2002).
42. Parris et al. (2019).
43. Episode 2-1, "MADMAX" (October 27, 2017).
44. Parris et al. (2020).
45. Episode 2-9, "The Gate" (October 27, 2017).
46. Pozzoli et al. (2017).
47. Episode 1-4, "The Body" (July 15, 2016).
48. Parris et al. (2020).
49. Parris et al. (2020).
50. Parris et al. (2020).
51. Tenenbaum et al. (2012).
52. Episode 2-1, "MADMAX" (October 27, 2017).

53. Hutson et al. (2021).
54. Episode 3-4, "The Sauna Test" (July 4, 2019).
55. Polanin et al. (2012).
56. Morrison (2006).
57. Episode 1-8, "The Upside Down" (July 15, 2016).
58. Polanin et al. (2012).
59. Episode 4-1, "The Hellfire Club" (May 27, 2022).
60. Episode 4-5, "The Nina Project" (May 27, 2022).
61. Episode 3-8, "Battle of Starcourt" (July 4, 2019).
62. Episode 4-1, "The Hellfire Club" (May 27, 2022).

7. Missing Children and the Impact on Their Loved Ones

1. Episode 1-4, "The Body" (July 15, 2016).
2. Families of the Missing (n.d.).
3. Episode 1-1, "The Vanishing of Will Byers" (July 15, 2016).
4. Episode 1-1, "The Vanishing of Will Byers" (July 15, 2016).
5. Episode 1-2, "The Weirdo on Maple Street" (July 15, 2016).
6. Jasper (2006); Kutner (2016).
7. Jin (2020); Palmer (2012).
8. Sephton (2017).
9. International Centre for Missing and Exploited Children (2022).
10. National Crime Information Center (2020, 2022).
11. Baraković et al. (2014).
12. Boss & Greenberg (1984); Boss et al. (1990); Hollingsworth et al. (2016); Pasley & Ihinger-Tallman (1989).
13. Greco & Roger (2003); Heeke et al. (2015); Lenferink et al. (2019).
14. Kennedy et al. (2019).
15. Episode 1-3, "Holly, Jolly" (July 15, 2016)
16. Wayland et al. (2016).
17. Lenferink et al. (2017).
18. Kahneman & Miller (1986); McGraw et al. (2005); Medvec et al.(1995).
19. Carey et al. (2014).
20. Episodes 1-1, "The Vanishing of Will Byers," and 1-2, "The Weirdo on Maple Street" (both July 15, 2016).
21. Episode 1-5, "The Flea and the Acrobat" (July 15, 2016).
22. Hsu et al. (2015); Igbal & Dar (2015); Olatunji et al. (2013).
23. Episode 2-1, "MADMAX" (October 27, 2017).
24. Episode 2-5, "Dig Dug" (October 27, 2017).
25. Kang et al. (2014).
26. Episode 2-1, "MADMAX" (October 27, 2017).
27. Greenbaum et al. (2020).
28. Zgoba (2004).

8. Missing You: An Exploration into Missing Persons, Ambiguous Loss, and the Journey to Acceptance

1. De Lamartine (1820/2000).
2. Episode 1-4, "The Body" (July 15, 2016).
3. Episode 1-2, "The Weirdo on Maple Street" (July 15, 2016).

4. Kübler-Ross (1973).
5. Horowitz (1976).
6. Horowitz (1976).
7. Episode 1-1, "The Vanishing of Will Byers" (July 15, 2016).
8. Parks (1998).
9. Devan (1993).
10. Episode 1-4, "The Body" (July 15, 2016).
11. Devan (1993).
12. Isuru et al. (2021).
13. Episode 1-1, "The Vanishing of Will Byers" (July 15, 2016).
14. Wayland et al. (2016).
15. Hollander (2016).
16. Kajtazi-Testa et al. (2018).
17. Blaauw (2002).
18. Kubler-Ross (1973).
19. National Crime Information Center (2020, 2022).
20. James et al. (2008); Swanton et al. (1989).
21. Arenliu et al. (2019).
22. Finkelhor et al. (1990); Lampinen et al. (2012); Lewit et al. (1998).
23. Mitchell et al. (2003).
24. Rees (2011); Henderson et al. (1999); Sanchez et al. (2006); Thompson et al. (2012); Tucker et al. (2011).
25. Episode 1-1, "The Vanishing of Will Byers" (July 15, 2016).
26. Arenliu et al. (2019).
27. Finkelhor et al. (1990).
28. Episode 2-1, "MADMAX" (October 27, 2017).
29. Episode 1-8, "The Upside Down" (July 15, 2016).
30. Episode 3-8, "The Battle of Starcourt" (July 4, 2019).
31. Finkelhor et al. (1990).
32. Episode 1-1, "The Vanishing of Will Byers" (July 15, 2016).
33. Episode 1-8, "The Upside Down" (July 15, 2016).
34. DeYoung et al. (2003); Finkelhor et al. (1990).
35. Episodes 1-5, "The Flea and the Acrobat," and 1-6, "The Monster" (both July 15, 2016).
36. Flowers (2001).
37. Episode 1-1, "The Vanishing of Will Byers" (July 15, 2016).
38. Episode 1-1, "The Vanishing of Will Byers" (July 15, 2016).
39. Flowers (2001).
40. Horowitz (1976).
41. Lampinen et al. (2016).
42. Episode 2-5, "Dig Dug" (October 27, 2017).
43. Henderson et al. (1999).
44. James et al. (2008).
45. Kajtazi-Testa et al. (2018).
46. Episode 2-1, "MADMAX" (October 27, 2017).
47. Kajtazi-Testa et al. (2018).
48. Kajtazi-Testa et al. (2018).
49. Episode 1-2, "The Weirdo on Maple Street" (July 15, 2016).

50. Morewitz et al. (2016).
51. Episode 1-1, "The Vanishing of Will Byers" (July 15, 2016).
52. Hein et al. (2010).
53. Herrera et al. (2018).
54. Hein et al. (2010).
55. Dasgupta et al. (2004).
56. Episode 1-4, "The Body" (July 15, 2016).
57. Episode 1-4, "The Body" (July 15, 2016).
58. Morewitz et al. (2016).
59. Episode 2-1, "MADMAX" (October 27, 2017).
60. Davies (2020).
61. Morewitz et al. (2016).
62. Episode 2-1, "MADMAX" (October 27, 2017).
63. Azarian et al. (1999); Cohen (2007); Gabriel (1992); Porcelli et al. (2012).
64. Van der Kolk (1994).
65. Episode 2-1, "MADMAX" (October 27, 2017).
66. Pfaltz et al. (2013).
67. Tarling et al. (2004).
68. Testoni et al. (2020).
69. Episode 1-3, "Holly, Jolly" (July 15, 2016).
70. Episodes 1-3, "Holly, Jolly," and 1-7, "The Bathtub" (July 15, 2016); 2-9, "The Gate" (October 7, 2017).
71. For example, episodes 4-4, "Dear Billy," and 4-6, "The Dive" (May 27, 2022); 4-9, "The Piggyback" (July 1, 2022).
72. Boss (2006).
73. Boss (2006).
74. Testoni et al. (2020).
75. Episode 2-1, "MADMAX" (October 27, 2017).
76. Testoni et al. (2020).
77. Episode 1-7, "The Bathtub" (July 15, 2016).
78. Woolnough et al. (2016).
79. Episode 1-8, "The Upside Down" (July 15, 2016).
80. Holmes (2014).
81. Episode 2-2, "Trick or Treat, Freak" (October 27, 2017).

9. Lonely Things: Surviving Trauma and Loneliness with Some Help from Our Friends

1. Brown (2017).
2. Episode 2-7, "The Lost Sister" (October 27, 2017).
3. Episode 1-1, "The Vanishing of Will Byers" (July 15, 2016).
4. Episodes 1-6, "The Monster" (July 15, 2016); 2-5, "Dig Dug" (October 27, 2017).
5. Episodes 4-1, "The Hellfire Club," through 4-4, "Dear Billy" (May 27, 2022).
6. Episode 4-5, "The Nina Project" (May 27, 2022).
7. Luhmann et al. (2016); Shevlin et al. (2015).
8. Episode 3-1, "Suzie, Do You Copy?" (July 4, 2019).
9. Duek et al. (2021).
10. Much of season 3.
11. Cacioppo et al. (2014).
12. Xu & Roberts (2010).

13. Episode 3-2, "The Mall Rats" (July 4, 2019).
14. Episode 1-8, "The Upside Down" (July 15, 2016).
15. Schawbel (2017).
16. Luhmann et al. (2016).
17. Episode 1-8, "The Upside Down" (July 15, 2016).
18. Episode 2-1, "MADMAX" (October 27, 2017).
19. Episode 4-7, "The Massacre at Hawkins Lab" (May 27, 2017).
20. Schawbel (2017).
21. Cacioppo et al. (2009); Hawkley & Cacioppo (2003); Wilson et al. (2007).
22. Episode 2-5, "Dig Dug" (October 27, 2017).
23. Cacioppo & Hawkley (2009); Cacioppo et al. (2009).
24. Cacioppo & Hawkley (2009); Cacioppo et al. (2009).
25. Qualter et al. (2013).
26. Episode 1-5, "The Flea and the Acrobat" (July 15, 2016).
27. Hawkley & Cacciopo (2010).
28. Episode 1-5, "The Flea and the Acrobat" (July 15, 2016).
29. Episode 2-3, "The Pollywog" (October 27, 2017).
30. Throughout season 4.
31. Friedmann et al. (2006); Tate (2018).
32. Cacioppo et al. (2014); Hawkley & Cacioppo (2010).
33. Stickley & Koyanagi (2016).
34. Stickley & Koyanagi (2016).
35. Episode 2-5, "Dig Dug" (October 27, 2017).
36. Stickley & Koyanagi (2016).
37. Eisenberger (2012).
38. Coan et al. (2006).
39. Episode 2-9, "The Gate" (October 27, 2017).
40. Episode 2-1, "MADMAX" (October 27, 2017).
41. Bellosta-Batalla et al. (2020); Crespi (2015); Eppel & Lithgow (2014).
42. Coghlan (2013); Xu & Roberts (2010).
43. Episode 3-3, "The Case of the Missing Lifeguard" (July 4, 2019).
44. Episode 2-6, "The Spy" (October 27, 2017).
45. Friedmann et al. (2006); Tate (2018).
46. Coghlan (2013); Xu & Roberts (2010).
47. Episode 1-8, "The Upside Down" (July 15, 2016).

10. The Now-Memories: The Nostalgic Appeal of *Stranger Things*

1. Boym (2001), p. 9.
2. Episode 2-4, "Will the Wise" (October 27, 2017).
3. Hepper et al. (2021); Stefaniak et al. (2022); Weiss & Dube (2021).
4. Iyer & Jetten (2011); Milligan (2003); Pourtova (2013).
5. Sedikides et al. (2008).
6. Jiang et al. (2021).
7. Cheung et al. (2018).
8. Talarico & Rubin (2007).
9. Episode 1-4, "The Body" (July 15, 2016).
10. Episode 2-1, "MADMAX" (October 27, 2017).
11. Yang et al. (2021).

12. Adler & Hershfield (2012); Hershfield et al. (2013).
13. Pasupathi (2001).
14. Howe & Courage (1993).
15. Erikson & Erikson (1998).
16. Arnett (1999).
17. Munawar et al. (2018).
18. Episode 2-9, "The Gate" (October 27, 2017).
19. Berntsen & Rubin (2004).
20. Episode 1-1, "The Vanishing of Will Byers" (July 15, 2016).
21. Episode 2-2, "Trick or Treat, Freak" (October 27, 2017).
22. Episode 3-1, "Suzie, Do You Copy?" (July 4, 2019).
23. Erikson & Erikson (1998).
24. Episode 1-8, "The Upside Down" (July 15, 2016).
25. Episode 3-8, "The Battle of Starcourt" (July 4, 2019).
26. Episode 2-9, "The Gate" (October 27, 2017).
27. Episode 3-3, "The Case of the Missing Lifeguard (July 4, 2019). See Betz (2011); Gillespie & Crouse (2012); Lis et al. (2015).
28. Episode 1-2, "The Weirdo on Maple Street" (July 15, 2016).
29. Episode 3-1, "Suzie, Do You Copy?" (July 4, 2019).
30. Zapoleon (2021).
31. Anspach (1934), p. 381.
32. Boym (2001).
33. Episode 3-8, "The Battle of Starcourt" (July 4, 2019).
34. Peters (1985).
35. Episode 1-3, "Holly, Jolly" (July 15, 2016).
36. Episode 2-5, "Dig Dug" (October 27, 2017).
37. Episode 2-7, "The Lost Sister" (October 27, 2017).
38. Episode 2-9, "The Gate" (October 27, 2017).
39. McCann (1943).
40. Episodes 3-1, "Suzie, Do You Copy?" and 3-3, "The Case of the Missing Lifeguard" (both July 4, 2019).
41. Episode 3-4, "The Sauna Test" (July 4, 2019).
42. Henley (2017).
43. Ismail et al. (2020).
44. Episode 3-8, "The Battle of Starcourt" (July 4, 2019).
45. Sedikides et al. (2015).
46. Wildschut et al. (2010).
47. Episode 3-8, "The Battle of Starcourt" (July 4, 2019).
48. Beike et al. (2016).
49. Hartmann & Brunk (2019).
50. Hirsch & Spitzer (2002).

11. A Strange Feeling: Investigating Murray Bauman's Grand Conspiracy

1. Episode 2-5, "Dig Dug" (October 27, 2017).
2. Randi (2013).
3. Episode 2-6, "The Spy" (October 27, 2017).
4. Episodes 2-1, "MADMAX," 2-5, "Dig Dug" (both October 27, 2017); 3-5, "The Flayed" (July 4, 2019).

5. Van Prooijen & Mengdi (2021).
6. Van Prooijen & Mengdi (2021).
7. Casabianca & Pedersen (2021); Douglas & Sutton (2018); Hale (2016).
8. Pennycook et al. (2015).
9. Pastorino & Doyle-Portillo (2009), p. 257.
10. Episode 2-5, "Dig Dug" (October 27, 2017).
11. Prooijen (2019).
12. Episode 2-6, "The Spy" (October 27, 2017).
13. Episode 3-7, "The Bite" (July 4, 2019).
14. Episode 2-6, "The Spy" (October 27, 2017).
15. Nickerson (1998).
16. Aronson (2004).
17. Respectively, episodes 2-5, "Dig Dug," and 2-1, "MADMAX" (October 27, 2017).
18. Biner et al. (1998); Blackmore & Trościanko (1985); Griffiths et al. (2019).
19. Wabnegger et al. (2021).
20. Episode 2-1, "MADMAX" (October 27, 2017).
21. Aronson (2004).
22. Episode 2-5, "Dig Dug" (October 27, 2017).
23. Biddlestone et al. (2021).
24. Biddlestone et al. (2021).
25. Episode 3-6, "E Pluribus Unum" (July 4, 2019).
26. Episode 2-1, "MADMAX" (October 27, 2017).
27. Lincoln et al. (2014).
28. Galliford & Furnham (2017); Udachina (2017).
29. APA (2013).
30. APA (2013).
31. Veling et al. (2021).
32. Oller (2019).
33. APA (2013), p. 645.
34. Episode 3-5, "The Flayed" (July 4, 2019).
35. APA (2013).
36. APA (2013).
37. APA (2013), pp. 655–59.
38. APA (2013).
39. Episode 3-8, "The Battle of Starcourt" (July 4, 2019); 4-6, "The Dive" (May 27, 2022).

12. Shame, Survival, and Trauma Processing in the State We Call Fear

1. Fisher (2017).
2. Episode 1-1, "The Vanishing of Will Byers" (July 15, 2016).
3. Bowman (2010); Cardona & Taylor (2020); Gallagher et al. (2017); Garski & Mastin (2021); Scarlet (2017).
4. Franco et al. (2011); Greater Good Science Center (2011).
5. Campbell (1949).
6. Best (2020); Kidd & Castano (2013); Lee et al. (2014); Mar et al. (2010). Chapter coauthor/volume editor said a version of this in Langley (2022).
7. Mansfield (2007); Sagarin et al. (2002).
8. Broomhall et al. (2017); Markham & Miller (2006); Quelas et al. (2008).
9. Episode 4-4, "Dear Billy" (May 27, 2022).

10. Episode 2-4, "Will the Wise" (October 27, 2017).
11. Lanese & Dutfield (2021).
12. Episodes 1-1, "The Vanishing of Will Byers," and 1-2, "The Weirdo on Maple Street" (both July 15, 2016).
13. Goldstein (2010); Romero & Butler (2007).
14. Episode 2-6, "The Spy" (October 27, 2017).
15. Episode 2-3, "The Pollywog" (October 27, 2017).
16. Porges (2011).
17. Harvard Health (2020).
18. Frothingham (2021).
19. Eleven—episode 1-8, "The Upside Down" (July 15, 2016); Hopper—3-5, "The Flayed" (July 4, 2019); 4-7, "The Massacre at Hawkins Lab" (May 27, 2022); 4-9, "The Piggyback" (July 1, 2022); Billy—2-9, "The Gate" (October 27, 2017).
20. Episode 1-2, "The Weirdo on Maple Street" (July 15, 2016).
21. Thompson et al. (2014); Webster et al. (2016).
22. Episodes 1-1, "The Vanishing of Will Byers" (July 15, 2016); 2-8, "The Mind Flayer" (October 27, 2017); 4-7, "The Massacre at Hawkins Lab" (May 27, 2022).
23. Frothingham (2021) includes *fawn*, whereas Bracha et al. (2004) suggest *fright* as the fourth major reaction.
24. For example episode 2-4, "Will the Wise" (October 27, 2017).
25. Episode 3-6, "E Pluribus Unum" (July 4, 2019).
26. Episode 4-7, "The Massacre at Hawkins Lab" (May 27, 2022).
27. Episode 3-4, "The Sauna Test" (July 4, 2019).
28. Episodes 3-4, "The Sauna Test" (July 4, 2019); 4-9, "The Piggyback" (July 1, 2022).
29. Episodes 2-8, "The Mind Flayer" (October 27, 2017); 3-8, "The Battle of Starcourt" (July 4, 2019).
30. Mudrack & Mason (2013); Murray (2018); Platt et al. (2017); Thompson-Hollands et al. (2021).
31. Bailey & Brand (2017); Bryant (2007); Cubelli (2003).
32. Fisher (2017, 2021).
33. Episode 2-3, "The Pollywog" (October 27, 2017).
34. Audere & Soma (n.d.); TV Tropes (n.d.).
35. Episode 1-8, "The Mind Flayer" (July 15, 2016).
36. Mitchell & Steele (2021); Moskowitz & van der Hart (2020); Schimmenti (2018).
37. Respectively, episodes 2-2, "Trick or Treat, Freak," and 2-3, "The Pollywog" (October 27, 2017); 3-2, "The Mall Rats" (July 4, 2019).
38. Episode 2-3, "The Pollywog" (October 27, 2017).
39. Episodes 2-4, "Will the Wise," 2-5, "Dig Dug," 2-9, "The Gate" (all October 27, 2017).
40. *The NeverEnding Story* (1984 motion picture).
41. Respectively, episodes 2-5, "Dig Dug," and 2-6, "The Spy" (October 27, 2017); 3-8, "The Battle of Starcourt" (July 4, 2019).
42. Elison et al. (2006); Nathanson (1992).
43. Episode 2-1, "MADMAX" (October 27, 2017).
44. Episode 2-1, "MADMAX" (October 27, 2017).
45. Episode 2-2, "Trick or Treat, Freak" (October 27, 2017).
46. Episode 2-2, "Trick or Treat, Freak" (October 27, 2017).
47. Erikson & Erikson (1998).

48. Cuncic (2021).
49. Carey (2003); Olweus (1996).
50. Cuncic (2021).
51. Episode 1-2, "The Weirdo on Maple Street" (July 15, 2016).
52. Episode 1-2, "The Weirdo on Maple Street" (July 15, 2016).
53. Episode 1-2, "The Weirdo on Maple Street" (July 15, 2016).
54. Leeds (2013), p. 12.
55. Episode 1-3, "Holly, Jolly" (July 15, 2016).
56. American Psychiatric Association (2013).
57. Shapiro (2001); Shapiro (2012).
58. Respectively, episodes 1-4, "The Body" (July 15, 2016); 3-2, "The Mall Rats" (July 4, 2019).
59. Van der Kolk (2014).
60. Fisher (2017), p. 4.
61. Fisher (2017, 2021).
62. Episode 3-8, "The Battle of Starcourt" (July 4, 2019).
63. Broomhall et al. (2017); Markham & Miller (2006); Quelas et al. (2008).
64. Episode 4-4, "Dear Billy" (May 27, 2022).

13. Stranger Things in the First Episodes: Lessons from the Start

1. Meadow (1990).
2. Episode 2-3, "The Pollywog."
3. Liegner (1977).
4. Episode 1-1, "The Vanishing of Will Byers" (July 15, 2016).
5. Liegner (1977).
6. Freud (1900/2010, 1920/1961).
7. Luborsky & Crit-Christoph (1998).
8. Episode 1-5, "The Flea and the Acrobat" (July 15, 2016).
9. Episode 2-1, "MADMAX" (October 27. 2017).
10. *Dragon's Lair* (1983 video game).
11. Meadow (1990), p. 5.
12. Jung (1951), para. 126.
13. Freud (1920/1922).
14. S. Marianski (personal communication, July, 2019).
15. Episode 3-1, "Suzie, Do You Copy?" (July 4, 2019).
16. Goodman & Freeman (2015).
17. Tennyson (1850/1993).
18. Episode 4-1, "The Hellfire Club" (May 27, 2022).
19. Episode 4-9, "The Piggyback" (July 1, 2022).
20. Episode 4-4, "Dear Billy" (May 27, 2022).
21. Henderson (1964); Jung (1958).
22. Episode 4-6, "The Dive" (May 27, 2022).
23. Episode 4-6, "The Dive" (May 27, 2022).

14. The Strangest Things: Choice, Chances, and the *Dungeons & Dragons* of Life

1. Graeber & Wengrow (2021), p. 115.
2. Shakespeare (1623/1982). Written between 1599 and 1601, its First Folio publication was in 1623.
3. Jordan & Day (2015).

4. Will attempts to DM in episode 3-3, "The Case of the Missing Lifeguard" (July 4, 2019). Eddie—4-1, "The Hellfire Club" (May 27, 2022).

5. Such as the original D&D basic set (Holmes, 1977); 1st edition Advanced Dungeons & Dragons (Gygax, 1978); 5th edition D&D (Wizards RPG Team, 2014).

6. Episode 1-6, "The Monster" (July 15, 2016).

7. Wegner (2003).

8. Episode 3-8, "The Battle of Starcourt" (July 4, 2019).

9. Wegner & Wheatley (1999).

10. Jordan (2013).

11. Episode 1-2, "The Weirdo on Maple Street" (July 15, 2016).

12. Abramson et al. (1978).

13. Vollmayr & Gass (2013).

14. McLaurin (2005).

15. Brown et al. (2016).

16. Sorrenti et al. (2019).

17. Episode 3-8, "The Battle of Starcourt" (July 4, 2019).

18. Jordan (2020).

19. Episode 1-4, "The Body" (July 15, 2016).

20. Episode 2-3, "The Pollywog" (October 27, 2017).

21. Fortenberry (2013).

22. Diamond (2003).

23. Diamond (2003); Fortenberry (2013).

24. Diamond (2003).

25. *Back to the Future* (1985 motion picture).

26. Episode 3-7, "The Bite" (July 4, 2019).

27. Episode 3-7, "The Bite" (July 4, 2019). Episode 4-1, "The Hellfire Club" (May 27, 2002) supports his assertions regarding Tammy's singing.

28. Ivie (2019).

29. Bartsch (2012).

30. Bond (2021), p. 574.

31. Bond (2021).

32. Bond (2021).

33. Gillig & Murphy (2016).

34. Jordan & Ranade (2014).

35. Hommel et al. (2001).

36. Wegner (2003).

37. Episode 3-8, "The Battle of Starcourt" (July 4, 2019).

38. Sidhu & Carter (2021).

39. Sidhu & Carter (2021), p. 12.

40. Sidhu & Carter (2021), p. 9.

41. Sidhu & Carter (2021), p. 14.

42. Sidhu & Carter (2021), p. 14.

43. Sidhu & Carter (2021), p. 14.

44. Sidhu & Carter (2021), p. 15.

45. Shakespeare (1623/1982).

46. Episode 3-8, "The Battle of Starcourt" (July 4, 2019).

47. Episodes 4-6, "The Dive," and 4-7, "The Massacre at Hawkins Lab" (May 27, 2022).

48. Episode 4-1, "The Hellfire Club" (May 27, 2022).
49. Adler & Doherty (1985).
50. Adler & Doherty (1985).
51. Witt (1985).
52. Episode 4-9, "The Piggyback" (July 1, 2022).
53. Livingston (1982); Schwegman (1976).

15. It's All in the Game: How Fighting Fake Foes Teaches Us to Face Our Fears

1. Schaefer & Kaduson (1994), p. 66.
2. Episode 2-4, "Will the Wise" (October 27, 2017).
3. Bregman (2019).
4. Marks-Tarlow (2012).
5. Episode 2-3, "The Pollywog" (October 27, 2017).
6. Runcan et al. (2012).
7. Capurso & Ragni (2016).
8. Pliske et al. (2021).
9. Episode 1-2, "The Weirdo on Maple Street" (July 15, 2016).
10. Capurso & Ragni (2016).
11. Episode 2-8, "The Mind Flayer" (October 27, 2017).
12. Episode 2-4, "Will the Wise" (October 27, 2017).
13. Nagoski & Nagoski (2019).
14. Episode 3-8, "The Battle of Starcourt" (July 4, 2019).
15. Episode 3-3, "The Case of the Missing Lifeguard" (July 4, 2019).
16. Adams (2013).
17. Janisse & Corupe (2016). Episodes 4-2, "Vecna's Curse" (May 27, 2022), through 4-9, "The Piggyback" (July 1, 2022).
18. Scriven (2021).
19. Adams (2013).
20. Episode 2-8, "The Mind Flayer" (October 27, 2017).
21. Berger & Luckmann (1966).
22. White (2007).
23. Wright et al. (2020).
24. Episode 1-6, "The Monster" (July 15, 2016).
25. Chung (2013).
26. Episode 1-5, "The Flea and the Acrobat" (July 15, 2016).
27. Episode 1-1, "The Vanishing of Will Byers" (July 15, 2016).
28. Episode 1-6, "The Monster" (July 15, 2016).
29. Episode 1-2, "The Weirdo on Maple Street" (July 15, 2016).
30. Episode 2-6, "The Spy" (October 27, 2017).
31. Episode 3-8, "The Battle of Starcourt" (July 4, 2019).
32. Episode 1-2, "The Weirdo on Maple Street" (July 15, 2016).
33. Episode 2-3, "The Pollywog" (October 27, 2017).

Final Word: Finding

1. Interviewed by McClurg (2018).
2. Episode 3-8, "The Battle of Starcourt" (July 4, 2019).

3. Apparent deaths, respectively episodes 1-3, "Holly, Jolly" (July 15, 2016), Will's body seemingly discovered; Eleven—3-8, "The Upside Down" (July 15, 2016); Hopper—3-8, "The Battle of Starcourt" (July 4, 2019). Survival confirmed, Will—1-4, "The Body" (July 15, 2016); Eleven—2-1, "MADMAX" (October 27, 2017); Hopper—hinted in 3-8, "The Battle of Starcourt" (July 4, 2019), confirmed in 4-2, "Vecna's Curse" (May 27, 2022). Max's "death," revival, and coma—episode 4-9, "The Piggyback" (July 1, 2022).

4. Barb—episode 1-7, "The Bathtub" (July 15, 2016). The Flayed—3-6, "E Pluribus Unum" (July 4, 2019).

5. From *The Walking Dead Psychology: Psych of the Living Dead* (Langley, 2015) through *The Joker Psychology: Evil Clowns and the Women Who Love Them* (Langley, 2019).

6. Moynihan et al. (2018).

7. DeYoung & Buzzi (2003); Lenferink et al. (2018); Stevenson & Thomas (2018).

8. Linley & Joseph (2011); Tedeschi & Blevins (2015); Triplett et al. (2012); Wortmann (2009).

9. Calhoun et al. (2010); Frankl (1959/2006, 2010).

10. McCormack et al. (2021); Schippers & Ziegler (2019); Leider (2015); Weinberg (2013).

11. Brittani Oliver Sillas-Navarro (2022), from the first draft of her chapter in this book.

References

Abrams, D., Weick, M., Thomas, D., Colbe, H., & Franklin, K. M. (2011). On-line ostracism affects children differently from adolescents and adults. *British Journal of Developmental Psychology*, *29*(1), 110-123.

Abramson, L. Y., Seligman, M. E., & Teasdale, J. D. (1978). Learned helplessness in humans: Critique and reformulation. *Journal of Abnormal Psychology*, *87*(1), 49-74.

Adams, A. S. (2013). Needs met through role-playing games: A fantasy theme analysis of Dungeons & Dragons. *Kaleidoscope: A Graduate Journal of Qualitative Communication Research*, *12*, 69-86.

Adams, G., & Kurtis, T. (2015). Friendship and gender in cultural-psychological perspective: Implications for research, practice, and consultation. *International Perspectives in Psychology: Research, Practice, Consultation*, *4*(3), 182-194.

Adler, J., & Doherty, S. (1983, September 9). Kids: The deadliest game? *Newsweek*, *93*(10), 9.

Adler, J. M., & Hershfield, H. E. (2012). Mixed emotional experience is associated with and precedes improvements in psychological well-being. *PloS One*, *7*(4), e35633.

American Psychiatric Association. (2013). *Diagnostic and statistical manual of mental disorders* (5th ed.) [DSM-5]. American Psychiatric Association.

Andreou, E., Tsermentseli, S., Anastasiou, O., & Kouklari, E. C. (2021). Retrospective accounts of bullying victimization at school: Associations with post-traumatic stress disorder symptoms and post traumatic growth among university students. *Journal of Child & Adolescent Trauma*, *14*(1), 9-18.

Anspach, C. K. (1934). Medical dissertation on nostalgia by Johannes Hofer, 1688. *Bulletin of the Institute of the History of Medicine*, *2*(6), 376-391.

Arenliu, A., Shala-Kastrati, F., Avdiu, V. B., & Landsman, M. (2019). Posttraumatic growth among family members with missing persons from war in Kosovo: Association with social support and community involvement. *Omega: Journal of Death & Dying*, *80*(1), 35-48.

Arnett, J. J. (1999). Adolescent storm and stress, reconsidered. *American Psychologist*, *54*(5), 317-326.

Aronson, E. (2004). *The social animal* (9th ed.). Worth.

Arora, N. K. (2008). Social support in health communication. In W. Donsbach (Ed.), *The international encyclopedia of communication* (pp. 4725–4727). Blackwell.

Audere & Soma (n.d.). *The "squishy caster" fallacy*. Tabletop Builds. https://tabletopbuilds.com/the-squishy-caster-fallacy.

Azarian, A., Miller, T. W., McKinsey, L. L., Skriptchenko-Gregorian, V., & Bilyeu, J. (1999). Trauma accommodation and anniversary reactions in children. *Journal of Contemporary Psychotherapy*, *29*(4), 355-368.

Bagwell, C. L., & Schmidt, M. E. (2011). *Friendships in childhood and adolescence*. Guilford.

Bailey, T. D., & Brand, B. L. (2017). Traumatic dissociation: Theory, research, and treatment. *Clinical Psychology: Science & Practice*, *24*(2), 170-185.

Baraković, D., Avdibegović, E., & Sinanović, O. (2014). Posttraumatic stress disorder in women with war missing family members. *Psychiatria Danubina, 26*(4), 340-346.

Bartlett, M. (2017). Rose-coloured rear-view: 'Stranger Things' and the lure of a false past. *Screen Education, 85*, 16-25.

Bartsch, A. (2012). Emotional gratification in entertainment experience: Why viewers of movies and television series find it rewarding to experience emotions. *Media Psychology, 15*(3), 267-302.

Baumeister, R. F., & Leary, M. R. (1995). The need to belong: Desire for interpersonal attachments as a fundamental human motivation. *Psychological Bulletin, 117*(3), 497-529.

Beike, D. R., Brandon, N. R., & Cole, H. E. (2016). Is sharing specific autobiographical memories a distinct form of self-disclosure? *Journal of Experimental Psychology: General, 145*(4), 434-450.

Bellosta-Batalla, M., Blanco-Gandía, M. C., Rodríguez-Arias, M., Cebolla, A., Pérez-Blasco, J., & Moya-Albiol, L. (2020). Increased salivary oxytocin and empathy in students of clinical and health psychology after a mindfulness and compassion-based intervention. *Mindfulness, 11*(4), 1006-1017.

Bem, S. (1974). The measurement of psychological androgyny. *Journal of Consulting & Clinical Psychology, 42*(2), 155-162.

Bem, S. (1975). Sex role adaptability: One consequence of psychological androgyny. *Journal of Personality & Social Psychology, 31*(4) 634-643.

Berger, P., & Luckmann, T. (1966). *The social construction of reality: A treatise in the sociology of knowledge.* Doubleday.

Berke, D. S., Leone, R., Parrott, D., & Gallagher, K. E. (2020). Drink, don't think: The role of masculinity and thought suppression in men's alcohol-related aggression. *Psychology of Men & Masculinities, 21*(1), 36-45.

Berndt, T. J., & Perry, B. (1983). *Benefits of friendship interview.* Unpublished manuscript. University of Oklahoma.

Berntsen, D., & Rubin, D. C. (2004). Cultural life scripts structure recall from autobiographical memory. *Memory & Cognition, 32*(3), 427-442.

Best, J. (2020). Reading literary fiction: More empathy, but at what cost? *North American Journal of Psychology, 22*(2), 269-288.

Betz (2011). What fantasy role-playing games can teach your children (or even you). *British Journal of Educational Technology, 42*(6), E117-E121.

Bevens, C. L., & Loughan, S. (2019). Insights into men's sexual aggression toward women: Dehumanization and objectification. *Sex Roles, 81*(11-12), 713-730.

Biddlestone, M., Green, R., Cichocka, A., Sutton, R., & Douglas, K. (2021). Conspiracy beliefs and the individual, relational, and collective selves. *Social & Personality Psychology Compass, 15*(10), Artl e12649.

Blaauw, M. (2002). "Denial and silence" or "acknowledgement and disclosure." *International Review of the Red Cross, 84*(848), 764-784.

Bliss, S. (1995). Mythopoetic men's movements. In M. S. Kimmel (Ed.), *The politics of manhood: Profeminist men respond to mythopoetic men's movement (and the mythopoetic leaders answer).* Temple University Press.

Boatright-Horowitz, S. L., Marraccini, M. E., & Harps-Logan, Y. (2012). Teaching antiracism: College students' emotional and cognitive reactions to learning about White privilege. *Journal of Black Studies, 43*(8), 893-911.

Book, A. S., Visser, B. A., Blais, J., Hosker-Field, A., Methot-Jones, T., Gauthier, N. Y., Volk, A., Holden, R. R., & D'Agata, M. G. (2016). Unpacking more "evil": What is at the core of the dark tetrad? *Personality & Individual Differences, 90*, 269-272.

Bond, B. J. (2021). The development and influence of parasocial relationships with television characters: A longitudinal experimental test of prejudice reduction through parasocial contact. *Communication Research, 48*(4), 573-593.

Boss, P. (2006). *Loss, trauma, and resilience: Therapeutic work with ambiguous loss.* Norton.

Boss, P., & Greenberg, J. (1984). Family boundary ambiguity: A new variable in family stress theory. *Family Process, 23*(4), 535-546.

Boss, P., Caron, W., Horbal, J., & Mortimer, J. (1990). Predictors of depression in caregivers of dementia patients: Boundary ambiguity and mastery. *Family Process, 29*(3), 245-254.

Bowman, S. L. (2010). *The functions of role-playing games: How participants create community, solve problems, and explore identity.* McFarland.

Boym, S. (2001). *The future of nostalgia.* Basic.

Bracha, H. S., Ralston, T. C., Matsukawa, J. M., & Williams, A. E. (2004). Does "fight or flight" need updating? *Journal of Consultation & Liaison Psychiatry, 45*(5), 448-449.

Brannon, R., & Juni, S. (1984). A scale for measuring attitudes about masculinity. *Psychological Documents, 14*(1), 6-7.

Breen, L. J., & O'Connor, M. (2011). Family and social networks after bereavement: Experiences of support, change and isolation. *Journal of Family Therapy, 33*(1), 98-120.

Bregman, R. (2019). *Humankind: A hopeful history.* Little, Brown.

Brewer, M. B. (2003). Optimal distinctiveness, social identity, and the self. In M. Leary & J. Tangney (Eds.), *Handbook of self and identity* (pp. 480–491). Guilford.

Broomhall, A. G., Phillips, W. J., Hine, D. W., & Loi, N. M. (2017). Upward counterfactual thinking and depression: A meta-analysis. *Clinical Psychology Review, 55*, 56-73.

Brown, B. (2017, November/December). *High lonesome: Braving the quest for true belonging.* Psychotherapy Networker. https://psychotherapynetworker.org/magazine/article/1124/high -lonesome.

Brown, E. D., Seyler, M. D., Knorr, A. M., Garnett, M. L., & Laurenceau, J. P. (2016). Daily poverty-related stress and coping: Associations with child learned helplessness. *Family Relations, 65*(4), 591-602.

Bryant, R. A. (2007). Does dissociation further our understanding of PTSD? *Journal of Anxiety Disorders, 21*(2), 183-191.

Buerkle, C. W. (2019). Adam mansplains everything: White-hipster masculinity as covert hegemony. *Southern Communication Journal, 84*(3), 170-182.

Buhrmester, D., & Furman, W. D. (1986). The changing functions of friends in childhood: A neo-Sullivanian perspective. In V. J. Derlega & B. A. Winstead (Eds.), *Friendship and social interaction* (pp. 41–62). Springer.

Bukowski, W. M., Hoza, B., & Boivin, M. (1994). Measuring friendship quality during pre- and early adolescence: The development and psychometric properties of the friendship qualities scale. *Journal of Social & Personal Relationships, 11*(3), 471-484.

Burleson, B. R., & MacGeorge, E. L. (2002). Supportive communication. In M. L. Knapp & J. A. Daly (Eds.), *Handbook of interpersonal communication* (3rd ed., pp. 374–424). Sage.

Cacioppo, J. T., & Hawkley, L. C. (2009). Perceived social isolation and cognition. *Trends in Cognitive Science, 13*(10), 447-454.

Cacioppo, J. T., Fowler, J. H., & Christakis, N. A. (2009). Alone in the crowd: The structure and spread of loneliness in a large social network. *Journal of Personality & Social Psychology, 97*(6), 977-991.

Cacioppo, S., Capitanio, J. P., & Cacioppo, J. T. (2014). Toward a neurology of loneliness. *Psychological Bulletin, 140*(6), 1464-1504.

Calhoun, L. G., Cann, A., & Tedeschi, R. G. (2010). The posttraumatic growth model: Socio-cultural considerations. In T. Weiss & R. Berger (Eds.), *Handbook of posttraumatic growth: Research and practice* (pp. 1–23). Erlbaum.

Campbell, J. (1949). *The hero with a thousand faces.* Princeton University Press.

Capurso, M., & Ragni, B. (2016). Bridge over troubled water: Perspective connections between coping and play in children. *Frontiers in Psychology,* 7, Artl 1953.

Cardona, J., & Taylor, L. (2020). *The geek therapy playbook: How to use comics, games, and movies to understand each other and ourselves.* Geek Therapy Books.

Carey, T. A. (2003). Improving the success of anti-bullying intervention programs: A tool for matching programs with purposes. *International Journal of Reality Therapy, 22*(2), 16-23.

Carey, T., Gallagher, J., & Greiner, B. A. (2014). Post-traumatic stress and coping factors among search and recovery divers. *Occupational Medicine, 64*(1), 31-33.

Casabianca, S. S., & Pedersen, T. (2021, May 27). *Why do some people believe in conspiracy theories?* PsychCentral. https://psychcentral.com/blog/conspiracy-theories-why-people-believe.

Case, A., & Ngo, B. (2017). "Do we have to call it that?" The response of neoliberal multiculturalism to college antiracism efforts. *Multicultural Perspectives, 19*(4), 215-222.

Cass, V. (1979). Homosexual identity formation: A theoretical model. *Journal of Homosexuality, 4*(3), 219-235.

Chen, C., Yang, C., Chan, M., & Jimerson, S. R. (2020). Association between school climate and bullying victimization: Advancing integrated perspectives from parents and cross-country comparisons. *School Psychology, 35*(5), 311.

Cheung, W. Y., Wildschut, T., & Sedikides, C. (2018). Autobiographical memory functions of nostalgia in comparison to rumination and counterfactual thinking: Similarity and uniqueness. *Memory, 26*(2), 229-237.

Chow, R. M., Tiedens, L. Z., & Govan, C. L. (2008). Excluded emotions: The role of anger in antisocial responses to ostracism. *Journal of Experimental Social Psychology, 44*(3), 896-903.

Christakis, N. A., & Fowler, J. H. (2009). *Connected: The surprising power of our social networks and how they shape our lives.* Little, Brown.

Chung, T. (2013). Table-top role-playing game and creativity. *Thinking Skills & Creativity, 8,* 56-71.

Coan, J. A., Schaefer, H. S., & Davidson, R. J. (2006). Lending a hand: Social regulation of the neural response to threat. *Psychological Science, 17*(12), 1032-1039.

Coghlan, A. (2013). Healthy living can turn our cells' clock back. *Health, 219*(2935), 14.

Cohen, P. F. (2007). Anniversary reactions in the therapy group. *International Journal of Group Psychotherapy, 57*(2), 153-166.

Cohen, S., & Wills, T. A. (1985). Stress, social support, and the buffering hypothesis. *Psychological Bulletin, 98*(2), 310-357.

Collins, W. A., & Laursen, B. (2000). Adolescent relationships: The art of fugue. In C. Hendrick & S. Hendrick (Eds.), *SAGE sourcebook on close relationships* (pp. 59–70). SAGE.

Conley-Fonda, B., & Leisher, T. (2018). Asexuality: Sexual health does not require sex. *Sexual Addiction & Compulsivity, 25*(1), 6-11.

Constantinople, A. (1973). Masculinity-femininity: An exception to a famous dictum. *Psychological Bulletin, 80*(5), 389-407.

Crespi, B. J. (2016). Oxytocin, testosterone, and human social cognition. *Biological Reviews, 91*(2), 390-408.

Cross, W. E. (1991). *Shades of Black: Diversity in African-American identity.* Temple University Press.

Cubelli, R. (2003). Defining dissociations. *Cortex, 39*(2), 211-214.

Cuncic, A. (2021, May 27). *What is shame?* Verywell Mind. https://verywellmind.com/what-is-shame-5115076.

Dasgupta, N. (2004). Implicit ingroup favoritism, outgroup favoritism, and their behavioral manifestations. *Social Justice Research, 17*(2), 143-169.

David, D., & Brannon, R. (Eds.). (1976). *The forty-nine percent majority: The male sex role.* Addison-Wesley.

Davies, E. A. (2020). *Identifying and responding to the psychosocial support needs of young people when a loved one is a missing person* [Doctoral dissertation, The Australian Catholic University].

De Lamartine, A. (1820/2000). *Les Méditations Poétiques.* Ellipses.

De Loera-Brust, A. (2017, November 10). *The strange racial politics of "Stranger Things" America.* The Jesuit Review. https://americamagazine.org/arts-culture/2017/11/10/strange-racial-politics-stranger-things.

De Visser, R. O., & Smith, J. A. (2007). Alcohol consumption and masculine identity among young men. *Psychology & Health, 22*(5), 595-614.

De Vries, E., Kaufman, T. M., Veenstra, R., Laninga-Wijnen, L., & Huitsing, G. (2021). Bullying and victimization trajectories in the first years of secondary education: implications for status and affection. *Journal of Youth & Adolescence, 50*(10), 1-12.

Denworth, L. (2020). *Friendship: The evolution, biology, and extraordinary power of life's fundamental bond.* Norton.

Devan, G. S. (1993). Management of grief. *Singapore Medical Journal, 34*, 445-445.

DeYoung, R., & Buzzi, B. (2003). Ultimate coping strategies: The differences among parents of murdered or abducted, long-term missing children. *Omega: Journal of Death & Dying, 47*(4), 343-360.

Diamond, L. M. (2003). What does sexual orientation orient? A biobehavioral model distinguishing romantic love and sexual desire. *Psychological Review, 110*(1), 173.

DiAngelo, R. (2018). *White fragility: Why it's so hard for white people to talk about race.* Beacon.

Dobkin, P. L., Civita, M. D., Paraherakis, A., & Gill, K. (2002). The role of functional social support in treatment retention and outcomes among outpatient adult substance abusers. *Addiction, 97*(3), 347-356.

Douglas, K. M., & Sutton, R. M. (2018). Why conspiracy theories matter: A social psychological analysis. *European Review of Social Psychology, 29*(1), 256-298.

Duek, O., Spiller, T. R., Pietrzak, R. H., Fried, E. I., & Harpaz-Rotem, I. (2021). Network analysis of PTSD and depressive symptoms in 158,139 treatment-seeking veterans with PTSD. *Depression 7 Anxiety, 38*(5), 554-562.

Eisenberger, N. I. (2012). The pain of social disconnection: Examining the shared neural underpinnings of physical and social pain. *Nature Reviews Neuroscience, 13*(6), 421-434.

Eisenberger, N. I., Lieberman, M. D., & Williams, K. D. (2003). Does rejection hurt? An FMRI study of social exclusion. *Science, 302*(5643), 290-292.

Elison, J., Lennon, R., & Pulos, S. (2006). Investigating the compass of shame: The development of the Compass of Shame Scale. *Social Behavior & Personality, 34*(3), 221-238.

Emmerlink, P. J. H., Vanwesenbeck, I., van den Eijnden, R. J. J. M., & ter Bogt, T. F. M. (2016). Psychosexual correlates of sexual double standard endorsement in adolescent sexuality. *Journal of Sex Research*, *53*(3), 286-297.

Epel, E. S., & Lithgow, G. J. (2014). Stress biology and aging mechanisms: Toward understanding the deep connection between adaptation to stress and longevity. *Journals of Gerontology Series A: Biomedical Sciences & Medical Sciences*, *69*(Suppl_1), S10-S16.

Epstude, K., & Peetz, J. (2012). Mental time travel: A conceptual overview of social psychological perspectives on a fundamental human capacity. *European Journal of Social Psychology*, *42*(3), 269-275.

Ericksen, J. A. (1998). With enough cases, why do you need statistics? Revisiting Kinsey's methodology. *Journal of Sex Research*, *35*(2), 132-140.

Erikson, E. H., & Erikson, J. M. (1998). *The life cycle completed (extended version)*. Norton.

Eyuboglu, M., Eyuboglu, D., Pala, S. C., Oktar, D., Demirtas, Z., Arslantas, D., & Unsal, A. (2021). Traditional school bullying and cyberbullying: Prevalence, the effect on mental health problems and self-harm behavior. *Psychiatry Research*, *297*, Artl 113730.

Families of the Missing (n.d.). [Home page]. Families of the Missing. https://familiesofthemissing .org.

Favrid, P., Braun, V., & Rowney, C. (2017). "No girl wants to be called a slut!" Women, heterosexual casual sex and the sexual double standard. *Journal of Gender Studies*, *26*(5), 544-560.

Finkelhor, D., Hotaling, G., & Sedlak, A. (1990). *Missing, abducted, runaway, and thrownaway children in America, first report: Numbers and characteristics national incidence studies*. Office of Juvenile Justice & Delinquency Prevention.

Fisher, J. (2017). *Healing the fragmented selves of trauma survivors: Overcoming internal self-alienation*. Routledge.

Fisher, J. (2021). *Transforming the living legacy of trauma*. PESI.

Flowers, R. B. (2001). *Runaway kids and teenage prostitution: America's lost, abandoned, and sexually exploited children*. Praeger.

Ford, T. E., Buie, H. S., Mason, S. D., Olah, A. R., Breeden, C. J., & Ferguson, M. A. (2020). Diminished self-concept and social exclusion: Disparagement humor from the target's perspective. *Self & Identity*, *19*(6), 698-718.

Fornier, M. A., Zuroff, D. C., & Moskowitz, D. S. (2007). The social competition theory of depression: Gaining from an evolutionary approach to losing. *Journal of Social & Clinical Psychology*, *26*(7), 786-790.

Fortenberry, J. D. (2013). Puberty and adolescent sexuality. *Hormones & Behavior*, *64*(2), 280-287.

Fowler, S. L., & Geers, A. L. (2017). Does trait masculinity relate to expressing toughness? The effects of masculinity threat and self-affirmation among college men. *Psychology of Men & Masculinity*, *18*(2), 176-186.

Franco, Z. E., Blau, K., & Zimbardo, P. G. (2011). Heroism: A conceptual analysis and differentiation between heroic action and altruism. *Review of General Psychology*, *15*(2), 99-113.

Frankl, V. (1959/2006). *Man's search for meaning* (I. Lasch, Trans.). Beacon.

Frankl, V. (2010). *The feeling of meaninglessness: A challenge to psychotherapy and philosophy* (D. Hallowell, Trans.). Marquette University Press.

Fraser, G. (1991). The dissociative table technique: A strategy for working with ego states in dissociative disorders and ego state therapy. *Dissociation*, *4*(4), 205-213.

Freud, S. (1900/2010). The interpretation of dreams. In J. Strachey (Ed. & Trans.), *The standard edition of the complete psychological works of Sigmund Freud, volume IV: The interpretation of dreams (first part)* (pp. ix–627). Basic.

Freud, S. (1920/1922). *Beyond the pleasure principle* (C. J. M. Habback, Trans.). Bartleby.

Friedlander, L., Connolly, J., Pepler, D., & Craig, W. (2007). Biological, familial, and peer influences on dating in early adolescence. *Archives of Sexual Behavior, 36*(6), 821-830.

Friedmann, E., Thomas, S. A., Liu, F., Morton, P. G., Chapa, D., & Gottlieb, S. S. (2006). Relationship of depression, anxiety, and social isolation to chronic heart failure outpatient mortality. *American Heart Journal, 152*(5), 940.e1-940.e8.

Frodi, A. (1977). Sex differences in perception of a provocation, a survey. *Perceptual & Motor Skills, 44*(1), 113-114.

Frosh, S. (2010). *Psychoanalysis outside the clinic: Interventions in psychosocial studies.* Palgrave Macmillan.

Frothingham, M. B. (2021, October 6). *Fight, flight, freeze, or fawn: What this response means.* Simply Psychology. http://simplypsychology.org/fight-flight-freeze-fawn.html.

Fugitt, J. L., & Ham, L. S. (2018). Beer for "brohood": A laboratory simulation of masculinity confirmation through alcohol use behaviors in men. *Psychology of Addictive Behaviors, 32*(3), 358-364.

Gabriel, M. A. (1992). Anniversary reactions: Trauma revisited. *Clinical Social Work Journal, 20*(2), 179-192.

Galán, C. A., Stokes, L. R., Szoko, N., Abebe, K. Z., & Culyba, A. J. (2021). Exploration of experiences and perpetration of identity-based bullying among adolescents by race/ethnicity and other marginalized identities. *JAMA Network Open, 4*(7), e2116364-e2116364.

Gallagher, K., Starkman, R., & Rhoades, R. (2017). Performing counter-narratives and mining creative resilience: Using applied theatre to theorize notions of youth resilience. *Journal of Youth Studies, 20*(2), 216-233.

Galliford, N., & Furnham, A. (2017). Individual differences and beliefs in medical and political conspiracy theories. *Scandinavian Journal of Psychology, 58*(5), 422-428.

Garrett, S. (1987). *Gender.* Tavistock.

Garski, L. A., & Mastin, J. (2021). *Starship Therapise: Using therapeutic fanfiction to rewrite your life.* North Atlantic.

Gibson, H., Willming, C., & Holdnak, A. (2002). "We're Gators . . . not just Gator fans": Serious leisure and University of Florida football. *Journal of Leisure Research, 34*(4), 397-425.

Gillespie, G., & Crouse, D. (2012). There and back again: Nostalgia, art, and ideology in old-school Dungeons and Dragons. *Games & Culture, 7*(6), 441-470.

Gillig, T., & Murphy, S. (2016). Fostering support for LGBTQ youth? The effects of a gay adolescent media portrayal on young viewers. *International Journal of Communication, 10*, 23.

Glace, A. M., Dover, T. L., & Zatkin, J. G. (2021). Taking the black pill: An empirical analysis of the "incel." *Psychology of Men & Masculinities, 22*(2), 288-297.

Goldstein, D. S. (2010). Adrenal responses to stress. *Cellular & Molecular Neurobiology, 30*(8), 1433-1440.

Gomer, J., & Petrella, C. (2017). *How the Reagan administration stoked fears of anti-white racism: The origins of the politics of "reverse discrimination."* The Washington Post. https://washingtonpost.com/news/made-by-history/wp/2017/10/10/how-the-reagan-administration-stoked-fears-of-anti-white-racism.

Gooden, M. (2014). Using Nigrescence to recover from my mis-education as a "successful" African American male. *Journal of African American Males in Education, 5*(2), 111-133.

Gooden, T. (2019, July 25). *Chief, fighter, dad: Hopper's best moments on "Stranger Things."* Hypable. https://hypable.com/hopper-stranger-things-best-moments.

Goodman, D., & Freeman, M. (2015). *Psychology and the other.* Oxford University Press.

Graeber, D., & Wengrow, D. (2021). *The dawn of everything: A new history of humanity.* Penguin UK.

Graves, R. (2017, November 13). *Stranger Things and the Sinclairs.* The Witness. https://thewitnessbcc.com/stranger-things-sinclairs.

Greater Good Science Center. (2011, January 12). *Philip Zimbardo: What makes a hero?* [Video]. YouTube. https://www.youtube.com/watch?v=grMHzqtRm_8.

Greco, V., & Roger, D. (2003). Uncertainty, stress, and health. *Personality & Individual Differences, 34*(6), 1057-1068.

Greenbaum, J., Albright, K., & Tsai, C. (2020). Introduction to the special issue of *Child Abuse & Neglect: Global child trafficking and health, 100,* ArtID 1043321.

Grieve, R., March, E., & Van Doom, G. (2019). Masculinity may be more toxic than we think: The influence of gender roles on trait emotional manipulation. *Personality & Individual Differences, 138,* 157-162.

Gygax, G. (1978). *Players handbook.* TSR.

Halatsis, P., & Christakis, N. (2009). The challenge of sexual attraction within heterosexuals' cross-sex friendship. *Journal of Social & Personal Relationships, 26*(7), 919-937.

Hale, J. (2016). *Patterns: The need for order.* PsychCentral. https://psychcentral.com/lib/patterns-the-need-for-order#1.

Harris, J. (Ed). (2016). *The quotable Jung.* Princeton University Press.

Hartmann, B. J., & Brunk, K. H. (2019). Nostalgia marketing and (re-)enchantment. *International Journal of Research in Marketing, 36*(4), 669-686.

Harvard Health. (2020, July 6). *Understanding the stress response.* Harvard Health. https://health.harvard.edu/staying-healthy/understanding-the-stress-response.

Hawkley, L. C., & Cacioppo, J. T. (2003). Loneliness and pathways to disease. *Brain, Behavior, & Immunity, 17*(1), 98-105.

Hawkley, L. C., & Cacioppo, J. T. (2010). Loneliness matters: A theoretical and empirical review of consequences and mechanisms. *Annals of Behavioral Medicine, 40*(2), 218-227.

Hayes, F. W. (2017). Historical disaster and the new urban crisis. *Journal of African American Studies, 22*(1), 1-16.

Hayes, R. A., Wesselmann, E. D., & Carr, C. T. (2018). When nobody "likes" you: Perceived ostracism through paralinguistic digital affordances within social media. *Social Media & Society, 4*(3).

Heeke, C., Stammel, N., & Knaevelstrud, C. (2015). When hope and grief interact: Rates and risks of prolonged grief disorder among bereaved individuals and relatives of disappeared persons in Colombia. *Journal of Affective Disorders, 173,* 59-64.

Hein, G., Silani, G., Preuschoff, K., Batson, C. D., & Singer, T. (2010). Neural responses to ingroup and outgroup members' suffering predict individual differences in costly helping. *Neuron, 68*(1), 149-160.

Henderson, J. L. (1964). The process of individuation. In C. G. Jung & M.-L. von Franz (Eds.), *Man and his symbols.* Windfall.

Henderson, M., Kiernan, C., & Henderson, P. (1999, June). *The missing person dimension.* Paper presented at the Children and Crime: Victims and Offenders conference, Australian Institute of Criminology, Brisbane.

Hensums, M., Overbeek, G., & Jorgensen, T. D. (2022). Not one double standard but two? Adolescents' attitudes about appropriate sexual behavior. *Youth & Society, 54*(1), 23-42.

Hepper, E. G., Wildschut, T., Sedikides, C., Robertson, S., & Routledge, C. D. (2021). Time capsule: Nostalgia shields psychological well-being from limited time horizons. *Emotion, 21*(3), 644-664.

Herrera, F., Bailenson, J., Weisz, E., Ogle, E., & Zaki, J. (2018). Building long-term empathy: A large-scale comparison of traditional and virtual reality perspective-taking. *PloS One, 13*(10).

Hershfield, H. E., Scheibe, S., Sims, T. L., & Carstensen, L. L. (2013). When feeling bad can be good: Mixed emotions benefit physical health across adulthood. *Social Psychological & Personality Science, 4*(1), 54-61.

Hirsch, M., & Spitzer, L. (2002). "We would not have come without you": Generations of nostalgia. *American Imago, 59*(3), 253-276.

Hochstetler, A., Copes, H., & Forsyth, C. J. (2014). The fight: Symbolic expression and validation of masculinity in working class tavern culture. *American Journal of Criminal Justice, 39*(3), 493-510.

Hojat, M., & Moyer, A. (Eds.) (2016). *The psychology of friendship*. Oxford University Press.

Hollander, T. (2016). Ambiguous loss and complicated grief: Understanding the grief of parents of the disappeared in northern Uganda. *Journal of Family Theory & Review, 8*(3), 294-307.

Hollingsworth, W. L., Dolbin-MacNab, M. L., & Marek, L. I. (2016). Boundary ambiguity and ambivalence in military family reintegration. *Family Relations, 65*(4), 603-615.

Holmes, J. E. (1977). *Dungeons & dragons* [basic set]. TSR.

Holmes, L. (2014). "When the search is over: Reconnecting missing children and adults." *London: Missing People*, 8.

Hommel, B., Müsseler, J., Aschersleben, G., & Prinz, W. (2001). The theory of event coding (TEC): A framework for perception and action planning. *Behavioral & Brain Sciences, 24*(5), 849-878.

Horowitz, M. J. (1976). *Stress response syndromes*. Aronson.

Howe, M. L., & Courage, M. L. (1993). On resolving the enigma of infantile amnesia. *Psychological Bulletin, 113*(2), 305-326.

Hsu, K. J., Beard, C., Rifkin, L., Dillon, D. G., Pizzagalli, D. A., & Björgvinsson, T. (2015). Transdiagnostic mechanisms in depression and anxiety: The role of rumination and attentional control. *Journal of Affective Disorders, 188*, 22-27.

Huddleston, J., & Ge, X. (2003). Boys at puberty: Psychosocial implications. In C. Hayward (Ed.), *Gender differences at puberty* (pp. 113–134). Cambridge University Press.

Huffman, K., Dowdell, K., & Sanderson, C. A. (2017). *Psychology in action* (12th ed.). Wiley.

Hutson, E., Thompson, B., Bainbridge, E., Melnyk, B. M., & Warren, B. J. (2021). Cognitive-behavioral skills building to alleviate the mental health effects of bullying victimization in youth. *Journal of Psychosocial Nursing & Mental Health Services, 59*(5), 15-20.

Hyde, A., Drennana, J., Howletta, E., Carneyb, M., Butlera, M., & Lohan, M. (2012). Parents' constructions of the sexual self-presentation and sexual conduct of adolescents: Discourses of gendering and protecting. *Culture, Health, & Sexuality, 14*(8), 895-909.

Igbal, N., & Dar, K. A. (2015). Negative affectivity, depression, and anxiety: Does rumination mediate the links? *Journal of Affective Disorders, 181*, 18-23.

International Centre for Missing and Exploited Children. (2022). *Statistics*. Global Missing Children's Network. https://globalmissingkids.org/awareness/missing-children-statistics.

Ismail, S., Cheston, R., Christopher, G., & Meyrick, J. (2020). Nostalgia as a psychological resource for people with dementia: A systematic review and meta-analysis of evidence of effectiveness from experimental studies. *Dementia, 19*(2), 330-351.

Isuru, A., Bandumithra, P., & Williams, S. S. (2021). Locked in grief: A qualitative study of grief among family members of missing persons in southern Sri Lanka. *BMC Psychology, 9*, Artl 167.

Ivie, D. (2019, August 4). *Stranger Things 3's actors fought against Steve and Robin becoming a couple.* Vulture. https://vulture.com/2019/08/netflix-stranger-things-3-steve-robin-romance.html.

Iyer, A., & Jetten, J. (2011). What's left behind: Identity continuity moderates the effect of nostalgia well-being and life choices. *Journal of Personality & Social Psychology, 101*(1), 94-108.

James, M., Anderson, J., & Putt, J. (2008). *Missing persons in Australia.* Australian Institute of Criminology.

James, W. (1890/1950). *Principles of psychology* (Vol. 1). Dover.

Janisse, K., & Corupe, P. (Eds.). (2016). *Satanic panic: Pop-cultural paranoia in the 1980s* (2nd ed.). FAB Press.

Jasper, M. C. (2006). *Missing and exploited children: How to protect your child.* Oxford University Press.

Jenkins, H. (2012). *Textual poachers: Television fans and participatory culture* (2nd ed.). Routledge.

Jiang, T., Cheung, W. Y., Wildschut, T., & Sedikides, C. (2021). Nostalgia, reflection, brooding: Psychological benefits and autobiographical memory functions. *Consciousness & Cognition, 90*, 103107.

Jin, L. (2020, December 17). *The rise and fall of the missing children milk carton campaign.* Medium. https://medium.com/the-collector/the-rise-and-fall-of-the-missing-children-milk-carton -campaign-4e9228d34cb7.

Jones, W. H., & Carver, M. D. (1991). Adjustment and coping implications of loneliness. In C. R. Snyder & D. R. Forsyth (Eds.), *Handbook of clinical psychology: The health perspective* (pp. 395–415). Pergamon.

Jordan, J. S. (2013). The wild ways of conscious will: What we do, how we do it, and why it has meaning. *Frontiers in Psychology, 4*, 574.

Jordan, J. S. (2019). Wild stories: Science, consciousness, and the anticipatory narratives in which we live. *Journal of Consciousness Studies, 27*(3-4), 128-151.

Jordan, J. S., & Day, B. (2014). *Wild systems theory as a 21st century coherence framework for cognitive science.* Open MIND.

Jordan, J. S., & Ranade, E. (2014). Multiscale entrainment: A primer in prospective cognition for educational researchers. *Journal of Cognitive Education & Psychology, 13*(2), 147-162.

Jung, C. G. (1951/1959). *Aion: Researches into the phenomenology of the self.* Princeton University Press.

Jung, C. G. (1958). *Psyche & symbol.* Anchor.

Justman, S. (2021). The guilt-free psychopath. *Philosophy, Psychiatry, & Psychology, 28*(2), 87-104.

Kahneman, D., & Miller, D. T. (1986). Norm theory: Comparing reality to its alternatives. *Psychological Review, 93*(2), 136-153.

Kahneman, D., & Tversky, A. (1972). Subjective probability: A judgment of representativeness. *Cognitive Psychology, 3*(3), 430-454.

Kajtazi-Testa, L., & Hewer, C. J. (2018). Ambiguous loss and incomplete abduction narratives in Kosovo. *Clinical Child Psychology & Psychiatry, 23*(2), 333-345.

Kang, X., Li, L., Wei, D., Xu, X., Zhao, R., Jung, Y., Ying-ying, X., Li-ze, G., & Jiang, W. (2014). Development of a simple score to predict outcome for unresponsiveness wakefulness syndrome. *Critical Care, 18*(1), Artl R37.

Karakis, E. N., & Levant, R. F. (2012). Is normative male alexithymia associated with relationship satisfaction, fear of intimacy, and communication quality among men in relationships? *Journal of Men's Studies, 20*(3), 179-186.

Karren, K. (2014). *Mind/body health: The effects of attitudes, emotions, and relationships.* Pearson.

Kennedy, C., Dean, F. P., & Chan, A. Y. C. (2019). In limbo: A systematic review of psychological responses and coping among people with a missing loved one. *Journal of Clinical Psychology, 75*(9), 1544-1571.

Kennedy, C., Deane, F. P., & Chan, A. Y. C. (2021). Intolerance of uncertainty and psychological symptoms among people with a missing loved one: Emotion regulation difficulties and psychological inflexibility as mediators. *Journal of Contextual Behavioral Science, 21*, 48-56.

Kidd, D. C., & Castano, E. (2013). Reading literary fiction improves theory of mind. *Science, 342*(6156), 377-380.

Kim, J. L., Sorsoli, C. L., Collins, K., Zylbergold, B. A., Schooler, D., & Tolman, D. L. (2007). From sex to sexuality: Exposing the heterosexual script on primetime network television. *Journal of Sex Research, 44*(2), 145-157.

King, C. A. S. (1983/1987). *The words of Martin Luther King, Jr.* Newmarket.

Kinsey, A. (1948). *Sexual behavior in the human male.* Saunders.

Kinsey, A. (1953). *Sexual behavior in the human female.* Saunders.

Kiselica, M. S., Benton-Wright, S., & Englar-Carlson, M. (2016). Accentuating positive masculinity: A new foundation for the psychology of boys, men, and masculinity. In Y. J. Wong & S. R. Wester (Eds.), *APA handbook of men and masculinities* (pp. 123–143). American Psychological Association.

Klages, S. V., & Wirth, J. H. (2014). Excluded by laughter: Laughing until it hurts someone else. *Journal of Social Psychology, 154*(1), 8-13.

Klotz, S., & Whithaus, C. (2015). Gloria Anzaldúa's rhetoric of ambiguity and antiracist teaching. *Composition Studies, 43*(2), 72-91.

Kochenderfer-Ladd, B., & Skinner, K. (2002). Children's coping strategies: Moderators of the effects of peer victimization? *Developmental Psychology, 38*(2), 267.

Kübler-Ross, E. (1973). *On death and dying.* Tavistock.

Kumar, R. (2019, February 26). "We're all patriots in this house": American fantasies of colorblindness and border control in Stranger Things. *Refractory: A Journal of Entertainment Media.* https://refractory-journal.com/were-all-patriots-in-this-house-american-fantasies-of-colorblindness-and-border-control-in-stranger-things.

Kutner, M. (2016, August 10). *How "Stranger Things" captures '80s panic over missing kids.* Newsweek. https://newsweek.com/stranger-things-missing-children-netflix-488605.

Lamar, B. (2019, July 29). What's up with how "Stranger Things" treats its Black characters? [Opinion]. Shadow and Act. https://shadowandact.com/stranger-things-black-characters.

Lampinen, J. M., & Moore, K. N. (2016). Missing person alerts: Does repeated exposure decrease their effectiveness? *Journal of Experimental Criminology, 12*(4), 587-598.

Lampinen, J. M., Peters, C. S., Gier, V., & Sweeney, L. N. (2012). The psychology of the missing: Missing and abducted Children. In R. E. Holliday & T. A. Marche (Eds.), *Child forensic psychology: Victim and eyewitness testimony* (pp. 241–272). Palgrave Macmillan.

Lanese, N., & Dutfield, S. (2021, November 12). *Fight or flight: The sympathetic nervous system.* Live Science. https://livescience.com/65446-sympathetic-nervous-system.html.

Langley, T. (2016). Acknowledgments. In T. Langley (Ed.), *Game of Thrones psychology: The mind is dark and full of terrors* (pp. vii–xi). Sterling.

Langley, T. (2022). *Batman and psychology: A dark and stormy knight* (2nd ed.). Wiley.

Langley, T. (Ed.). (2015). *The Walking Dead psychology: Psych of the living dead.* Sterling.

Langley, T. (Ed.). (2019). *The Joker psychology: Evil clowns and the women who love them.* Sterling.

Larson, R., Richards, M. H., Moneta, G., Holmbeck, G., & Duckett, E. (1996). Changes in adolescents' daily interactions with their families from ages 10 to 18: Disengagement and transformation. *Developmental Psychology, 32*(4), 744-754.

Lash, J. P. (1997). *Helen and teacher: The story of Helen Keller and Anne Sullivan Macy.* Da Capo.

Leary, M. R., Springer, C., Negel, L., Ansell, E., & Evans, K. (1998). The causes, phenomenology, and consequences of hurt feelings. *Journal of Personality & Social Psychology, 74*(5), 1225-1237.

Lee, K., Talwar, V., McCarthy, A., Ross, I., Evans, A., & Arruda, C. (2014). Can classic moral stories promote honesty in children? *Psychological Science, 25*(8), 1630-1636.

Leeds, A. M. (2013). *Strengthening the self: Principles and procedures for creating successful treatment outcomes for adult survivors of neglect and abuse.* EMDRIA. https://emdria.org/learning-class /strengthening-the-self-principles-and-procedures-for-creating-successful-treatment -outcomes-for-adult-survivors-of-neglect-and-abuse.

Leider, R. J. (2015). *The power of purpose: Find meaning, live longer, better* (3rd ed.). Berrett-Koehler.

Lenferink, L. I. M., de Keijser, J., Piersma, E., & Boelen, P. A. (2018). I've changed, but I'm not less happy: Interview study among nonclinical relatives of long-term missing persons. *Death Studies, 42*(6), 346-355.

Lenferink, L. I. M., de Keijser, J., Wessel, I., & Boelen, P. A. (2018). Cognitive-behavioral correlates of psychological symptoms among relatives of missing persons. *International Journal of Cognitive Therapy, 11*(3), 311-324.

Lenferink, L. I. M., Eisma, M. C., de Keijser, J., & Boelen, P. A. (2017). Grief rumination mediates the association between self-compassion and psychopathology in relatives of missing persons. *European Journal of Psychotraumatology, 8*(Suppl 6), ArtID 1378052.

Levant, R., Allen, P., & Lien, M-C. (2014). Alexithymia in men: How and when do emotional processing deficiencies occur? *Psychology of Men & Masculinity, 15*(3), 324-334.

Lewit, E. M., & Baker, L. S. (1998). Missing children. *The Future of Children, 8*, 141-151.

Lieberman, M. D. (2013). *Social: Why our brains are wired to connect.* Crown.

Liegner, E. (1977). The first interview in modern psychoanalysis. *Modern Psychoanalysis, 2*(1), 55-66.

Lincoln, T. M., Stahnke, J., & Moritz, S. (2014). The short-term impact of a paranoid explanation on self-esteem: An experimental study. *Cognitive Therapy & Research, 38*(4), 397-406.

Link. N. F., Sherer, S. E., & Byrne, P. N. (1977). Moral judgment and moral conduct in the psychopath. *Canadian Psychiatric Association Journal, 22*(7), 341-346.

Linley, P. A., & Joseph, S. (2011). Meaning in life and posttraumatic growth. *Journal of Loss & Trauma, 16*(2), 150-159.

Lis, E., Chiniara, C., Biskin, R., & Montoro, R. (2015). Psychiatrists' perceptions of role-playing games. *Psychiatric Quarterly, 86*(3), 381-384.

Livingstone, Ian (1982). *Dicing with dragons: An introduction to role-playing games* (Revised ed.). Routledge.

Lowy. (1991). Yuppie racism: Race relations in the 1980s. *Journal of Black Studies, 21*(4), 445-464.

Lozenski, B. (2018, March). On the mythical rise of White Nationalism and other stranger things. *Journal of Language & Literacy Education.* http://jolle.coe.uga.edu/wp-content /uploads/2018/03/SSO-March-2018_Lozenski_Final.pdf.

Luborsky, L. (1998). The Relationship Anecdotes Paradigm (RAP) interview as a versatile source of narratives. In L. Luborsky & P. Crits-Christoph (Eds.), *Understanding transference: The core conflictual relationship theme method* (pp. 109–120). American Psychological Association.

Luhmann, M., Bohn, J., Holtmann, J., Koch, T., & Eid, M. (2016). I'm lonely, can't you tell? Convergent validity of self- and informant ratings of loneliness. *Journal of Research in Personality, 61,* 50-60.

Maccoby, E. E. (1990). Gender and relationships: A developmental account. *American Psychologist, 45*(4), 513-520.

MacDonald, G., & Leary, M. R. (2005). Why does social exclusion hurt? The relationship between social and physical pain. *Psychological Bulletin, 131*(2), 202-223.

Maier, S. F., & Seligman, M. E. (2016). Learned helplessness at fifty: Insights from neuroscience. *Psychological Review, 123*(4), 349-367.

Maki, V. (2019, November 14). *Stranger Things' Billy Hargrove is most definitely a queer coded character.* Comics Beat. https://comicsbeat.com/stranger-things-billy-hargrove-queer-coded -character.

Mansfield, P. R. (2007). The illusion of invulnerability. *BMJ Clinical Research, 334*(7602), 1020.

Mar, R. A., Tackett, J. L., & Moore, C. (2010). Exposure to media and theory-of-mind development in preschoolers. *Cognitive Development, 25*(1), 69-78.

Markham, K. D., & Miller, A. K. (2006). Depression, control, and counterfactual thinking: Functional for whom? *Journal of Social & Clinical Psychology, 25*(2), 210-227.

Marks-Tarlow, T. (2012). The play of psychotherapy. *American Journal of Play, 4*(3), 352-377.

Marsh, H., Nagengast, B., Morin, A., Parada, R., Craven, R., & Hamilton, L. (2011). Construct validity of the multidimensional structure of bullying and victimization: An application of exploratory structural equation modeling. *Journal of Educational Psychology, 103*(3), 701-732.

Matos, K., O'Neill, O., & Lei, X. (2018). Toxic leadership and the masculinity contest culture: How "win or die" cultures breed abusive leadership. *Journal of Social Issues, 74*(3), 500-528.

McCain, J., Gentile, B., & Campbell, W. K. (2015). A psychological exploration of engagement in geek culture. *PLoS One, 10,* e0142200.

McCann, W. H. (1943). Nostalgia: A descriptive and comparative study. *Pedagogical Seminary & Journal of Genetic Psychology, 62*(1), 97-104.

McClurg, J. (2018, March 27). *#BookmarkThis: Kidnap victim Elizabeth Smart says she's proud to be a survivor.* USA Today. https://usatoday.com/story/life/books/2018/03/27/bookmarkthis -kidnap-victim-elizabeth-smart-says-shes-proud-survivor/464293002.

McCormack, L., Ballinger, S., Valentine, M., & Swaab, L. (2021). Complex trauma and post-traumatic growth: A bibliometric analysis of research output over time. *Traumatology* (advance online publication). https://onlinelibrary.wiley.com/doi/10.1002/jcad.12143.

McFarland, M. (2017, October 31). *How "Stranger Things 2" cloaks racial tension in the heartland.* Salon. https://salon.com/2017/10/31/how-stranger-things-2-cloaks-racial-tension-in-the -heartland.

McGraw, A. P., Mellers, B. A., & Tetlock, P. E. (2005). Expectancies and emotions of Olympic athletes. *Journal of Experimental Social Psychology, 41*(4), 438-446.

McLaurin, S. L. (2005). *Childhood experiences of sibling abuse: An investigation into learned helplessness* [Doctoral dissertation, Virginia Polytechnic Institute and State University].

Meadow, P. (1990). Treatment beginnings. *Modern Psychoanalysis, 15*(1), 3-10.

Medvec, V. H., Madey, S. F., & Gillovich, T. (1995). When less is more: Counterfactual thinking and satisfaction among Olympic medalists. *Journal of Personality & Social Psychology, 69*(4), 603-610.

Mell-Taylor, A. (2019, August 23). *The (metaphorical) blackface of Stranger Things.* Alex Has Opinions. https://alexhasopinions.medium.com/the-metaphorical-blackface-of-stranger -things-8768a0d58d75.

Midgett, A., & Doumas, D. M. (2019). Witnessing bullying at school: The association between being a bystander and anxiety and depressive symptoms. *School Mental Health, 11*(3), 454-463.

Milligan, M. J. (2003). Displacement and identity discontinuity: The role of nostalgia in establishing new identity categories. *Symbolic Interaction, 26*(3), 381-403.

Mitchell, N., Biehal, F., & Wade, J. (2003). *Lost from view: A study of missing people in the UK.* The Policy Press.

Mitchell, S., & Steele, K. (2021). Mentalising in complex trauma and dissociative disorders. *European Journal of Trauma & Dissociation, 5*(3), ArtID 100168.

Morewitz, S. J., & Colls, C. S. (2016). Missing persons: An introduction. In S. J. Morewitz & C. S. Colls (Eds.), *Handbook of missing persons* (pp. 1–5). Springer, Cham.

Morrison, B. (2006). School bullying and restorative justice: Toward a theoretical understanding of the role of respect, pride, and shame. *Journal of Social Issues, 62*(2), 371-392.

Moskowitz, A., & van der Hart, O. (2020). Historical and contemporary conceptions of trauma-related dissociation: A neo-Janetian critique of models of divided personality. *European Journal of Trauma & Dissociation, 4*(2), ArtID 100101.

Moules, N. J., Estefan, A., Laing, C. M., Schulte, F., Guilcher, G. M. T., Field, J. C., & Strother, D. (2017). "A tribe apart": Sexuality and cancer in adolescence. *Journal of Pediatric Oncology Nursing, 34*(4), 295-308.

Moynihan, M., Pitcher, C., & Saewyc, E. (2018). Interventions that foster healing among sexually exploited children and adolescents: A systematic review. *Journal of Child Sexual Abuse: Research, Treatment, & Program Innovations for Victims, Survivors, & Offenders, 27*(4), 403-423.

Mudrack, P. E., & Mason, E. (2013). Dilemmas, conspiracies, and Sophie's choice: Vignette themes and ethical judgments. *Journal of Business Ethics, 118*(3), 639-653.

Munawar, K., Kuhn, S. K., & Haque, S. (2018). Understanding the reminiscence bump: A systematic review. *PloS One, 13*(12), e0208595.

Murray, H. L. (2018). Survivor guilt in posttraumatic stress disorder clinic sample. *Journal of Trauma & Loss, 23*(7), 600-607.

Nagoski, E., & Nagoski, A. (2019). *Burnout: The secret to unlocking the stress cycle.* Ballantine.

Nail, P. R., Simon, J. B., Bihm, E. M., & Beasley, W. H. (2016). Defensive egoism and bullying: Gender differences yield qualified support for the compensation model of aggression. *Journal of School Violence, 15*(1), 22-47.

Nathanson, D. (1987). A timetable for shame. In D. Nathanson (Ed.), *The many faces of shame* (pp. 1–63). Guilford.

Nathanson, D. L. (1992). *Shame and pride.* Norton.

National Crime Information Center (2020). *NCIC Missing person and unidentified person statistics for 2018.* https://fbi.gov/file-repository/2018-ncic-missing-person-and-unidentified-person -statistics.pdf/view.

National Crime Information Center (2022). *2021 Missing and unidentified person statistics.* National Crime Information Center.

Nickerson, R. S. (1998). Confirmation bias: A ubiquitous phenomenon in many guises. *Review of General Psychology, 2*(2), 175-220.

Norton, M. I., & Sommers, S. R. (2011). Whites see racism as a zero-sum game that they are now losing. *Perspectives on Psychological Science, 6*(3), 215-218.

Olatunji, B. O., Naragon-Gainey, K., & Wolitzky-Taylor, K. B. (2013). Specificity of rumination in anxiety and depression: A multimodal meta-analysis. *Clinical Psychology: Science & Practice, 20*(3), 225-257.

Oller, J. (2019, July 8). *Call now! Stranger Things sets up hilarious answering machine Easter egg.* SyFy. https://syfy.com/syfy-wire/stranger-things-answering-machine-easter-egg.

Olweus, D. (1993). *Bullying at school: What we know and what we can do.* Blackwell.

Olweus, D. (1996). Bullying or peer abuse in school: Intervention and prevention. In G. Davis, S. Lloyd-Bostock, M. McMurran, & C. Wilson (Eds.), *Psychology, law, and criminal justice: International developments in research and practice* (pp. 248–263). De Gruyter.

Osei-Opare, N. (2020). *Around the world, the U.S. has long been a symbol of anti-black racism.* The Washington Post. https://washingtonpost.com/outlook/2020/06/05/around-world-us-has -long-been-symbol-anti-black-racism.

Pak, G. (2020). *Stranger Things: The bully* (V. Favoccia, Illus.). Dark Horse.

Palmer, B. (2012, April 20). *Why did children start showing up on milk cartons?* Slate. https://slate.com /news-and-politics/2012/04/etan-patz-case-why-did-dairies-put-missing-children-on-their -milk-cartons.html.

Parkes, C. M. (1998). Coping with loss: Bereavement in adult life. *BMJ, 316*(7134), 856-859.

Parr, H., Stevenson, O., & Woolnough, P. (2016). Searching for missing people: Families living with ambiguous absence. *Emotion, Space, & Society, 19*, 66-75.

Parris, L., Jungert, T., Thornberg, R., Varjas, K., Meyers, J., Grunewald, S., & Shriberg, D. (2020). Bullying bystander behaviors: The role of coping effectiveness and the moderating effect of gender. *Scandinavian Journal of Psychology, 61*(1), 38-46.

Parris, L., Varjas, K., Meyers, J., Henrich, C., & Brack, J. (2019). Coping with bullying: The moderating effects of self-reliance. *Journal of School Violence, 18*(1), 62-76.

Pasley, B. K., & Ihinger-Tallman, M. (1989). Boundary ambiguity in remarriage: Does ambiguity differentiate degree of marital adjustment and interaction? *Family Relations, 38*(1), 46-52.

Pastorino, E., & Doyle-Portillo, S. (2009). *What is psychology?* (2nd ed.). Thomas Learning.

Pasupathi, M. (2001). The social construction of the personal past and its implications for adult development. *Psychological Bulletin, 127*(5), 651-672.

Patchin, J. W., & Hinduja, S. (2006). Bullies move beyond the schoolyard: A preliminary look at cyberbullying. *Youth Violence & Juvenile Justice, 4*(2), 148-169.

Patz, K. (2012, April 20). *Etan Patz: A brief history of the "missing child" milk carton campaign.* Time. https://newsfeed.time.com/2012/04/20/etan-patz-a-brief-history-of-the-missing-child -milk-carton-campaign.

Pennycook, G., Cheyne, J. A., Barr, N., Koehler, D. J., & Fugelsang, J. A. (2015). On the reception and detection of pseudo-profound bullshit. *Judgment & Decision Making, 10*(6), 549-563.

Peters, R. (1985). Reflections on the origin and aim of nostalgia. *Journal of Analytical Psychology, 30*(2), 135-148.

Pfaltz, M. C., Michael, T., Meyer, A. H., & Wilhelm, F. H. (2013). Reexperiencing symptoms, dissociation, and avoidance behaviors in daily life of patients with PTSD and patients with panic disorder with agoraphobia. *Journal of Traumatic Stress, 26*(4), 443-450.

Plass, P. S. (2007). Secondary victimizations in missing child events. *American Journal of Criminal Justice, 32*(1-2), 30-44.

Platt, M. G., Luoma, J. B., & Freyd, J. J. (2017). Shame and dissociation in survivors of high and low betrayal trauma. *Journal of Aggression, Maltreatment, & Trauma, 26*(1), 34-39.

Pliske, M. M., Stauffer, S. D., & Werner-Lin, A. (2021). Healing from adverse childhood experiences through therapeutic powers of play: "I can do it with my hands." *International Journal of Play Therapy, 30*(4), 244-258.

Polanin, J. R., Espelage, D. L., & Pigott, T. D. (2012). A meta-analysis of school-based bullying prevention programs' effects on bystander intervention behavior. *School Psychology Review, 41*(1), 47-65.

Pollock, G. (2006). *Psychoanalysis and the image.* Blackwell.

Porcelli, P., Fava, G. A., Rafanelli, C., Bellomo, A., Grandi, S., Grassi, L., Pasquini, P., Picardi, A., Quartesan, R., Rigatelli, M., & Sonino, N. (2012). Anniversary reactions in medical patients. *Journal of Nervous & Mental Disease, 200*(7), 603-606.

Pourtova, E. (2013). Nostalgia and lost identity (J. Sklyanyn, Trans.). *Journal of Analytical Psychology, 58*(1), 34-51.

Preece, D. (2017). Establishing the theoretical components of alexithymia via factor analysis: Introduction and validation of the attention-appraisal model of alexithymia. *Personality & Individual Differences, 119,* 341-352.

Price, J., Sloman, L., Gardner, R., Gilbert, P., & Rodhe, P. (1994). The social competition hypothesis of depression. *British Journal of Psychiatry, 164*(3), 309-315.

Prudom, L. (2017, November 7). *There's only one logical explanation for Billy's behavior on 'Stranger Things.'* Mashable. https://mashable.com/article/billy-steve-stranger-things-2-ship-gay -character.

Qualter, P., Rotenberg, K., Barrett, L., Henzi, P., Barlow, A., Stylianou, M., & Harris, R. A. (2013). Investigating hypervigilance for social threat of lonely media. *Journal of Abnormal Child Psychology, 41*(2), 325-338.

Quelas, A. C., Power, M. J., Juhos, C., & Senos, J. (2008). Counterfactual thinking and functional differences in depression. *Clinical Psychology & Psychotherapy, 15*(5), 352-365.

Randi, J. (2013, October 23). *No amount of belief makes something a fact.* [Status update]. Facebook.

Rees, G. (2011). *Still running 3: Early findings from our third national survey of young runaways.* The Children's Society.

Reitman, D., & Drabman, R. S. (1997). The value of recognizing our differences and promoting healthy competition: The cognitive behavioral debate. *Behavior Therapy, 28*(3), 419-429.

Renfro, K. (2017, November 8). *'Stranger Things 2' actor reveals the challenges of filming a major fight scene: 'That was a really messed up day.'* Insider. https://insider.com/stranger-things-2 -hopper-eleven-mike-fight-scenes-2017-11.

Reysen, S., Plante, C. N., Roberts, S. E., & Gerbasi, K. C. (2016). Optimal distinctiveness and identification with the furry fandom. *Current Psychology, 35*(4), 638-642.

Ribot, T. (1896/2018). *Las psychologie des sentiments.* Hachette Livre-BNF.

Riggio, R. E. (2014, October 21). *The top ten things that make horror movies scary.* Psychology Today. https://psychologytoday.com/us/blog/cutting-edge-leadership/201410/the-top-ten -things-make-horror-movies-scary.

Ritchey, K. (2014). Black identity development. *Vermont Connection, 35,* 99-105.

Riva, P., & Eck, J. (2016). The many faces of social exclusion. In P. Riva & J. Eck (Eds.), *Social exclusion: Psychological approaches to understanding and reducing its impact* (pp. ix–xv). Springer.

Riva, P., Montali, L., Wirth, J. H., Curioni, S., & Williams, K. D. (2017). Chronic social exclusion and evidence for the resignation stage: An empirical investigation. *Journal of Social & Personal Relationships, 34*(4), 541-564.

Roberts, N. P., Roberts, P. A., Jones, N., & Bisson, J. I. (2015). Psychological interventions for post-traumatic stress disorder and comorbid substance use disorder: A systematic review and meta-analysis. *Clinical Psychology Review, 38*, 25-38.

Romero, L. M., & Butler, L. K. (2007). Endocrinology of stress. *International Journal of Comparative Psychology, 20*(2-3), 89-95.

Rudert, S. C., Hales, A. H., Greifeneder, R., & Williams, K. D. (2017). When silence is not golden: Why acknowledgment matters even when being excluded. *Personality & Social Psychology Bulletin, 43*(5), 678-692.

Runcan, P. L., Petracovschi, S., & Borca, C. V. (2012). The importance of play in the parent-child interaction. *Procedia—Social & Behavioral Sciences, 46*, 795-799.

Sagarin, B. J., Cialdini, R. B., Rice, W. E., & Sema, S. B. (2002). Dispelling the illusion of invulnerability: The motivations and mechanisms of resistance to persuasion. *Journal of Personality & Social Psychology, 83*(2), 526-541.

Salmon, S., Turner, S., Taillieu, T., Fortier, J., & Afifi, T. O. (2018). Bullying victimization experiences among middle and high school adolescents: Traditional bullying, discriminatory harassment, and cybervictimization. *Journal of Adolescence, 63*, 29-40.

Sanchez, R. P., Waller, M. W., & Greene, J. M. (2006). Who runs? A demographic profile of runaway youth in the United States. *Journal of Adolescent Health, 39*(5), 778-781.

Satir, V. (1988). *The new peoplemaking*. Science & Behavior Books.

Schaefer, C. E., & Kaduson, H. (1994). *The quotable play therapist: 238 of the all-time best quotes on play and play therapy*. J. Aronson.

Scarlet, J. (2017). *Superhero therapy: Mindfulness skills to help teens and young adults deal with anxiety, depression, and trauma*. Instant Help.

Schawbel, D. (2017, October 7). *Vivek Murthy: How to solve the work loneliness epidemic*. Forbes. https://forbes.com/sites/danschawbel/2017/10/07/vivek-murthy-how-to-solve-the-work-loneliness-epidemic-at-work/?sh=1d10e6f37172.

Schelfhout, S., Bowers, M. T., & Hao, Y. A. (2021). Balancing gender identity and gamer identity: Gender issues faced by Wang "Baize" Xinyu at the 2017 Hearthstone summer championship. *Games & Culture, 16*(1), 22-41.

Schimmenti, A. (2018). The trauma factor: Examining the relationships among different types of trauma, dissociation, and psychopathology. *Journal of Trauma & Dissociation, 19*(5), 552-571.

Schippers, M. C., & Ziegler, N. (2019). Life crafting as a way to find purpose and meaning in life. *Frontiers in Psychology, 10*, ArtID 2778.

Schwartz, M., & Galperin, L. (2002). Hyposexuality and hypersexuality secondary to childhood trauma and dissociation. *Journal of Trauma & Dissociation, 3*(4), 107-120.

Schwartz, R. (2013). *Internal family systems therapy* (2nd ed.). Guilford.

Schwegman, D. (1976, February). Statistics regarding classes: (Additions)—bards. *The Strategic Review, 2*(1), 11.

Scriven, P. (2021). From tabletop to screen: Playing Dungeons and Dragons during COVID-19. *Societies, 11*(4), 125.

Seabrook, R. C., Ward, L. M., & Giaccardi, S. (2019). Less than human? Media use, objectification or women, and men's acceptance of sexual aggression. *Psychology of Violence, 9*(5), 536-545.

Sedikides, C., Wildschut, T., Arndt, J., & Routledge, C. (2008). Nostalgia: Past, present, and future. *Current Directions in Psychological Science, 17*(5), 304-307.

Sedikides, C., Wildschut, T., Routledge, C., & Arndt, J. (2015). Nostalgia counteracts self-discontinuity and restores self-continuity. *European Journal of Social Psychology*, *45*(1), 52-61.

Sephton, C. (2017, May 4). *Missing children cases that shocked the world: What happened next?* Sky News. https://news.sky.com/story/missing-children-cases-that-shocked-the-world-what-happened-next-10859345.

Shakespeare, W. M. (1623/1982). *Hamlet, prince of Denmark*. In *The illustrated Stratford Shakespeare* (pp. 799–831). Chancellor.

Shamsian, J. (2017, October 18). *Netflix has a special word for people who binge watch an entire season of TV right after it drops*. Insider. https://insider.com/netflix-binge-race-watch-tv-show-24-hours-2017-10.

Shantz, C. U., & Hobart, C. J. (1989). Social conflict and development: Peers and siblings. In T. J. Berndt & G. W. Ladd (Eds.), *Peer relations in child development* (pp. 71–94). Wiley.

Shapiro, F. (2001). *Eye movement desensitization and reprocessing: Basic principles, protocols, and procedures* (2nd ed.). Guilford.

Shapiro, F. (2012). *Getting past your past: Take control of your life with self-help techniques from EMDR therapy*. Harmony/Rodale.

Shaw, B. A., Krause, N., Chatters, L. M., Connell, C. M., & Ingersoll-Dayton, B. (2004). Emotional support from parents early in life, aging, and health. *Psychology & Aging*, *19*(1), 4-12.

Shea, L., Thompson, L., & Bleiszner, R. (1988). Resources in older adults' old and new friendships. *Journal of Social & Personal Relationships*, *5*(1), 83-96.

Shevlin, M., McElroy, E., & Murphy, J. (2015). Loneliness mediates the relationship between childhood trauma and adult psychopathology: Evidence from the adult psychiatric morbidity survey. *Social Psychiatry & Psychiatric Epidemiology*, *50*(4), 591-601.

Sidhu, P., & Carter, M. (2021). Pivotal play: Rethinking meaningful play in games through death in Dungeons & Dragons. *Games & Culture*, *16*(8), 1044-1064.

Skalski, S., & Pochwatko, G. (2020). Gratitude is female: Biological sex, socio-cultural gender versus gratitude and positive orientation. *Current Issues in Personality Psychology*, *8*(1), 1-9.

Smith, A., & Williams, K. D. (2004). R U There? Effects of ostracism by cell phone messages. *Group Dynamics: Theory, Research, & Practice*, *8*(4), 291-301.

Smith, B. N., Vaughn, R. A., Vogt, D., King, D. W., King, L. A., & Shipherd, J. C. (2013). Main and interactive effects of social support in predicting mental health symptoms in men and women following military stressor exposure. *Anxiety, Stress & Coping*, *26*(1), 52-69.

Smith, D. G., Xiao, L., Bechara, A. (2012). Decision making in children and adolescents: Impaired Iowa gambling task performance in early adolescence. *Developmental Psychology*, *48*(4), 1180-1187.

Smith, T. W. (1991). A critique of the Kinsey Institute/Roper Organization National Sex Knowledge Survey. *Public Opinion Quarterly*, *55*(3), 449-457.

Smith. J. (2013). Between colorblind and colorconscious: Contemporary Hollywood films and struggles over racial representation. *Journal of Black Studies*, *44*(8), 779-797.

Solsman, J. E. (2019, October 16). *Stranger Things is Netflix's most-watched show (as far as we know): The company reveals how much we binge its originals like Money Heist, Tall Girl, Secret Obsession and Unbelievable*. c|net. https://cnet.com/news/stranger-things-is-netflix-most-watched-show-as-far-as-we.know.

Somerville, L. H. (2013). The teenage brain: Sensitivity to social evaluation. *Current Directions in Psychological Science*, *22*(2), 121-127.

Sorrenti, L., Spadaro, L., Mafodda, A. V., Scopelliti, G., Orecchio, S., & Filippello, P. (2019). The predicting role of school Learned helplessness in internalizing and externalizing problems. An exploratory study in students with Specific Learning Disorder. *Mediterranean Journal of Clinical Psychology*, 7(2), 1-14.

Stapley, L. A., & Murdock, N. L. (2020). Leisure in romantic relationships: An avenue for differentiation of self. *Personal Relationships*, 27(1), 76-101.

Stefaniak, A., Wohl, M. J. A., Blais, J., & Pruysers, S. (2022). The I in us: Personality influences the expression of collective nostalgia. *Personality & Individual Differences*, 187, ArtID 111392.

Sterlin, S. (2020, December 4). *Stranger Things: Hopper's 5 best traits (& 5 worst)*. ScreenRant: https://screenrant.com/netflix-stranger-things-hopper-best-worst-traits.

Stevens, E., Jason, L. A., Ram, D., & Light, J. (2015). Investigating social support and network relationships in substance use disorder recovery. *Substance Abuse*, 36(4), 396-399.

Stevenson, E., & Thomas, S. D. M. (2018). A 10-year follow-up study of young people reported missing to the police for the first time in 2005. *Journal of Youth Studies*, 21(10), 1361-1375.

Stickley, A., & Koyanagi, A. (2016). Loneliness, common mental disorders and suicidal behavior: Findings from a general population survey. *Journal of Affective Disorders*, 197, 81-87.

Stillman, T. F., Baumeister, R. F., Lambert, N. M., Crescioni, A. W., DeWall, C. N., & Fincham, F. D. (2009). Alone and without purpose: Life loses meaning following social exclusion. *Journal of Experimental Social Psychology*, 45(4), 686-694.

Substance Abuse and Mental Health Services Administration. (2014). *Trauma-informed care in behavioral health services*. US Department of Health and Human Services.

Sue, D. W. (2010). Microaggressions, marginality, and oppression: An introduction. In D. W. Sue (Ed.), *Microaggressions and marginality: Manifestation, dynamics, and impact* (pp. 3–22). Wiley.

Swanton, B., & Wilson, P. (1989). Research brief: Missing persons. *Australian Institute of Criminology: Trends & Issues in Criminal Justice* (17). Australian Institute of Criminology.

Symister, P., & Friend, R. (2003). The influence of social support and problematic support on optimism and depression in chronic illness: A prospective study evaluating self-esteem as a mediator. *Health Psychology*, 22(2), 123-129.

Szücs, A., Szanto, K., Adalbert, J., Wright, A. G. C., & Clark, L. (2020). Status, rivalry, and admiration-seeking in narcissism and depression: A behavioral study. *PloS One*, 15(12), ArtID e02453588.

Talarico, J. M., & Rubin, D. C. (2007). Flashbulb memories are special after all; in phenomenology, not accuracy. *Applied Cognitive Psychology*, 21(5), 557-578.

Tarling, R., & Burrows, J. (2004). The nature and outcome of going missing: The challenge of developing effective risk assessment procedures. *International Journal of Police Science & Management*, 6(1), 16-26.

Tate, N. (2018, May 4). *Loneliness rivals obesity, smoking as health risk*. WebMD. https://webmd.com/balance/news/20180504/loneliness-rivals-obesity-smoking-as-health-risk.

Tedeschi, R. G., & Blevins, C. L. (2015). From mindfulness to meaning: Implications for the theory of posttraumatic growth. *Psychological Inquiry*, 26(4), 373-376.

Tenenbaum, L. S., Varjas, K., Meyers, J., & Parris, L. (2011). Coping strategies and perceived effectiveness in fourth through eighth grade victims of bullying. *School Psychology International*, 32(3), 263-287.

Tennyson, A. (1850/1993). In memoriam A. H. H. In A. H. Abrams, G. H. Ford, & C. T. Christ (Eds.), *The Norton anthology of English literature* (6th ed., Vol. 2, pp. 1084–1132). Norton.

Terrizzi, J., & Shook, N. (2018). On the origin of shame: Does shame emerge from an evolved disease-avoidance architecture? *Frontiers in Behavioral Neuroscience.* https://frontiersin.org/articles/10.3389/fnbeh.2020.00019/full.

Testoni, I., Franco, C., Palazzo, L., Iacona, E., Zamperini, A., & Wieser, M. A. (2020). The endless grief in waiting: A qualitative study of the relationship between ambiguous loss and anticipatory mourning amongst the relatives of missing persons in Italy. *Behavioral Sciences, 10*(7), 110.

Thepostarchive. (2016, January 17). *The Negro in American culture.* [Video]. YouTube. https://youtube.com/watch?v=jNpitdJSXWY.

Thompson, E. (2017, November 3). *Some Stranger Things fans really want Steve and Billy to make out.* Cosmopolitan. https://cosmopolitan.com/entertainment/tv/a13148667/billy-steve-shipping-stranger-things.

Thompson, K. L., Hannan, S. M., & Miron, L. R. (2014). Fight, flight, and freeze: Threat sensitivity and emotion dysregulation in survivors of chronic childhood maltreatment. *Personality & Individual Differences, 69*, 28-32.

Thompson, S. J., Cochran, G., & Barczyk, A. N. (2012). Family functioning and mental health in runaway youth: Associations with posttraumatic stress syndrome. *Journal of Traumatic Stress, 25*(5), 598-601.

Thompson-Hollands, J., Marx, B. P., Lee, D. J., & Sloan, D. M. (2021). Longitudinal change in self-reported peritraumatic dissociation during and after a course of posttraumatic stress disorder treatment: Contributions of symptom severity and time. *Psychological Trauma: Theory, Research, Practice, & Policy, 13*(6), 665-672.

Tomkins, S. (1962). *Affect imagery consciousness. The positive affects* (Vols. 1-2). Springer.

Triplett, K. N., Tedeschi, R. G., Cann, A., Calhoun, L. G., & Reeve, C. L. (2012). Posttraumatic growth, meaning in life, and life satisfaction in response to trauma. *Psychological Trauma: Theory, Research, Practice, & Policy, 4*(4), 400-410.

Trollo, J. (2017, November 25). *Father-child relationships on "Stranger Things."* Psychology Today. https://psychologytoday.com/us/blog/its-all-about-the-dads/201711/father-child-relationships-stranger-things.

Tucker, J. S., Edelen, M. O., Ellickson, P. L., & Klein, D. J. (2011). Running away from home: A longitudinal study of adolescent risk factors and young adult outcomes. *Journal of Youth & Adolescence, 40*(5), 507-518.

Turner, S. E. (2014). *The colorblind screen: Television in post-racial America.* New York University Press.

TV Tropes (n.d.). *Squishy wizard.* TV Tropes. https://tvtropes.org/pmwiki/pmwiki.php/Main/SquishyWizard.

Udachina, A., Bentall, R. P., Varese, F., & Rowse, G. (2017). Stress sensitivity in paranoia: Poor-me paranoia protects against the unpleasant effects of social stress. *Psychological Medicine, 47*(16), 2834-2843.

Vaes, J., Paladino, P., & Puvia, E. (2011). Are sexualized women complete human beings? Why men and women dehumanize sexually objectified women. *European Journal of Social Psychology, 41*(6), 774-785.

Van der Kolk, B. A. (1994). The body keeps the score: Memory and the evolving psychobiology of posttraumatic stress. *Harvard Review of Psychiatry, 1*(5), 253-265.

Van der Kolk, B. A. (2014). *The body keeps the score: Brain, mind, and body in the healing of trauma.* Viking.

Van Prooijen, J. (2019). Belief in conspiracy theories: Gullibility or rational skepticism? In J. P. Forgas & R. F. Baumeister (Eds.), *The social psychology of gullibility: Fake news, conspiracy theories, and irrational beliefs* (pp. 319–332). Routledge Taylor & Francis.

Van Prooijen, J., & Song, M. (2021). The cultural dimension of intergroup conspiracy theories. *British Journal of Psychology*, *112*(2), 455-473.

Van Zantvliet, P. I., Ivanova, K., & Verbakel, E. (2020). Adolescents' involvement in romantic relationships and problem behavior: The moderating effect of peer norms. *Youth & Society*, *54*(4), 574-591.

Veling, W., Sizoo, B., van Buuren, J., van den Berg, C., Sewbalak, W., Pijnenborg, G. H. M., Boonstra, N., Castelein, S., & van der Meer, L. (2021). Zijn complotdenkers psychotisch? Een vergelijking tussen complottheorieën en paranoïde wanen (Are conspiracy theorists psychotic? A comparison between conspiracy theories and paranoid delusions). *Tijdschrift Voor Psychiatrie*, *63*(11), 1-7.

Verhulst, J. (1984). Limerence: Notes on the nature and function of passionate love. *Psychoanalysis & Contemporary Thought*, *7*(1), 115-138.

Verkuyten, M., & Masson, K. (1996). Culture and gender differences in the perception of friendship by adolescents. *International Journal of Psychology*, *31*(5), 207-217.

Vidourek, R. A., King, K. A., & Merianos, A. L. (2016). School bullying and student trauma: Fear and avoidance associated with victimization. *Journal of Prevention & Intervention in the Community*, *44*(2), 121-129.

Vollmayr, B., & Gass, P. (2013). Learned helplessness: Unique features and translational value of a cognitive depression model. *Cell & Tissue Research*, *354*(1), 171-178.

Wabnegger, A., Gremsl, A., & Schienle, A. (2021). The association between the belief in coronavirus conspiracy theories, miracles, and the susceptibility to conjunction fallacy. *Applied Cognitive Psychology*, *35*(5), 1344-1348.

Wajsblat, L. L. (2012). Positive androgyny and well-being: A positive psychological perspective on gender role variance. *Dissertation Abstracts International, Section B: The Sciences & Engineering*, *72*(8-B), 5019.

Walton, M. T., Lykins, A. D., & Bhullar, N. (2016). Sexual arousal and sexual activity frequency: Implications for understanding hypersexuality. *Archives of Sexual Behavior*, *45*(4), 777-782.

Wayland, S., Maple, M., McKay, K., & Glassock, G. (2016). Holding on to hope: A review of the literature exploring missing persons, hope and ambiguous loss. *Death Studies*, *40*(1), 54-60.

Webster, V., Brough, P., & Daly, V. (2016). Fight, flight, or freeze: Common responses for follower coping with toxic leadership. *Stress & Health*, *32*(4), 346-354.

Wegner, D. M. (2017). *The illusion of conscious will*. MIT Press.

Wegner, D. M., & Wheatley, T. (1999). Apparent mental causation: Sources of the experience of will. *American Psychologist*, *54*(7), 480-492.

Weinberg, C. M. (2013). Hope, meaning, and purpose: Making recovery possible. *Psychiatric Rehabilitation Journal*, *36*(2), 124-125.

Weinstein, N., Ryan, W. S., DeHaan, C. R., Przybylski, A. K., Legate, N., & Ryan, R. M. (2012). Parental autonomy support and discrepancies between implicit and explicit sexual identities: Dynamics of self-acceptance and defense. *Journal of Personality & Social Psychology*, *102*(4), 815-832.

Weiss, K. J., & Dube, A. (2021). Whatever happened to nostalgia (the diagnosis)? *Journal of Nervous & Mental Disease*, *209*(9), 622-627.

Wesselmann, E. D., & Williams, K. D. (2017). Social life and social death: Inclusion, ostracism, and rejection in groups. *Group Processes & Intergroup Relations, 20*(5), 693-706.

Wesselmann, E. D., Williams, K. D., Ren, D., & Hales, A. H. (2021). Ostracism and solitude. In R. J. Coplan, J. Bowker, & L. J. Nelson (Eds.), *The handbook of solitude: Psychological perspectives on social isolation, social withdrawal, and being alone* (2nd ed., pp. 209–223). Wiley-Blackwell.

White, M. (2007). *Maps of narrative practice.* Norton.

Widiger, T. A., & Crego, C. (2021). Psychopathy and the lack of guilt. *Philosophy, Psychiatry, & Psychology, 28*(2), 109-111.

Wiese, A. (2004). *Places of their own: African American suburbanization in the twentieth century.* University of Chicago Press.

Wildschut, T., Sedikides, C., Routledge, C., Arndt, J., & Cordaro, F. (2010). Nostalgia as a repository of social connectedness: the role of attachment-related avoidance. *Journal of Personality & Social Psychology, 98*(4), 573-586.

Wilhelm, H. (2017). The surprising joy of Stranger Things: A good, non-angry, non-political TV show is hard to find. *National Review, 69*(21), 24-25.

Willer, R., Rogalin, C. L., Conlon, B., & Wojnowicz, M. T. (2013). Overdoing gender: A test of the masculine overcompensation thesis. *American Journal of Sociology, 118*(4), 980-1022.

Williams, K. D. (2009). Ostracism: A temporal need-threat model. In M. P. Zanna (Ed.), *Advances in experimental social psychology* (Vol. 41, pp. 275–314). Academic Press.

Williams, K. D., & Nida, S. A. (2009). Is ostracism worse than bullying? In M. J. Harris (Ed.), *Bullying, rejection, and peer victimization: A social cognitive neuroscience perspective* (pp. 279–296). Springer.

Williams, K. D., Govan, C. L., Croker, V., Tynan, D., Cruickshank, M., & Lam, A. (2002). Investigations into differences between social and cyberostracism. *Group Dynamics: Theory, Research, & Practice, 6*(1), 65-77.

Wilson, R. S., Krueger, K. R., Arnold, S. E., Schneider, J. A., Kelly, J. F., Barnes, L. L., Tang, Y., & Bennett, D. A. (2007). Loneliness and risk of Alzheimer disease. *Archives of General Psychiatry, 64*(2), 234-240.

Wing Sue, D., & Sue, D. (2019). *Counseling the culturally diverse: Theory and practice* (8th ed.). Wiley.

Witt, H. (1985, January 27). Fantasy game turns into deadly reality. *Chicago Tribune*, C3, 81.

Wizards RPG Team (2014). *D&D player's handbook.* Wizards of the Coast.

Wolf, W., Levordashka, A., Ruff, J. R., Kraaijeveld, S., Lueckmann, J. M., & Williams, K. D. (2015). Ostracism Online: A social media ostracism paradigm. *Behavior Research Methods, 47*(2), 361-373.

Wong, Y. J., Owen, J., & Shea, M. (2012). A latent class regression analysis of men's conformity to masculine norms and psychological distress. *Journal of Counseling Psychology, 59*(1), 176-183.

Woolnough, P. S., Alys, L., & Pakes, F. (2016). Mental health issues and missing adults. In K. S. Greene & L. Alys, *Missing persons* (pp. 99–112). Routledge.

Wortmann, J. H. (2009). Religion-spirituality and change in meaning after bereavement: Qualitative evidence for the meaning making model. *Journal of Loss & Trauma, 14*(1), 17-34.

Wright, J. C., Weissglass, D. E., & Casey, V. (2020). Imaginative role-playing as a medium for moral development: Dungeons & Dragons provides moral training. *Journal of Humanistic Psychology, 60*(1), 99-129.

Wrzus, C., Hanel, M., Wagner, J., & Neyer, F. J. (2013). Social network changes and life events across the life span: A meta-analysis. *Psychological Bulletin, 139*(1), 53-80.

Xu, J., & Roberts, R. E. (2010). The power of positive emotions: It's a matter of life or death—subjective well-being and longevity over 28 years in a general population. *Health Psychology*, *29*(1), 9-19.

Yang, Z., Sedikides, C., Izuma, K., Wildschut, T., Kashima, E. S., Luo, Y. L., Chen, J., & Cai, H. (2021). Nostalgia enhances detection of death threat: Neural and behavioral evidence. *Scientific Reports*, *11*(1), 1-8.

Yao, Z., & Enright, R. (2021). Developmental cascades of hostile attribution bias, aggressive behavior, and peer victimization in preadolescence. *Journal of Aggression, Maltreatment & Trauma*, *31*(1), 1-19.

Zapoleon, G. (2021). *Guy Zapoleon's 2021 10-year music cycle update*. AllAccess. https://allaccess.com/consultant-tips/archive/32506/guy-zapoleon-s-2021-10-year-music-cycle-update.

Zevnik, A. (2017). Postracial society as social fantasy: Black communities trapped between racism and a struggle for political recognition. *Political Psychology*, *38*(4), 621-635.

Zgoba, K. (2004). The Amber Alert: The appropriate solution to preventing child abduction? *Journal of Psychiatry & Law*, *32*(1), 71-88.

Zhu, Y., Guan, X., & Li, Y. (2015). The effects of intergroup competition on prosocial behaviors in young children: A comparison of 2.5–3.5-year-olds with 5.5–6.5-year-olds. *Frontiers in Behavioral Neuroscience*, *12*, ArtID 16.

Index

About the Editor

Travis Langley, PhD, distinguished professor of psychology at Henderson State University, has been a child abuse investigator, courtroom expert, *Wheel of Fortune* game show champion, and popular keynote speaker for the American Psychological Association, Amazon, and other organizations. Author and editor of fourteen books, he speaks regularly at events throughout the world, discussing the psychology of heroism and the power of story in people's lives. *The New York Times*, *The Wall Street Journal*, *Saturday Evening Post*, CNN, MTV, and hundreds of other outlets have interviewed him and covered his work. He has also appeared as an expert in documentary programs such as *Necessary Evil*, *Legends of the Knight*, *Superheroes Decoded*, *Pharma Bro*, *AMC Visionaries: Robert Kirkman's Secret History of Comics*, and Hulu's *Batman & Bill*.

Follow Travis Langley as **@Superherologist** on Instagram and Twitter or **@DrTravisLangley** on Facebook. Join him as he investigates the best and worst in human nature through his *Psychology Today* blog, "Beyond Heroes and Villains," and through the Popular Culture Psychology page at **Facebook.com/ThePsychGeeks**.

CPSIA information can be obtained
at www.ICGtesting.com
Printed in the USA
JSHW021658070723
44388JS00001B/1